I. A. HOROWITZ

and

GEOFFREY MOTT-SMITH

POINT COUNT CHESS

An Accurate Guide to WINNING CHESS

With a Foreword by Samuel Reshevsky

SIMON AND SCHUSTER   NEW YORK

1960

LIBRARY OF CONGRESS CATALOG CARD NUMBER: 60-6092
MANUFACTURED IN THE UNITED STATES OF AMERICA
PRINTED BY THE MURRAY PRINTING CO., FORGE VILLAGE, MASS.
BOUND BY GEO. MCKIBBIN & SONS, NEW YORK

Foreword

WHEN I was a child prodigy many years ago, chess players were amazed at the ease and accuracy of my play against the veritable giants of chessdom. To be perfectly frank, I was no less amazed, and I have thought about this over and over again. What was it that I had which has been variously described as talent or genius or the divine afflatus which enabled me to select the proper move or line in a given situation? The answer to this question, of course, should prove enlightening. I discovered that I had the happy faculty of being able to spot weak and strong points in a position merely by a glance at its contour. Having done so, I could go on to the next step and enhance my strong points, while surveying my weak ones and/or contain my opponent's strong points and exploit his weak ones.

I fear that I cannot account for this fortuitous bounty. I do know, however, that the foundation of chess logic is the perception of weak and strong points on the board or projected a few moves from possibility to reality. *Point Count*

Chess exactly coincides with my reflections on this matter. Not only does it define the salient features, but also it evaluates them. It is unique in the annals of chess literature in that it is the first and only book that does so. Indeed, it is a great stride forward in bringing the essential ideas to the ordinary player.

SAMUEL RESHEVSKY

Contents

POINT COUNT CHESS

1.   The Point Count Method

POINT COUNT is a coined term borrowed from the game of bridge. There, it is an evaluation of the cards based upon the experience of leading masters. The count of each hand is high, average or low, depending upon the chance of the deal. In chess, however, the element of chance is at an absolute minimum. The players begin even, and any and all advantages are attained by sheer skill. These advantages, from the gross material ones to the small and often subtle positional pluses, yield a determinable appraisal which can be translated into units of points. And these points must be earned—they are not furnished or withheld by a whim of fate. This book tells you how to earn them.

Purpose of the Point Count

The average chess player is familiar with a few guiding principles. He soon discovers the relative value of the men, and his first concept is to steal a profit, relying more or less on his opponent's obtuseness or his own guile, or resorting to what he considers to be a clever bit of horse-trading. As he progresses and his horizon enlarges, he rejects these tricky designs for sounder ones. He learns to bring out his men, possibly to control the center. Unfortunately, one or two elementary ideas often remain the sum and substance of his knowledge.

What he needs is a systematic method of augmenting his understanding. It is not enough to know, for example, what a queen or a rook is worth, or, for that matter, the complete table of relative values of the chessmen. While this information is essential, it is hardly sufficient for forming gainful plans.

Nor is it enough to obtain a scattered knowledge about any other factors in chess without grasping their interrelationships. We have observed a player actually parting with a piece—a whole piece, mind you—merely for the purpose of avoiding doubled pawns! He had been warned against the horrendous evils of weak pawn structure but forgot (or never fully realized) the absurdity of giving up nine or ten points represented by the piece in order to avoid incurring the one minus point of the doubled pawns. Similarly, we have seen players sacrifice scads of material for the purpose of maintaining the center, or refuse to move an attacked piece for fear of losing a tempo. These unprofitable trades, in a game where successful trading is of the essence, can be put in proper focus by a more accurate idea of what you are giving up for what you are getting. Distorted ideas such as those illustrated above are more widespread than is generally supposed and pinpoint the need for a systematic Point Count.

Winning with the Point Count

What, then, will the Point Count do for you? First of all, it will see you safely through the normal vicissitudes of a game of chess. It will enable you to play more surely and forcefully in the light of a precise guide. No longer will you be stumped by a paucity of things to do. Rather, each position will open up with rich possibilities for action, enabling you to steer the game into channels familiar and favorable to you. Even "masterly inactivity" will be thought of more as watchful waiting than dull passivity. We must not suppose that the Point Count will do away with experience, intuition, genius; but genius itself can create only through the medium of rules and techniques, pretty much as a musician requires a knowledge of notes and musical structure before he can compose a symphony. The watchword, therefore, will be: Appraise, act, win!

To illustrate what Point Count can do for you, examine the

four following positions, selected at random from the text. Check the material and positional values and then determine what plan you would pursue if you were playing these games. Bear in mind that where strategy predominates the game does not necessarily conclude with a crusher, though the plan you inaugurate may very well do so. Then compare your ideas with those of the text.

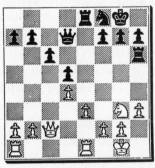

NO. 152. *Minority Attack*
White to move

NO. 167. *Rook on the Seventh*
White to move

Solution appears on page 216.   Solution appears on page 239.

NO. XB. *After 23 . . .*
K – N2

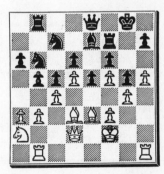

NO. XIIB. *After 23 KPxB*

Solution appears on page 324.   Solution appears on page 329.

The Importance of Strategy

This book offers a systematic treatment and evaluation of the strategy of chess as distinguished from tactics. Many books have been written on chess tactics, few on strategy. In many sources you can find explanations of the minor tactics—the pin, the fork and so on—as well as of major tactics—the sacrificial attack leading to checkmate or the gain of material.

It is axiomatic that a tactical combination can work only when based on a sufficient *strategical advantage.* In other words, a combination may intensify but cannot create a winning superiority: the advantage must be there initially to admit of a winning combination.

Most of what you can read about strategy is contained in asides to the discussion of tactics. There is a natural reason for this preoccupation with tactics. A winning advantage is useless if you do not know how to capitalize on it. Even to hold equality you must continually detect and parry your opponent's short threats. At every move you must be alert to see whether there is a tactical threat more urgent than the remoter strategical considerations. For example, after

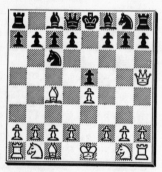

1 P – K4	P – K4
2 B – B4	N – QB3
3 Q – R5	

NO. A. *Black to move*

it is useless to weigh the merits of 3 . . . N – K3 and 3 . . . B – B4. Both are good developing moves, serving long-term strategical purposes. But both are tactically faulty: if you want to play on, you must parry White's threat of 4 QxBP mate.

Nevertheless, there are times in a game when you are not faced with any immediate threat, and where, therefore, the choice of a move may be more difficult because less restricted. Here you have need of strategic judgment. And, even in meeting short threats, trifling though they may be, you must choose the answer that best serves your long-range plan.

The process of improving your chess game is essentially a matter of adding to the list of positions that you *fully understand*. In other words, you must sharpen your power of evaluation. To pick the right move you must examine the positions that can result from various moves and thus discover which position will be the most favorable to you.

One is reminded in this connection of Spielmann's well-known comment on Alekhine's virtuosity. "Given Alekhine's positions, I could see the brilliancies as well as Alekhine," said Spielmann, "but my trouble is that I can't reach the positions." Aye, there's the rub—to get the sort of game that will enable you to win. We believe the Point Count will be an effective instrument for accomplishing just that, though you will assuredly not gain a "Master's degree" without experience and study.

Many of the strategical factors are no doubt familiar to you through the catch-phrases "control of the center," "the two bishops," "the outside passed pawn" and so on. This book undertakes to give a comprehensive list of these factors, to explain how to determine their merits and to provide a simple system of evaluation.

POSITIONAL POINT COUNT TABLE

Plus Points

Control of the center	Rook(s) on the seventh rank
Pawn on fourth *v.* pawn on third	Passed pawn
Mobile pawn wing	Outside passed pawn
Strong outpost station	Protected passed pawn
Superior development	Advanced pawn
Greater space	Qualitative pawn majority
Bishop-pair	Advanced chain
Bishop *v.* knight	Advanced salient
Half-open file	Better king position
Control of useful open file	Offside pawn majority

Minus Points

WEAK PAWNS

Backward pawn	Hanging pawns
Doubled pawn	Hanging phalanx
Isolated pawn	Crippled majority wing

WEAK SQUARES

"Weak-square complex"	King held in center
Holes	Cramped position
Compromised king-side	Bad bishop

The Arithmetic of the Point Count

The Point Count Table is given in full above. Read it over and over until you are thoroughly familiar with it.

On the basis of pretested experience, each of the positional factors there listed is rated as one point. If the human mind were capable of a sufficiently intricate calculus, then in a given position a strong outpost station, for example, might be seen to be worth, not one point, but nine tenths of a point, while in other circumstances the same outpost might be figured as exceeding the value of one point by a small fraction. Such refinements, however, are neither possible nor necessary, and for all practical purposes it is quite satisfactory to deal in full points, plus or minus.

Need we stress once again that the Point Count System is not presented to you as the "solution" of chess? The game is too profound for that; it is not ticktacktoe, and no mind has plumbed the depths of the events on the sixty-four squares. This is as it should be, for the very uncertainties and mysteries of the game provide its greatest charm. To "solve" chess would be to kill it— and what chess player would relish that? But if the Point Count System will not give you what has been denied the world champion—namely, total mastery—it can and does act like a rudder on a ship, performing an indispensable function even if not synonymous with the entire science of navigation. Here you are handed a powerful weapon. By its means you will be able to plan for victory.

The by-product of Point Count, incidentally, may be of greater value than the net of its pluses and minuses. It is the assimilation by the learner of the varying ideas which form the strategic base of the chess game.

To apply the system, examine the positions of your forces and your opponent's forces. Credit yourself with one point for every item due you on the *plus* list and deduct one for every due liability on the *minus* list. Do the same for your opponent's position. Then compare his net score with yours. The difference measures the strategic superiority, if any, that one of you enjoys.

Here are two examples to illustrate this simple arithmetic.

No. 1 is the position after

QUEEN'S GAMBIT

1	P – Q4	N – KB3
2	N – KB3	P – K3
3	P – B4	P – Q4
4	N – B3	B – N5
5	B – N5	BxNch
6	PxB	

NO. 1. *Black to move*

Without plunging at once into a discussion of strategic motifs, which will be examined in detail in the following chapters, let us simply say at this juncture that White counts one plus point for having the bishop-pair (for definition of "bishop-pair" and other terms, see Glossary) less one point for impaired queen-side pawns, a net of zero. Black counts one plus for the qualitative majority of pawns on the queen-side, less one for a bad bishop, again a net of zero. The game is even.

No. 2 is the position after

KING'S GAMBIT

1 P – K4	P – K4
2 P – KB4	PxP

NO. 2. *White to move*

White is entitled to a point for center superiority (two center pawns against one), another for the half-open king bishop file and a third for lead in development. This last point consists of more than the initial lead that is always White's by virtue of his first move. It is foreseeable, and experience proves, that White can bring out his minor pieces rapidly to good posts (N – KB3, N – QB3, B – QB4), whereas the Black minor pieces will be somewhat constricted (N – KB3 has to reckon with P – K5 and the Black king bishop cannot advance yet beyond the second rank). Further, if Black wants to save his advanced pawn, he must expend one or two turns in pawn moves at the expense of piece moves.

Thus, White has three countable points. What does Black have? Nothing on our list! But he has an extra pawn.

We know from experience that position No. 2 is an even game. From this instance and many others, we conclude that THREE POINTS ARE EQUIVALENT TO A PAWN.

Four net points certainly constitute a winning advantage, allowing for a slim surplus margin, since a master would ordinarily find three points sufficient.

In view of the three material points assigned to a pawn, we evaluate the other men approximately as follows:

MATERIAL POINT COUNT

Pawn = Three points	**Rook** = Fifteen points
Knight = Nine points	**Queen** = Twenty-seven points
Bishop = Nine points	**King** = Nine points

It will be seen that each 16-man army totals 126 points.

Since the loss of a single pawn without compensation is so serious as to be well-nigh fatal, the loss of a piece, with its tremendous Point Count, is entirely catastrophic unless heavy counterbalancing advantages are present in the position.

The king is included in the table even though it is not subject to capture because, on a relatively peaceful board, it is both a powerful offensive and defensive unit.

The bishop, as a rule, is stronger than a knight. Because of numerous exceptions detailed in the text, it is rated on a par, subject to modification according to specific circumstance.

The Strategic Plan

Why use the Point Count?

We have previously indicated one answer. In order to choose between two plausible moves, you have to be able to assess properly the different positions that may result from each. A second and equally important answer is that accurate assessment of the present positions is the basis of a strategical plan.

We need hardly point out that you cannot play chess from move to move; you must follow some general plan.

Let us examine Nos. 1 and 2 to see how the mere recognition of the points indicates the proper strategical plans.

A plan should naturally try to capitalize plus points and eliminate or neutralize minus points. In No. 1, after completing his development, Black should try to advance pawns on the queenside, perhaps ultimately to get a passed pawn, and as soon as possible to give scope to his bad bishop. White, upon getting out his pieces, should try to work up a king-side attack with his two bishops, plus his more advanced center pawns (which do not yet give him a countable point for "center control" but give him the edge toward acquiring it). Similarly, in No. 2 White should try to work up an attack on Black's most vulnerable square, his KB2, by moving B – B4, and also by trying to force off the advanced Black king bishop pawn so that his rook can operate on the file. If Black loses this pawn, he will have nothing but minuses to show for 2 . . . PxP; therefore he should try to maintain it or to gain equivalent compensation. Experience has shown that his "mobile pawn wing" (P – KN4 – N5) cannot be ignored, and his lag in development can be repaired by an early P – Q4, even at the cost of a pawn.

Scope of the Point Count

It cannot be too much emphasized that the Point Count is intended to be used when strategic considerations are uppermost. It cannot be expected to give a true picture when tactical urgencies supervene, as during the discharge of accumulated advantages by a combination.

Look at No. 3A. White has an overwhelming material superiority: a queen against a bishop. He also has a protected passed pawn, plus a queen-side majority of pawns as soon as he captures the Black weakling on his QB4. Black has minuses for his weak isolated pawns, and also for the wretched deployment of his pieces—his knight goes lost as soon as attacked, for it can neither retreat nor be defended.

Thus White has a lead of four points in position and the equivalent of about eighteen points in material. But—he happens to be checkmated.

Torre *v.* Alekhine 1922

NO. 3A. *Black has moved*

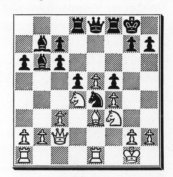

NO. 3B. *Black to move*

The absurdity arises because we have applied the Point Count where it is not intended: at the end of a sacrificial mating combination. If we go back to the position just before Black launched his combination, we will see that the Point Count yields a true appraisal.

The earlier position is No. 3B. Here we would credit White with a point for his protected passed pawn and another for his outpost at Q4, with possibly a debit for a somewhat bad bishop. Black counts plus points for his bishop-pair, outpost knight, mobile queen-side pawns and superior development (all his pieces are active, bearing upon the center or king-side, whereas White's only aggressive piece is his queen knight, while his queen rook as yet does nothing). At first sight, then, we judge that Black is two or three points ahead. When we examine the points dynamically (see p. 14 for a definition of this term), we see that his lead is even greater. His outpost knight is unassailable, whereas the White outpost can be expelled by P – QB4. The mobile Black pawns are, indeed, an acute menace, supported as they are by three minor pieces and a rook, whereas the White center pawns are stopped. The passed pawn is but a remote asset, far from realization because Black strongly controls the squares from which its advance might otherwise be supported.

On this reassessment, we would conclude that Black's net plus is so great that he probably can evolve a combination for a quick win. And he did: *1* . . . P – B4; *2* N – N3, P – B5; *3* N(N3) – Q4, P – B4; *4* N – K2, followed, after some preparation, by P – Q5 and a queen sacrifice by QxN (at KR3).

"Pictorial" and "Dynamic" Points

As we see from No. 3B, the points are not actually all of equal value. White's passed pawn has no fighting force at the moment, whereas Black's two bishops are very much "present and voting." Even the same point may have different values in different circumstances. Black's outpost knight would be worth more than White's even if the latter could be maintained, because it is farther advanced. But White's point for an outpost is obviously transient, for the knight can be immediately ousted.

However, the valuation of each point as one plus or minus will yield an accurate assessment, most of the time, if you are careful to count the points dynamically rather than pictorially.

That means, look at more than the static picture presented by the White and Black pieces. Look ahead a few moves to see whether an advantage is enduring or transient, real or an optical illusion.

You are not asked to make an exhaustive analysis of all possible lines of play. Far from it! You are asked merely to keep in mind the broad lines of the battle, plus the immediate tactical situation. The latter you have to examine anyhow to choose your next move. Your purpose as to the Point Count is to avoid gross errors, such as counting the bishop-pair in your favor when you intend or can be forced to swap one bishop for a knight, or counting that you have control of an open file when your opponent can immediately challenge it.

The difference between the "pictorial" and the "dynamic" count will be illustrated by No. 4.

Saemisch *v*. Nimzovich   1923

NO. 4. *White to move*

White has a knight for two pawns. Since a knight is generally worth three pawns, White has a material superiority of one pawn, which is a point superiority of three. Black has a point for control of the king bishop file. That leaves White with a net of two. We might deduct another point because he seems to control less space than does Black. So much for the "pictorial" count: White is one ahead.

Now look at it dynamically. What move will you make for White? If you try every possible piece move, you will discover that every one leads to the loss of a piece. The only safe moves are pawn moves, and after White exhausts them he will have to hurl himself on the sword. The fact is that, dynamically, there is only one point to be counted, since it is decisive: the White cramp. In No. 4 White resigned.

Before and After

To reap the benefit of the Point Count, apply it to positions *before they arise*. Project the future position in your mind.

Let us compare two positions, Nos. 5A and 5B.

Prins *v.* Kinzl   1955

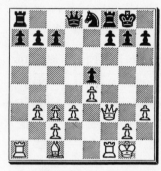

NO. 5A. *White to move*   NO. 5B. *White to move*

In No. 5A, the game appears to be even. Black is a tempo ahead in development, since all his minor pieces are out while the White queen bishop is still at home. But White has given the tempo to get an edge in the center by P – KB4.

In No. 5B White can count a decided center superiority which will turn into full control when he can advance his pawns, plus two half-open files, plus bishop *v.* knight, plus a big lead in development (his rooks already stand on the open files; his bishop can reach the strong square R3 in one move; the Black knight is "undeveloped"). By our precepts, White is ahead 4–0, so he has a won game.

What Black player would want to turn No. 5A into No. 5B? Yet a player did, by the following moves:

1 P – KR3	BxKN	4 RPxN	BxN
2 QxB	N – QR4	5 PxB	N – K1
3 B – N3	NxB	6 PxP	PxP

We can conclude only that Black forgot to examine the resultant position.

The road to chess mastery is not to forget! Apply the Point

Count faithfully a few moves ahead of time, and you will avoid such debacles as this.

Winning a Won Game

Proverbially the hardest game to win is a "won game." The reason is, perhaps, that you incline to think that a won game will play itself. Not so: you still have to make tactical calculations just as at any other time.

Since the Point Count does not deal with tactics, it cannot tell you how to win a won game. But we cannot resist pointing out that tactical problems often solve themselves if you keep in mind at all times your *strategical objectives*. From that viewpoint you often uncover the best of parries to a threatened adverse move— which is to perceive a reason why your opponent cannot profitably make it!

For example, in No. 5B, the Point Count has suggested White's logical line of play—to advance his mobile queen-side pawns, taking command of the center and threatening to smash up the Black queen-side. The natural first step is P – Q4, but at the moment it seems to lose a pawn. Does it, though? Looking at his other assets, White discovers a reason why Black cannot play PxP, so . . .

| 7 | P – Q4! | Q – K2 |

If 7 . . . PxP, then 8 B – R3, N – Q3; 9 P – K5 winning the exchange.

| 8 | R – R5 | P – KB3 |
| 9 | PxP | P – QB4 |

If 8 . . . PxP, then 9 RxKP, RxQ; 10 RxQ, etc.

| 10 | Q – Q3 | K – R1 |

If 10 . . . P – QN3; 11 Q – Q5ch.

| 11 | Q – Q5 | |

White wins a pawn and still keeps his great positional advantage.

2.   Pawn Formations

IN military usage, "strategy" refers to measures of preparation for battle, such as the mobilization and deployment of troops. "Tactics" refers to maneuvers executed during and as part of a battle. In chess, the two terms have analogous meanings.

Chess strategy is concerned with long-range plans based on the more enduring features of positions. Now, the least transient feature of any position is the *pawn formation*, which changes at a slower pace than the positions of the pieces. It is not surprising, therefore, that in the Point Count (or any other method of weighing strategic factors) fully half of the points arise from aspects of the pawn formation.

Criteria of Pawn Moves

The move of a pawn differs in an important way from the move of a piece: it is not retractable. Every pawn move makes a permanent change in the position. You should weigh every contemplated pawn move by these criteria:

SAFETY of the pawns themselves from attack and capture.

COMMAND of squares on which your opponent might otherwise post pieces advantageously.

SPACE created for the deployment of your pieces.

MOBILITY of your pawns to penetrate the opponent's territory and spearhead an attack.

The pawn is paralleled only by the knight in that its move necessarily abandons the guard of squares previously guarded. Under the criterion of COMMAND, consider not only the new squares that a pawn will guard after its advance but also the squares it relinquishes. A pawn thrust into enemy territory may be intrinsically desirable yet inadvisable because of the "holes" it leaves at home.

Probably in no phase of chess can you get something for nothing. Certainly in a pawn move you have to "give to get." This does not at all mean that you should be a Timid Soul, afraid to extend your front line. It does mean that you should weigh each pawn advance to be sure that you do not give away more than you get.

Definitions

The following terms are used in describing pawn structures:

The PHALANX comprises two or more pawns on the same rank and adjacent files, as the White pawns in No. 6.

The CHAIN comprises two or more pawns on a diagonal across adjacent files, as the Black pawns in No. 6.

NO. 6. A. *Chain* B. *Phalanx*

NO. 7.
A. *Salient*
B. *Reverse Salient*

The SALIENT comprises three pawns in a V pointing forward, as the White pawns in No. 7.

The REVERSE SALIENT comprises three pawns in a V pointing backward, as the Black pawns in No. 7.

NO. 8.
Backward Pawns

The BACKWARD PAWN is one that cannot be guarded by a fellow pawn and cannot advance without being susceptible to capture by an enemy pawn, as the Black queen knight pawn in No. 8. The White queen bishop pawn is not backward, although it cannot advance without loss, since it can be guarded by P – QN3. Pawns on their home squares are sometimes exempted from the definition, since they cannot be guarded by fellow pawns anyhow, but one under actual restraint, as the king pawn in No. 8, may well be called backward. The king knight pawns in No. 8, though neither can be guarded by a fellow nor advanced without loss, are not regarded as backward, for the reason that both are shielded from frontal and forward-diagonal attack.

The DOUBLED PAWN comprises two pawns of the same color on the same file, as the queen bishop pawns in No. 9.

NO. 9.
A. *Isolated Pawn*
B. *Doubled Pawn*
C. *Hole*

The ISOLATED PAWN (or *isolani*) is a pawn that cannot be guarded by another because the pawns on the adjacent files have disappeared, as the queen rook pawn in No. 9.

A HOLE, in the narrowest sense, is a square in front of an unmoved pawn, no longer guarded by any adjacent pawn, as Black's KN3 in No. 9. But the term is broadly applied to any square in one's own territory from which an adverse piece cannot be expelled by a pawn.

HANGING PAWNS are a group (usually a phalanx) susceptible to frontal attack and in some danger of capture. The question whether pawns hang or not depends on the dynamics of the particular position. See Chapter 10, page 114.

A STOPPED PAWN is one whose advance is halted by an enemy pawn directly ahead of it on the file. In No. 6 the queen pawns are stopped.

A BLOCKADED PAWN is one whose forward advance is prevented by an enemy piece directly ahead of it on the file.

The Center

The CENTER comprises the four squares Q4, Q5, K4, K5. In No. 10 the center is indicated by the solid black square.

NO. 10. A. *Center*
B. *Subcenter*

The twelve other squares adjacent to these central four comprise the SUBCENTER.

One strategic purpose dominates the opening and, usually, all of the early play until the issue is settled—that is, control of the center.

The importance of the center is obvious. A piece standing there has its maximum range and may attack both enemy wings simultaneously. The lateral shift of pieces to defend a threatened wing is much impeded if the enemy controls the center. In extreme cases, a drive forward in the center may split the enemy forces into two groups, each impotent to help the other.

The question "How do you gain control of the center?" leaps to mind. It would seem that the answer is to be found in tactics. Yet, as we shall show, the path to the answer lies through strategy. There is a previous question to be answered, "What constitutes control of the center?" After you have studied the factors in this matter, you will know a great deal about the tactics necessary to gain control.

White and Black begin a game on equal terms, except that

White, having the first move, is a tempo ahead in development. There is no formula, however, by which either side can gain undisputed control of the center. The proper aim is more modest: to maintain *at least equality* in the center. This means that you should aim

A] To exclude enemy pieces from taking permanent posts in the center. If total exclusion is impossible, through the dissolution of central pawns, the aim becomes

B] To gain at least as many, or as effective, piece-posts in the center as does your opponent.

Center Control by Pawns

What may be called the normal course to effect aim [A] is to advance one or both of your center pawns to the fourth rank. Thus you exclude enemy pieces from the fifth-rank squares guarded by your pawns. The great preponderance of games in fact begin with *1* P – K4 or *1* P – Q4. Most of the others begin with the advance of a subcenter pawn, *1* P – QB4 or *1* P – KB4, followed soon by a central advance.

The strongest formation of two pawns for offensive purposes is the phalanx, which attacks four squares on the next rank. If a phalanx pawn is attacked by an enemy pawn, it may have choice of PxP or advancing to form a chain. Enduring advantages are due, above all, to the acquisition of such options.

The chain is essentially a defensive formation: the advanced pawn is guarded by the other. It obviously has less offensive power than the phalanx, since it leaves squares of one color unguarded.

White, by virtue of his first move, is often able to form a central phalanx early, whereas Black, to challenge it, can form only a chain. Here are some opening possibilities:

French Defense: 1 P – K4, P – K3; *2* P – Q4, P – Q4; *3* N – QB3.

Philidor's Defense: 1 P – K4, P – K4; *2* N – KB3, P – Q3; *3* P – Q4.

King's Indian Defense: 1 P – Q4, N – KB3; *2* P – QB4, P – KN3; *3* N – QB3, B – N2; *4* N – B3, P – Q3; *5* P – K4.

Against all three defenses, White's best line is to form the fourth-rank phalanx immediately.

What Center Control is NOT

Let us clear away two possible misconceptions.

First, occupation of the center by pawns does NOT represent control of the center. You want central squares as posts or avenues for your *pieces*. Your own pawns in the center exclude your pieces as effectively as would enemy pawns. No; occupation of the center by pawns is a means to an end. To gain control of the center you have first got to fight the enemy pawns that try to exclude you.

This is not to deprecate central advances. On the contrary, your chances of winning the fight are the better, as a rule, the more pawns you can bring to bear on central squares, and the farther your pawns can penetrate safely into the enemy half of the board.

Second, the possession of a fourth-rank phalanx opposed only by a chain does NOT represent control of the center. But it does afford the better chance of winning that control.

Center Liquidation

If all the pawns disappear from the king file and queen file, the pieces take over the center fight. Development and time become the governing factors. A slight lead in development becomes magnified. A player who has established an early lead will therefore strive to liquidate the center while his opponent stoutly resists.

The same "open game" characteristics are often observable when the center becomes stabilized, as by the formation of stopped chains which neither side can well break up.

In considering a pawn advance that may lead to a swap or to stabilization of the center, give due regard to the present status and future prospects of your piece development. For example:

Center Game: 1 P – K4, P – K4; 2 P – Q4.

By analogy, with the French Defense and Philidor's Defense,

White may argue, "Why shouldn't I form the phalanx while I can?" But then follows 2 . . . PxP; 3 QxP, N – QB3. Black gains a tempo in development, the importance of which is that he can soon enforce P – Q4 if he pleases and so equalize the center command. Thus 2 P – Q4, while not actually bad, is inferior to other moves (as 2 N – KB3, 2 B – B4, etc.) because it gives away White's initial advantage.

Pawn on Fourth v. Pawn on Third

In view of what has just been said, the reader may well ask what is the percentage for White in P – Q4 in the given lines of the French Defense and Philidor's Defense. Black can play PxP, just as in the Center Game.

After White recaptures with the knight the position is No. 11

 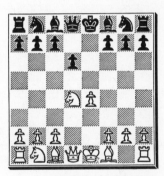

NO. 11. *French Defense*   NO. 12. *Philidor's Defense*

or No. 12. White has a center pawn on the fourth rank *v.* a Black center pawn on the third rank. The difference is a superiority for White in center command that many times has helped White to acquire other advantages and eventually to win the game. Dr. Tarrasch went so far as to proclaim the pawn on fourth *v.* pawn on third a winning advantage in itself. While this view has been shown to be too extreme, it is a fact that the more restricted side faces a long uphill battle.

The only reliable equalizer is to get the third-rank pawn to the fourth or to liquidate the enemy fourth-rank pawn. In No. 11,

Black cannot move P – K4 without loss until he has brought guards to bear on K4, but White can pile up attackers faster. Thus, if 4 . . . N – QB3; 5 N – KB3, what next? After 5 . . . B – Q3 White has choice among B – QN5, Q – K2, NxB followed by B – KB4, and even P – B4 (preparing P – Q5). In No. 12, if Black plays 4 . . . P – Q4 (at cost of a tempo) he faces further loss of time after 5 PxP, QxP; 6 N – QB3, B – QN5; 7 Q – Q3 followed by B – K3 and O – O – O. If instead 4 . . . N – KB3; 5 N – QB3, Black's problem is not only to enforce P – Q4 but also to neutralize White's possible reply P – K5.

A picture significantly different from Nos. 11 and 12 is presented by No. 13, which arises in the

Scotch Game: 1 P – K4, P – K4; *2* N – KB3, N – QB3; *3* P – Q4, PxP; *4* NxP.

NO. 13. *Scotch Game*

Black can eventually move . . . P – Q4 because White's king knight is loose. The attack on this knight, indeed, permits Black to delay P – Q4 in favor of piece play: 4 . . . B – B4; 5 B – K3, Q – B3, etc. If White retreats his knight from Q4, he gives away his initial tempo; if White plays NxN, Black recaptures with the knight pawn and can soon play P – Q4.

Thus White's 3 P – Q4 leads merely, if Black so wills, to liquidation of the center. Such an early liquidation is almost invariably in Black's favor, since it relieves him of any development cramp. The Scotch Game, though better for White than the Center Game, is regarded as objectively inferior to the Ruy Lopez and other lines in which the center tension is longer maintained.

Two Against One

In connection with the King's Gambit (No. 2) we said that after 2 . . . PxP White has two pawns in the center against Black's one. We indicated that this is a countable point in the system.

The realizable value of this point, however, varies widely in different positions.

In the King's Gambit, we see that White can immediately capitalize his two-against-one: he can complete his center phalanx by P – Q4 and maintain a good grip on the center. The fact is that Black is well-advised to play an early P – Q4, even at cost of a pawn, to break up the phalanx and also to let out his queen bishop.

The situation is somewhat different in the

Sicilian Defense: 1 P – K4, P – QB4; 2 N – KB3, P – Q3; 3 P – Q4, PxP; 4 NxP.

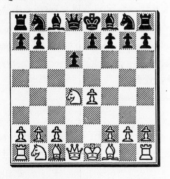

NO. 14. *Sicilian Defense*

White must sooner or later dispute Black's command of his Q4, and the simpler course is to do it sooner, as shown.

Now Black has two-for-one in the center, plus a half-open queen bishop file. His general plan is to bring a rook to this file, advance his queen-side pawns in a minority attack (see p. 215), and support the operation (if feasible) by fianchettoing his king bishop.

White's assets in No. 14 are the pawn on fourth *v.* pawn on third, the half-open queen file, and greater space for development. His natural plan is to get his pieces out quickly, castle, and advance his king-side pawns.

It may seem strange to grant both sides points for their central pawn formation—but that is how it is!

White's pawn on the fourth is of *immediate* value. It restrains Black's center pawns and so somewhat cramps his bishops. The Black two-for-one is of *potential* value. It may enable him later to swap off White's king pawn and remain with greater center control through his own remaining pawn. He cannot play 4 . . . P – Q4 (5 B – N5ch! gives White a gain of material) and White can quickly mass pieces to restrain the queen pawn (N – QB3, B – QB4, also queen and rook on the queen file). Experience corroborates that the realization of Black's assets is a lengthy process; White's king-side attack hits first. Short Sicilian games are mostly won by White; long ones by Black.

A hazard of the retarded two-for-one center is that the opponent, by a wing advance, may threaten to smash it up. In the Sicilian, White often moves P – KB4, establishing a wing phalanx that largely devalues the Black center. A typical position is shown in No. 31, page 52. White threatens P – K5 or P – B5 according to circumstances, and in either case Black's center is a target of attack rather than a source of strength.

SUMMARY

The possession of a phalanx *v.* a chain in the center is NOT a countable point. But it does afford the better prospect of gaining center control.

Count one point for a center pawn on the fourth rank opposed only by a pawn on its third rank. Count one point for having two center pawns against one. In both cases, be ready to discount the point if it is remote rather than immediate, transient rather than permanent. Examine the dynamics of the position sufficiently to form a judgment on this character.

3. *Advanced Chains and Salients*

AN *advanced* pawn group, as we here use the term, is one that has encroached on enemy territory—that is, whose vanguard pawn has reached at least the fifth rank.

White, as we have said, can often form a central phalanx on the fourth, while Black can oppose only by a chain. Thereafter, Black usually has no option but to try to maintain his single pawn on the fourth, or to bring up a subcenter pawn. To play PxP would leave White with pawn on fourth *v.* pawn on third.

White's advantage is mainly that he has a real option between PxP and an advance to change the phalanx into a chain. So long as he can defer the decision, Black has got to be prepared to meet the tactical consequences of either course.

The French Defense Chains

The main line of the French Defense begins

1 P – K4		P – K3
2 P – Q4		P – Q4
3 N – QB3		N – KB3
4 B – KN5		B – K2

NO. 15A. *White to move*

Since Black now threatens to win the king pawn, White must make a decision. The swap PxP is safe but unenterprising, since it gives Black equality in the center at once. The defense of the king pawn by B – Q3 allows Black, by PxP, to force two minor-piece swaps, easing his game greatly. The sharpest line is P – K5, leading to No. 15B:

5 P – K5   KN – Q2
6 BxB   QxB

NO. 15B. *White to move*

Does White now have "control of the center" countable as a point? Well, the purpose of this chapter is to investigate that question. To anticipate, the answer is "No!"

When opposing chains are stopped, one of them is bound to be more advanced than the other. The advanced chain enjoys greater space, which may or may not be worth a point. But the issue of center control remains in abeyance until the subcenter fight is decided.

Attacking an Advanced Chain

In No. 15B Black must promptly attack the White chain, to weaken if not to destroy it. Its cramping effect is otherwise unendurable. We can generalize: an advanced chain (or salient) invites attack, and in many instances the opponent must attack it quickly to avoid strangulation.

Now, the most effective attack on a chain is on its *base*, the pawn at the rear. The threat is to leave the *van* pawn isolated and defenseless.

Black's natural counter in No. 15B is P – QB4, and his pieces are poised to support this thrust at once. White has one tempo to initiate a defense of his queen pawn. Several plans have been tried. One is 7 N – N5, vacating QB3 for the queen bishop pawn. Black has then to stop NxBPch. White therefore gets time to play P – QB3, N – QR3 – B2, etc., in order to maintain a pawn at his Q4.

But this is not a manual of openings. You can study the intricacies of the French Defense elsewhere. We wish merely to indicate the strategic lines consequent from No. 15B.

Capitalizing an Advanced Chain

White's pawn at K5 cramps the Black king-side. The natural way to capitalize this situation is to throw forward the White king-side pawns: P – KB4, P – KN4, P – KB5. The effect may be to compromise the castled king if Black plays O – O, or to open a file for White penetration, or merely to weaken the Black pawn structure. In any event, White is likely to benefit from the known fact that a cramped pawn wing usually needs more pieces for defense than for attack, because the cramp prevents the defenders from operating at full capacity.

The force of the pawn at K5 is illustrated by the following game, in which White apparently abandons his Q4 to concentrate on the wing advance.

Continuing from No. 15B:

7	P – B4	P – QR3
8	N – B3	P – QB4
9	PxP	NxBP
10	B – Q3	NxBch

Black cannot have his cake and eat it too. If he lets the bishop live, it menaces his king-side. But the capture brings reinforcement to the White center.

11	PxB!	N – B3
12	Q – Q2	O – O
13	O – O	B – Q2
14	R – B2	Q – B4
15	R – QB1	

White delays P – Q4 in order not to cede Black his QB5 as an outpost station.

15	. . . .	Q – R2
16	P – Q4	

Now Black cannot try to get his knight to B5 by N – R4 because then White wins a pawn by NxP.

16 . . . .   N – K2

NO. 15C. *White to move*

White is now ready to resume the king-side push, and Black belatedly goes to the defense.

17	P – KN4	QR – B1
18	R – Q1	R – B5
19	Q – Q3	KR – B1?
20	N – KN5	N – N3

Forced, since P – KN3 obviously fails against Q – R3. Now if at once *21* P – B5 Black gets counterplay by NxKP.

21   Q – K3   P – R3

Suicide, but nothing avails.

22 NxBP!	KxN
23 P – B5	N – K2
24 PxPch	KxP
25 QxPch	PxQ
26 R – B6 mate	

The Insecure Chain

The foregoing game shows the triumph of an advanced chain (and its logical follow-up) over the counterattack. To balance the picture, here is an instance of the defeat of the chain.

Kopylov *v.* Taimanov   1949

1 P – QB4	N – KB3
2 N – KB3	P – B3
3 P – Q4	P – Q4
4 P – K3	B – B4
5 Q – N3	Q – N3

NO. 16. *White to move*

(Parenthetically, let us say that this is a typical position in which neither side wants to play QxQ, because the resulting half-open file outweighs the doubled pawn.)

It is probable that White, at his next move, suffered an attack of "chess blindness," thinking the exchange of queens was forced.

6 P – B5?

After 6 . . . QxQ, White would indeed have a queen-side bind and Black could not hope to enforce P – K4 to weaken the White chain. But— ·

6 . . . .   Q – B2!

The *reductio ad absurdum.* In a few moves Black can enforce P – K4, after which (if White plays PxP) White's pawn at QB5 goes lost, or Black moves P – K5 and establishes an impregnable advanced chain. The actual continuation was

7	N – B3	QN – Q2
8	B – Q2	P – K4

and Black, already having the upper hand, eventually won. Another instance of an unwise advance arose in No. 17.

Shiva *v.* Szabo   1955

NO. 17. *Black to move*

At the moment White has an imposing phalanx on the fourth, more space, and an outpost knight. But he cannot keep all these points: the Black pawns are yet to be heard from.

1	. . . .	P – Q3
2	N – Q3	P – Q4
3	P – B5	

White hopes to keep the Black bishops locked up. His salient looks powerful but is not. White had nothing better than *3* Q – N3.

3	. . . .	P – QR4!

Of course! The merit of an advanced chain or salient depends on whether it can survive the attack on its base. The reply that White should have examined first of all was 3 . . . P – QR4; had he done so, he would have discovered that the position of his queen compromises him badly.

4	Q – N3

Either pawn capture costs White some material.

4		RPxP
5 QxNP		QN – Q2
6 N – R4		PxP!

For if 7 QxB, RxN; 8 QxP, RxQP.

7 N(4)xP		B – R3
8 B – N5		NxN
9 PxN		

Now Black controls the center while White has two weak
isolated pawns.

The Chain in the King's Gambit Declined

When Black declines the King's Gambit, White has a
chance to form an advanced chain by P – KB5, if he wishes. The
merit of the move depends on (a) whether the chain is safe
against the counterattack, P – Q4, etc., and (b) whether the king
bishop pawn exerts any real pressure, as by threat of P – B6 or
of a pawn storm (P – KN4 – N5, etc.).

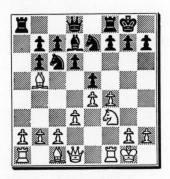

Capablanca v. Allies   1914

NO. 18. *White to move*

In No. 18, White has a choice between PxP and P – B5 to lay
the foundation for a king-side attack. Both moves are good; White
(Capablanca) actually chose P – B5. We can see that the move
is both safe and useful. Though Black can move P – Q4 immediately, White can cheerfully let Black play PxP, for White can

easily defend his K4. The king bishop pawn cramps Black's queen bishop, which in turn blocks the operation of heavy pieces in the center. If Black delays P – Q4, White can stop it forever by P – QB4, even though he thereby makes his own bishop "bad." (Capablanca did just that! For a discussion of the "bad" bishop, see page 203 in Chapter 17.)

The continuation was

1	P – B5	P – B3	5	Q – K1	Q – K1
2	B – B4ch	K – R1	6	Q – R4	N – Q1
3	P – QR3	B – K1	7	B – R2	B – B2
4	B – K6	B – R4	8	P – B4!?	

Shortly afterward White played P – KN4 – N5, and the regulation king-side attack won.

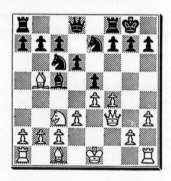

Alapin v. Rubinstein   1908

NO. 19. *White to move*

Contrast No. 18 with No. 19. In the latter, also, White played P – B5. But what a difference! The move is suspect on its face, for (a) Black's queen bishop is not on the board to be cramped; (b) Black's P – Q4 can be backed up by heavy pieces quickly, since his center is not obstructed, and in fact his minor pieces are ideally posted; (c) Black threatens N – Q5, which at the very least will get rid of White's king bishop; (d) White is too undeveloped to dream of a quick king-side pawn storm. The continuation was

1 P – B5?	N – Q5
2 Q – N3	NxB

It is well known that 2 . . . NxPch; 3 K – Q1, NxR is not good for Black; the White attack is too strong.

3 NxN	P – KB3

Having got rid of the White king bishop, Black can make this move without serious weakening. Then in case of B – R6 he can defend by R – B2. No longer having the means for an attack, White has to get rid of Black's king bishop, which bores into his middle.

4 B – K3	BxB
5 QxB	P – Q4!
6 O – O	P – B3
7 N – R3	Q – N3!

How the picture has changed since the ill-advised 9 P – B5! Now Black has the central phalanx, White has merely an over-extended chain. After the forced swap of queens, Black doubles rooks on the queen file, opens it when he pleases, and crashes through the White center.

The Chain on Q5

The possibility of forming a chain with its van on Q5 arises in various openings. Let us apply the principle of evaluation to some of these cases.

No. 20 arose from a King's Gambit Declined. The position has a superficial resemblance to No. 19, with the vital difference that here White has achieved P – Q4, forming a triple phalanx. The continuation was

1 P – Q5	N – N1
2 B – Q3	

We can see that the advance is powerfully cramping. Black's natural counter, P – KB4, is prevented. White, indeed, threatens

Rubinstein *v*. Salwe   1907

NO. 20. *White to move*

to set up a reverse salient by P – KB5, since the flank attacks on it by P – QB3 and P – KN3 can safely be met by P – QB4 and P – KN4 (if nothing better offers). Black can give himself an out-post station (see Chapter 12) at K4 by PxP, but cannot well move N – K4 until he has backed up the knight by one more piece, else White's NxN will force PxN, plugging the station and also masking White's backward king pawn. Virtually the only tactical calculation White has to make in weighing *1* P – Q5 is to see that his backward king pawn will not be a serious weakness.

2		PxP	5 N – B4		QN – Q2
3 BxP		N – KB3	6 NxB		RPxN
4 QN – Q2		B – N5	7 O – O		

White's center is strong; he has much greater space.

Tarrasch *v*. Teichmann   1905

NO. 21. *White to move*

No. 21 is a regular position in an old defense to the Ruy Lopez. White (Tarrasch) proceeds to show that it is unsatisfactory.

1 P – Q5!

Superficially attractive, since it gains a tempo and leaves Black momentarily very cramped. Yet the move requires rather precise calculation that White's queen-side pawn storm will become menacing before Black can do any harm on the king-side. Thus, to enforce P – KB4 with the threat of P – B5, Black has got to play N – KN1, R – KB1, and K – R1, at the very least. White has time for N – R2, P – B3, and B – B2, after which his position is proof against sudden shocks, and no piece necessary to his queen-side operations has had to withdraw. In the actual play, Black made no effort at a king-side counterattack but tried to stop the queen-side advance.

1	. . . .	N – Q1
2	P – B4	P – QR4
3	P – N3	

A necessary preliminary to P – R3 and P – N4. If at once 3 P – R3, then P – R5 prevents White from ever getting a pawn to QN4.

3	. . . .	P – N3
4	P – R3	N – N2
5	P – N4	R -- R2

Preparing to double rooks. White immediately guards his QR1 to prevent Black from getting command of the file.

6	Q – B3	N – N1
7	N – Q2	KR – R1
8	P – B3	

Black has for the moment prevented the break P – B5 but has thus renounced all hope of a king-side counter. White has the means to strengthen his position (by bringing rooks to the queen

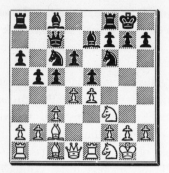

NO. 22. *White to move*

bishop file) while Black has not. White won in a protracted game, keeping the upper hand all the way.

No. 22 arises in another line of the Ruy Lopez. Here P – Q5 confers no advantage on White—he cannot follow up with a queen-side pawn storm. The move is not actually bad but is un-enterprising. Black has a clear-cut strategic objective, which he can reach—to enforce P – KB4. The preparation is long-winded: N – K1, P – KN3, N – KN2, B – Q2, and (if necessary) Q – QB1. Since White might move B – R6 after P – KN3 and then pluck off the knight after N – N2, Black may choose to preface P – KN3 with P – KB3, N – Q1 – B2 so as to stop B – R6. The process eventually may bring five pieces to bear on KB4.

No. 23 arises from the Giuoco Piano. White has the usual edge of center phalanx *v.* chain. An attempt to capitalize it by P – Q5 is futile. In two moves Black can attack the chain by P – KB4.

NO. 23. *White to move*

White is far from being able to storm the queen-side with his pawns; here the Black king bishop is a powerful counterattacker, anyhow. The effect of White's P – Q5 would be to open the line for this bishop, close the line for the White king bishop and leave White with a precarious chain. The proper course for White in No. 23 is to maintain the center tension, develop his pieces and jockey for position.

Salient v. Reverse Salient

A moot question is: which is stronger, a central salient or reverse salient? Most experienced players will probably vote for the salient. But the matter is arguable. The salient is the more frequent, if only because easier to achieve.

Stumpers *v.* Bouwmeester   1955

NO. 24. *White to move*

In the crucial case where a salient and a reverse salient are directly opposed, as in No. 24, one is necessarily more advanced than the other. Analysis will show, we believe, that the more advanced formation, whichever type it is, usually has the edge. Thus in No. 24 White has more space; Black consequently has a more restricted development.

Nevertheless, there is a peculiarity of this formation that favors the reverse salient. The flank attacks by White pawns will hit the *van* of the Black reverse salient, whereas the flank attacks by Black pawns will hit the *base* of the White salient. The attack on the base of a chain is generally more serious than the attack on the van.

This slight edge enjoyed by the reverse salient can overcome the opposing point for greater space only in special circumstances. The present game shows how it can happen.

1 P – QR3	R – B1

White aims for P – QN4 and Black for P – KB4. Perhaps White has already gone astray. The opening of lines against his castled king seems more dangerous than his queen-side counter.

2 P – QN4	N – K1
3 R – N1	

Here is spotlighted the inferiority of the frontal attack. By 3 PxP, PxP, White can establish a protected passed pawn and also somewhat weaken the defense of Black's forward pawns: yet these gains are trifling compared to Black's gain of the "eternal square" Q3 for his knight, whence it hits both bases of the White phalanx. Hence White defers PxP until he can muster a raiding party on the queen-side. But then he is constrained to take defensive measures on the king-side—starting them too late.

3	P – N3
4 R – B1	P – KR3
5 N – K1	Q – K2
6 P – N3	P – B4
7 P – B4	KPxP!

If White retakes on B4 with a piece, Black will have a mighty outpost station on his K4. If 8 NPxP, then PxKP, and White is left with an isolated pawn on an open file. In either case Black has gained an important point and has nullified White's initial superiority in space.

No doubt White could have retained his advantage; nevertheless, the game shows that the reverse salient has more bite than you might think!

SUMMARY

An advanced chain, salient or reverse salient is countable as a point for greater space. You must often discount this point, however, because you can foresee that it is transient.

Like the fourth-rank phalanx, the advanced group does not represent control of the center but usually is an edge toward establishing control. The issue is not settled until the opponent's flank pawns have had their day. If your advanced group survives the flank attack, you are then entitled to count one point for center control.

In extreme cases, where your advanced pawns achieve a permanent bind, you are entitled to debit your opponent one point for his cramped position.

4. *The Advanced Pawn*

IN the last chapter we saw that an advanced chain or salient does not necessarily spell center control, though it usually does imply greater space. In this chapter we consider the question of *when* an advanced formation is countable as center control.

The question hinges primarily on the influence exerted by the advanced pawn. If that influence is sufficiently great, and if the pawn itself is sufficiently secure, then it spells center control.

The matter of *influence* is qualitative, not quantitative. At maximum, a pawn affects three squares, guarding two and plugging a third (against the advance of an enemy pawn). This number is trifling as compared with the average scope of a piece. But the pawn control of a single vital square may outweigh the command of many nonessential squares.

The Benoni Pawn at Q5

Against 1 P – Q4, the Benoni Defense of 1 . . . P – QB4 attempts to swap a wing pawn for an adverse center pawn (with a potential advantage that we have discussed in connection with the Sicilian Defense and the King's Gambit). White moves 2

P – Q5 (no other move is worth a moment's consideration) and the position is No. 25.

The advanced pawn prevents the development of Black's queen knight at B3, wherefore it has to come out at R3, an inferior post, or at Q2, blocking the queen bishop. The Black queen pawn can advance no farther than Q3 in order to let out the queen-side minor pieces, with the result that the king bishop is practically compelled to come out at KN2.

Efforts to dislodge White's advanced pawn by N – KB3, P – K3, etc., are clearly futile, since the pawn can be supported quickly by P – QB4, N – QB3, P – K4, and already is guarded by the queen.

From this cursory analysis of No. 25 we would conclude that White already, at the second move, has *control of the center.* Although the Black center pawns are yet to have their word, we judge that they cannot break the cramp—and experience has not

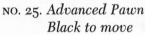

NO. 25. *Advanced Pawn*
          Black to move

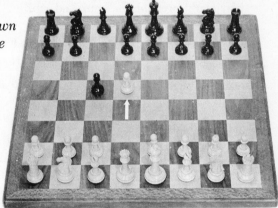

yet upset that verdict, though the Benoni Defense continues to be tried by venturesome souls.

To show how the cursory analysis of No. 25 is borne out, we give the beginning of two crucial games. In the first, Black tries to relieve his center cramp by swapping his king pawn for the White queen bishop pawn, but then White's early P – KB4 establishes the long-lasting threat of P – K5 to create a mighty phalanx on the fifth. In the second game, Black swaps his king pawn against the White king bishop pawn, hoping thereby to secure the outpost station K4 for a knight, but does not succeed.

Taimanov *v*. Trifunovich   1957

1 P – Q4	N – KB3
2 P – QB4	P – B4
3 P – Q5	P – K3
4 N – QB3	PxP
5 PxP	P – Q3
6 P – K4	P – KN3
7 P – B4	

NO. 26A. *Black to move*

This may be regarded as the normal position in one line of the defense. White may already have a won game, though Black's play could probably be improved by 7 . . . P – QR3; 8 P – QR4, B – N2.

| 7 . . . . | B – N2 |
| 8 B – N5ch | KN – Q2 |

Unfortunately, QN – Q2 loses a piece to 9 P – K5 with threat of P – K6.

| 9 B – Q3 | |

Or 9 P – QR4. The idea is to preserve the king bishop against 9 . . . P – QR3 followed by P – QN4.

9	O – O
10 N – B3	N – R3
11 O – O	

NO. 26B. *Black to move*

Now Black is in a bad way. His minor pieces, other than the king bishop, cannot find good posts anywhere; he cannot prevent P – K5 in the long run; even his queen pawn can be menaced by the White knights.

Teschner *v.* Fuderer   1957

1 P – Q4	P – QB4
2 P – Q5	P – K4
3 P – K4	P – Q3
4 P – KB4	

NO. 27A. *Black to move*

In this "normal position" of another Benoni line, 4 . . . PxP has been tried, without conspicuous success, except that in a match game Bogolyubov *v.* Alekhine there followed 5 BxP, Q – R5ch; 6 P – N3, Q – K2, and White let himself be bluffed, playing 7 N – QB3 instead of 7 N – KB3 (for if 7 . . . QxPch, then 8 K – B2! and quickly brings his king rook to the king file). Fuderer tries another plan to keep his K4 open as an outpost station.

4	N – Q2
5 N – KB3	P – KN3
6 PxP	NxP

Black's plan depends on the fact that White cannot now plug the outpost square, for if 7 NxN, Q – R5ch.

| 7 B – N5ch | B – Q2 |
| 8 BxBch | QxB |

Consistent would have been 8 . . . NxB, despite the dangerous loss of time.

9 NxN   PxN
10 O – O

NO. 27B. *Black to move*

Black's position may be tenable, but White certainly has marked
advantage in his protected passed pawn and the half-open king
bishop file through which he can fight against the attempt to
undermine his king pawn by P – KB4.

Black P – Q5 against the English

Against the English Opening, Black may try to get a kind
of Benoni with colors reversed, thus:

1 P – QB4   P – K3
2 P – KN3   P – Q4
3 N – KB3   P – Q5

NO. 28A. *White to move*

Compare the position with No. 25. Suppose that in No. 25 the
Black king knight stood at B3, the king knight pawn at N3, and

it were still *Black's turn to move*. He would be two tempos farther
along in the attack against the advanced pawn. Well, that is precisely White's situation in No. 28A—and the reason why Black's
3 . . . P – Q5 in the English is dubious. The following two typical continuations show how quickly White can frustrate Black's
bid for center control.

4 B – N2	N – QB3
5 O – O	P – K4
6 P – Q3	

NO. 28B. *Black to move*

| 6 . . . . | N – B3 |
| 7 P – QN4! | |

Black must accept the proffered pawn, else it goes on to N5,
displacing the knight, and the Black king pawn is loose.

7	BxP
8 NxKP	NxN
9 Q – R4ch	

Thus White regains his piece and has swapped his queen knight
pawn for the Black king pawn, an advantageous transaction in
itself, here enhanced by the weakening of the advanced queen
pawn.

The other game continued from No. 28B:

6	P – QR4
7 P – K3	B – K2
8 PxP	PxP
9 N – R3!	

Black is compelled to capture this knight, for on QN5 it would
be too strong.

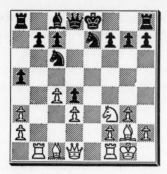

Heinicke *v.* Stahlberg   1955

9 . . . .   BxN
10 PxB   KN – K2
11 R – N1

NO. 28C. *Black to move*

White has by far the better game: the bishop-pair, the half-open file, while Black suffers a queen-side cramp and his queen pawn is shaky. The price that White has paid—the doubled isolated pawn—is small.

P – Q5 in the Ruy Lopez

Comparison of No. 28A with No. 25 suggests that P – Q5 is the less likely to exert a real bind, the later the move is made. This proposition is generally true. In No. 22 we have seen a White P – Q5 late in a Ruy Lopez. We have noted that Black is not inconvenienced; on the contrary, locking of the center allows him to indulge in long-winded preparation for P – KB4. However, P – Q5 is safe—the supporting pawn at White's K4 can be maintained—and the move avoids the immediate opening of the center, if that is White's purpose.

In some analogous positions, P – Q5 to keep the center closed is positively weak. An instance is No. 29. Black threatens BxN,

Yates *v.* Rubinstein   1922

NO. 29. *White to move*

compelling White to compromise his king-side by PxB since QxB
would lose the queen pawn. In the present game, White tried

| 1 | P – Q5 | N – QR4 |
| 2 | B – B2 | P – B3! |

The vital difference between this position and No. 22 is that
here Black can attack the advanced pawn with his queen bishop
pawn. If 3 PxP, Black is left with two-to-one in the center, and
his backward queen pawn can soon advance.

3	P – KR3	BxN
4	QxB	PxP
5	PxP	N – B5

White has a bad game. His queen pawn is virtually isolated,
and the disappearance of his king pawn allows Black to play
P – KB4 quickly, with a virulent attack. This game and others
have led to the conclusion that if, just prior to the position of
No. 29, White wants to move P – Q4 (instead of P – Q3), he must
first play P – KR3 to avoid the pin of his king knight.

Securing an Outpost Station

An important function that an advanced pawn may serve
is to secure a square for an outpost (see Chapter 12). In No. 30
the game continued

Gruenfeld *v.* Lokvenc   1926

NO. 30. *White to move*

| 1 | P – K5 | N – Q4 |

The White advance leaves the queen pawn backward and
abandons the guard of Q5; these concessions are trifling against

the nailing down of Q6. So important is this square that White is already entitled to count a point for full control of the center.

2 N – K4	R – B2
3 P – KN3	B – K1
4 N – Q6	

Manifestly, this outpost is far more menacing than the Black outpost on Q4.

4	N – N3
5 B – N3	N – QB1
6 N – K4	

The White outpost has been ousted—for the moment. But his gross weakness at Q3 has forced Black to "develop backward." Even the king knight cannot be maintained on the third rank (against P – KR4 – R5). White will soon be able to break through against the castled king (N – R4, P – KB4 – B5, etc.).

A similar example of "giving" to get an outpost station is No. 90, p. 129.

P – K5 to Chase the King Knight

The strongest single piece for defense of the castled king is a knight at B3. The prelude to an attack is often to chase this knight from its post.

No. 31 is typical of many positions that fairly cry out for P – K5.

Keres *v.* Szabo   1955

NO. 31. *White to move*

The game continued

1 P – K5	PxP		
2 NxN	PxN		
3 PxP	N – Q2		
4 P – KR4			

The isolated king pawn looks shaky. Black cannot capture it at once (for then QxQ would win a piece) but in the long run its protection may be difficult. No matter! The immediate effect—driving back the king knight—is devastating. Black's king-side is laid bare to an attack for which avenues lie open to all the White pieces, whereas the Black pieces are woefully cramped by the lowly pawn.

4 : . . .	R – N1	7 BxB	RxB
5 Q – K3	R – K1	8 R – N3	R – K1
6 R – R3	Q – R4		

At last threatening to capture the king pawn. Of course 8 . . . NxP or QxP was impossible because of the eventual R – Q8ch and mate.

9 RxN!

White can afford to give up the exchange to save his advanced pawn, which still splits off the Black queen-side pieces from his beleaguered king-side. After five more moves Black resigned.

(9 . . . BxR; 10 B – Q3, P – KR3? 11 Q – B4, K – B1; 12 RxP! KxR; 13 Q – B6ch, K – B1; 14 B – N6 and mate next move.)

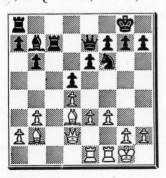

Zukertort v. Blackburne   1883

NO. 32. *White to move*

The ominous P – K5 set the stage for Zukertort's famous brilliancy against Blackburne. From No. 32 the continuation was

1	P – K4	QR – QB1
2	P – K5	N – K1
3	P – B4	

Already threatening P – B5.

3	. . . .	P – N3
4	R – K3	P – B4
5	PxP e.p.	NxP

Black seems to have come off unscathed, for now he threatens N – K5, breaking the force of the attack by cutting off White's king bishop. If White then plays BxN, the disappearance of his bishop lays open his QB2 to invasion by the Black rooks. But Zukertort had prepared his "immortal combination" beginning with *6* P – B5 and won after a blaze of fireworks. (*6* P – B5, N – K5; *7* BxN, PxB; *8* PxNP, R – B7; *9* PxPch, K – R1; *10* P – Q5ch, P – K4; *11* Q – N4, R(1) – B4; *12* R – B8ch, KxP; *13* QxPch, K – N2; *14* BxPch, KxR; *15* B – N7ch, Resigns.)

P – K5 in the French Defense

In the chief line of the French Defense, White moves P – K5, chasing the Black king knight from KB3 (No. 15). In view of the examples above, does this move mean capture of the center? We have already answered this question: it does not. No. 15B differs from the above examples in several important respects:

A] White will have to develop before he can press a kingside attack. Black will have time to prepare a defense and is the better able to do this because at the moment his pieces stand *uncommitted*.

B] Black can immediately launch the normal attack against the White chain (P – QB4). White will be kept busy for a while merely defending his pawns.

c] Black has not yet castled; his option as to where to put his king is an important defensive resource.

That the pawn at K5 can turn into a liability is illustrated in No. 33. Black has duly moved P – QB4 and made one exchange. White has omitted the reinforcement P – KB4; Black can afford to strike the van pawn by

Kitto *v.* Wallace 1955

NO. 33. *Black to move*

1 . . . .   P – B3

If 2 PxP, the White queen pawn remains isolated, and the backwardness of the Black king pawn is insufficient compensation— though this is the better line for White.

2	P – KR4	PxP
3	P – R5	KN – K2
4	PxP	Q – B2

No doubt White permitted the displacement of his queen pawn on the principle that at K5 the pawn is not isolated; perhaps some time White will be able to follow up with P – KB4. But that time is far away! Black's prompt attack on the advanced pawn prevents the White king knight from moving away to clear the path for P – KB4.

5	B – KB4	N – B4
6	B – Q3	N – N5
7	NxN	

White could isolate the Black queen pawn by BxN but would then be in trouble, e.g., 7 BxN, PxB; 8 QN – Q4, Q – B5 with the dire threat of N – Q6ch.

7	BxNch
8 K – B1	O – O

Black has pressure on the king bishop file, plus a protected passed pawn. White resigned a dozen moves later, just ahead of checkmate, his king pawn going lost as a matter of course during the attack.

The Pawn at K5 by Capture

In many opening variations you can post a knight (at least temporarily) on your K5, supported by your queen pawn on the fourth. Your opponent is faced with the question: Is the knight more, or less, bearable than the pawn that will replace it if he captures your outpost?

The answer must be sought mainly in two factors:

A] What is the relative state of development? Will you be able to support your advanced pawn by P – KB4? If so, can you continue with a regulation king-side pawn storm?

B] If he captures, then plays P – KB3 to remove your advanced pawn, will he gain by the file opening or will you gain from the loosening of his king-side pawns?

Euwe v. Bogolyubov   1928

NO. 34. *Black to move*

A typical Queen's Gambit position in which these questions arise is No. 34. The average player would move *1* . . . B – N2 on the principle "If that's no good, my game is no good"—and he

would be right! The actual Black player (Bogolyubov), perhaps
from an excess of his notorious optimism, went in for

1	NxN?
2 PxN	N – Q2
3 B – KB4!	B – N2
4 N – K2	Q – N1
5 N – Q4	

and Black has a miserable game. His queen bishop is bad; he is
going to have to compromise his king-side pawns after Q – R5; if
he plays P – KB3 to get rid of the cramping pawn, the line and
square openings benefit White, not to mention that Black's king
pawn is *en prise*. The displacement of White's queen pawn has
been a boon to him by giving him an "eternal square" for his
knight.

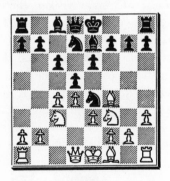

Tarrasch *v.* Von Sheve   1894

NO. 35. *Black to move*

Compare this position with No. 35. Black has just made the
mistake of moving N(B3) – K5. White plays NxN. The comment
by Tarrasch is: "Black is left with a weak king pawn which requires protection. If it is to be maintained permanently . . . P –
KB4 must be played, but then P – B3 renews the attack. Black
must capture, whereupon the king knight file is opened for White.
The result is a combined and irresistible attack with both rooks,
queen, and queen bishop against KN7." All of which came to
pass.

The diametric difference between NxN in No. 34 and in No. 35 comes about from the present posts and future prospects of the pieces. In No. 35 the Black queen bishop is still locked behind its own pawns; in No. 34 the White queen bishop is outside its pawns. In No. 34 the capture gives White access to his Q4; in No. 35 the White queen bishop pawn denies Black access to his Q4. In No. 34 Black has castled; in No. 35, White has not. Indeed, in No. 35 White played O – O – O so as to preserve the freedom of his king-side pawns to advance without exposing his own king.

The Pawn at KB5 by Capture

When the king pawn arrives at KB5 by a capture, it usually is weaker than would be the original king bishop pawn advanced to B5, for (a) the latter can be backed up by rooks on the file, and (b) the capture *away from the center* may weaken center control. Still, the advanced doubled pawn may on occasion be strong. An obvious case is No. 36. Black moves *1 . . . N – B5!* and the outpost is powerful. If 2 BxN, PxB, the pawn restricts the White king knight and nails down the holes around the White king, while the disappearance of White's queen bishop aggravates the danger. The advanced pawn is clearly safe from capture.

Dus-Chotimirsky *v.* Capablanca, 1925   Alekhine *v.* Capablanca, 1914

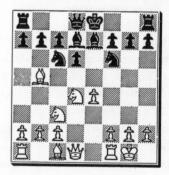

NO. 36. *Black to move*   NO. 37. *White to move*

A picture on the other side is No. 37. In this regular Ruy Lopez position, White experimented with

1	N – B5	BxN
2	PxB	O – O

It seems likely that the advanced pawn cannot be adequately defended by pieces alone; P – KN4 will be necessary sooner or later. Therefore P – KN4 should be played immediately, and White should quickly regroup his pieces to support a king-side pawn storm. This will involve some danger to his own king, for Black has no weaknesses and is well developed. Undoubtedly he can work out strong counterplay through the center. If White is unwilling to face that prospect, he should not have played 1 N – B5.

White actually shrank from the positional necessities (Alekhine, no less!) and continued

3	R – K1	N – Q2
4	N – Q5	B – B3
5	P – QB3	N – N3
6	NxBch	QxN
7	BxN	PxB

Perhaps White should have saved his king bishop for defense of his pawn on B5—but then Black would have had another knight with which to attack it. The exchange doubles a Black pawn, which White hopes will be as weak as his own. But, as one would expect, the hope was frustrated. The waif at B5 presently went lost, and with it, the game.

SUMMARY

Count one point for an advanced pawn that is reasonably safe and either cramps the opponent's development or prevents his occupation of a square vital to his defense against an attack.

5. *Delayed Central Pawn Advances*

WE have repeatedly warned that you cannot count a point for "control of the center" merely because you have a fourth-rank phalanx, or an advanced chain or salient. Control depends on the outcome of the fight when your opponent's pawns "are heard from."

This advice is the more necessary because it is feasible, in certain opening variations, to establish a sufficient control of the center by pieces alone before advancing either center pawn. The delayed pawn advances are then particularly powerful.

The English Opening

A regular line of the English Opening is

1	P – QB4	N – KB3
2	P – KN3	P – K3
3	B – N2	P – Q4
4	N – KB3	PxP

For comment on *4* . . . P – Q5 see No. 28.

5	Q – R4ch	B – Q2
6	QxBP	B – B3
7	O – O	QN – Q2
8	Q – B2	B – K2?

The bishop belongs on Q3 to support P – K4, without which Black gives White too free a hand in the center.

Filip *v.* Euwe 1955

9 N – B3	O – O
10 R – Q1	N – N3

NO. 38. *White to move*

Black controls only his Q4; White controls the other three center squares by pieces alone. The advance of his central pawns, long delayed, now gives him an overwhelming center.

11 P – K4	Q – B1
12 P – Q4	

The Benoni Defense

A regular position of the Benoni is brought about thus:

1 P – Q4	N – KB3	5 PxP	P – Q3
2 P – QB4	P – K3	6 N – B3	P – KN3
3 N – KB3	P – B4	7 P – KN3	
4 P – Q5	PxP		

The fianchetto, with delay of P – K4 and P – KB4, is one of the two main lines against the Benoni. The other line, illustrated in No. 26A, involves making both these pawn advances as early as possible and therefore delaying N – KB3.

Florian *v.* Kluger 1955

7	B – N2
8 B – N2	O – O
9 O – O	R – K1
10 N – Q2	

NO. 39A. *Black to move*

The center control is balanced: White controls the light squares and Black the dark. But White still has two unmoved pawns available to dispute Black's share. Black has the usual difficulty in developing his queen-side. The queen bishop, particularly, is a problem. Black's plan to swap it off seems plausible but turns out poorly in this game.

10	P – N3
11 P – QR4	

The "reception committee" goes into action!

11	B – QR3
12 N – N5	BxN
13 PxB	QN – Q2
14 P – R3	

There is no rush about the central pawn advances, since they cannot be prevented. White forestalls N – N5.

14	P – QR4

In order, at least, to release the queen rook from guarding the pawn. Naturally White does not capture e.p., for then with P – QN4 and Q – N3 Black would gain some space.

15 R – K1	R – QB1
16 R – R4	

Smothering the hope of counterplay based on P – B5.

NO. 39B. *Black to move*

16	N – R4
17 P – KN4	KN – B3
18 P – B4	N – B1
19 P – K4	KN – Q2
20 N – B4	

Tableau! White's center is overwhelming; against an eventual P – K5 Black is helpless.

The Giuoco Pianissimo

Though you are advised to count a point for pawn on fourth *v.* pawn on third (e.g., No. 11), you must realize that this point is often transient. It disappears if the third-rank pawn can advance without loss to the fourth. Even though the advance be long delayed, the advantage enjoyed meanwhile by the fourth-rank pawn may be merely "pictorial."

One of the most memorable of delayed pawn advances occurred in Steinitz *v.* Tchigorin, 1892, our No. 40. Steinitz, as White, often adopted the restrained pawn formation: K4, Q3, QB3. The present game opened as a Ruy Lopez, but this pawn formation may be regarded as characteristic of the Giuoco Pianissimo rather than of the Ruy. Keeping his center pawns intact (except for swap of the king pawn for the queen pawn), Steinitz had posted his bishops to rake the Black king-side and had opened the king rook file. Finally, after a delay of twenty moves,

Steinitz *v.* Tchigorin   1892

NO. 40. *White to move*

1 P – Q4!

The advance is now murderous. Black is compelled to capture.

1	PxP
2 NxP	BxN

Again Black must capture—with the bishop. If he plays NxN the game ends suddenly by *3* RxPch, KxR; *4* Q – R1ch, B – R3; *5* QxB mate.

3 RxB!   NxR

White recaptures with the rook to save his bishop for the last recapture—with a fatal check. He threatens 4 R(4) – KR4, threatening both RxPch and B – Q4. The only alternative to 3 . . . NxR is R – K2, but this does not save Black for long. After the text move, White is mated by a combination beginning 4 RxPch.

The King's Indian

Delay in the advance of a center pawn, the better to prepare it, is a feature of a number of modern opening variations. Much played in recent tournaments is the King's Indian Defense:

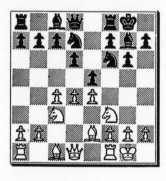

1	P – Q4	N – KB3
2	P – QB4	P – KN3
3	N – QB3	B – N2
4	P – K4	P – Q3
5	N – B3	O – O
6	B – K2	QN – Q2
7	O – O	P – K4

NO. 41. *White to move*

The effect of Black's preparations for P – K4 is that White cannot long maintain the center tension: he will soon have to release it by PxP or P – Q5. Black has the means to increase his own pressure on the center, particularly the king pawn by R – K1 and Q – K2. With the removal of the White queen pawn, Black gains his K4 or QB4 as an outpost station.

Numerous Black successes with this defense have led to its adoption, on occasion, by White with a move in hand. It is then the King's Indian Attack:

1 N – KB3	N – KB3
2 P – KN3	P – Q4
3 B – N2	B – B4
4 O – O	P – K3

NO. 42. *White to move*

White now prepares to enforce P – K4.

5 P – Q3	P – B3
6 QN – Q2	QN – Q2
7 Q – K1	P – KR3
8 P – K4	

The Colle System

We have remarked that White, by virtue of his first move, can establish a fourth-rank phalanx at once, if he wishes, while Black can form only a chain against it. In the Colle System, White lets Black form the phalanx, the better to prepare his own thrust against it.

1 P – Q4	P – Q4
2 N – KB3	N – KB3
3 P – K3	

This is a voluntary loss of a tempo, since the pawn is to go to K4 later.

3	P – B4
4 P – B3	P – K3
5 B – Q3	B – Q3

The neophyte should observe that 5 . . . P – B5 here (and in analogous positions) would be a mistake. White can soon move P – K4; Black is compelled to take (else P – K5), and his pawn at QB5 is then precariously posted.

Colle *v.* O'Hanlon   1930

6 QN – Q2	QN – Q2
7 O – O	O – O
8 R – K1	R – K1

NO. 43. *White to move*

The positions are nearly symmetrical, but White comes first with P – K4. The effect of his extensive preparation is evident:

9 P – K4	QPxP
10 NxP	NxN
11 BxN	

The White king bishop, king knight and queen stand poised for a quick king-side attack based on the elimination of the defensive knight at KB3. The half-open king file will enable White to post his knight on K5, where it (or the pawn that takes its place in the event of its capture) will be supported by the rook.

The correct move in the present position is *11 . . .* N – B3. The peril for Black inherent in the position is illustrated by the brilliancy prize game Colle *v.* O'Hanlon:

11	PxP?
12 BxPch!	KxB
13 N – N5ch	K – N3

If K – N1, Q – R5 wins in a hurry.

| 14 P – KR4 | R – R1 |
| 15 RxPch | N – B3 |

If PxR, Q – Q3ch leads to mate.

| 16 P – R5ch and wins | |

For if *16 . . .* RxP; then *17* Q – Q3ch, K – R3; *18* Q – R7 mate.

Hypermodernism and Its Dangers

The plan of delaying a center-pawn advance until it is thoroughly prepared, especially by fianchetto of both bishops, has proved so fascinating that it has acquired a name, "hypermodernism." Carried to excess, the plan can be self-defeating; the opponent may be able to set up an impregnable center. At all events, if you let your opponent advance his center pawns unopposed, you must at every move make sure that you retain the possibility of smashing back at them and gaining your fair share of space. To show the negative side of the case fairly, we have selected two games played by leading exponents of hypermodernism.

1	N – KB3	P – Q4
2	P – B4	P – QB3
3	P – QN3	

With 3 P – Q4 White can go into a favorable variation of the Slav Defense. But Reti was intent on the idea of keeping the diagonal open for his fianchettoed queen bishop—and this game was hailed as important to theory in showing that the idea is probably impractical.

3	B – B4	6	B – N2		P – K3
4 P – N3	N – B3	7	O – O		B – Q3
5 B – KN2	QN – Q2	8	P – Q3		

Consistent, but inferior to P – Q4.

Reti *v.* Dr. Lasker   1924

8		O – O
9 QN – Q2		P – K4

NO. 44. *White to move*

The verdict of analysis is that Black has a better game than he can expect to get after an early P – Q4 by White. He has the center phalanx, and White must continually reckon with its advances. His queen bishop is out in the open, instead of locked in at home as it is in so many of the queen pawn openings. (Black won the game, but we cannot attribute the victory to his slight edge after move 9. Tactical errors were made by both sides in the very difficult midgame.)

	1	P – QB4	P – KB4
	2	P – QN3	P – K4

The classicist Mieses says, "If you give me the center I'll take it!"

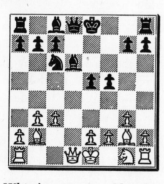

Nimzovich *v.* Mieses   1920

3	N – QB3	N – KB3
4	B – N2	P – Q4!
5	PxP	NxP
6	P – N3	NxN
7	PxN	B – Q3
8	B – N2	N – B3

NO. 45. *White to move*

White's prospects of breaking the Black phalanx are dim. Thus, if P – K4, the opening of the king bishop file will profit Black after O – O, Q – B3, etc. White has nothing better than restrained development (P – K3 and N – K2). In the long run Black's advantages (center control, superior development, mobile king-side pawns) should triumph. Realizing this, White tries to create mere tactical difficulties for Black.

9	Q – Q5	Q – K2
10	P – K4	B – K3
11	Q – N5	O – O!
12	QxNP	

If White does not take the pawn he has nothing to show for his increased lag in development.

12	B – Q2
13 Q – R6	QR – N1
14 N – B3	

No doubt with the idea that if PxP, then N – Q2 and gains the outpost station K4. But Black's lead is now so overwhelming that he can embark on a sacrificial combination.

14 . . . . N – N5! and wins

(15 PxN, BxPch; 16 N – Q2, B – N4; 17 QxP, BxNch; 18 KxB, Q – Q3ch; 19 K – B2, B – Q6ch; 20 K – B3, R – N3; 21 Q – R5, Q – Q5ch; 22 K – Q2, QxPch; 23 KxB, R – Q1ch; 24 Q – Q5ch, RxQch; 25 PxR, P – K5ch; 26 K – B3, Q – K6ch; 27 K – B2, Q – Q6ch; 28 K – B1, R – N4; 29 B – QR3, RxQP; 30 B – B1, Q – K6ch; 31 K – B2, R – Q7ch; 32 K – N1, R – Q8ch; 33 K – N2, Q – Q7 mate.)

Too Much Preparation

An instructive example of a center advance postponed too long is No. 46A. Here both sides have developed in hypermodern fashion, keeping the queen pawns at home. It is now high time for White to strike with P – Q4. Instead, he hopes to improve his position by another preparatory move:

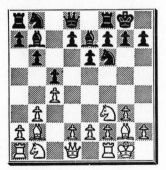

Shainswit v. Denker   1939

NO. 46A. *White to move*

1 N – B3?	P – Q4!
2 PxP	NxP

White must capture; he cannot stand P – Q5. Black recaptures with the knight to avoid the hanging pawns that might result from 2 . . . PxP; 3 P – Q4.

3 N – K5	NxN
4 PxN	BxB

5 KxB	Q – B2

NO. 46B. *White to move*

If we examine No. 46B dynamically, we see that White will have to expend three moves merely to consolidate his loose forces: one to retreat the knight, one to get the queen off the open file, and P – QB4 to get his bishop back into the game. Black, meanwhile, can make three forward-looking moves: B – B3, N – B3 and R – Q1. The upshot of White's *1* N – B3 (instead of P – Q4) has thus been, not a pawn weakness in the center, but a marked lag in development.

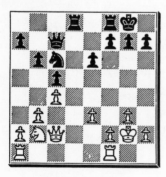

6 P – QB4	B – B3
7 N – Q3	BxB
8 NxB	N – B3
9 P – K3	QR – Q1
10 Q – B2	

NO. 46C. *Black to move*

The White knight is poorly placed—except for one purpose, dispute of the queen file. Thus, if Black doubles rooks to try to hold the file, 10 . . . R – Q2; 11 KR – Q1, KR – Q1; 12 RxR, the reply . . . QxR is useless because of 13 R – Q1. Black therefore ignores the file and plays his trump card—his mobile pawn wing in conjunction with the White king-side holes.

10 . . . .   P – KN4!

Threatening P – N5 followed by N – K4 – B6. White might have tried 11 P – KR3 or even P – B4; his actual move is hopeless.

11	Q – K4?	R – Q7
12	N – Q3	Q – Q3
13	QR – Q1	

Losing a piece, but if the knight retreats Black plays P – B4 and N – K4 with an overwhelming position.

13	. . . .	P – B4
14	Q – B3	P – N5
15	Q – B4	QxN
	Resigns	

SUMMARY

If your opponent allows you a free hand in the center, do not assume that you control it merely because your pawns occupy it. You may have to reckon with a strongly prepared, though delayed, counterthrust.

If you yourself delay a center advance, the better to prepare it, watch your timing! Don't overprepare!

6. *The Mobile Pawn Wing*

THE classic pattern of a direct attack against the castled king, as laid down by Philidor, Anderssen, Morphy et al., consists in pawn advances to batter the pawns in front of the enemy king, supported and eventually supplanted by pieces that utilize the lines thus opened. Many instances are seen in the games we cite elsewhere, notably Nos. 18 and 32.

Now, when both players castle on the same side, a wing-pawn advance by one player against the other's king leaves his own king exposed. Why, it may be asked, does he not imperil himself even more than his opponent? We cannot dismiss the hazard in denuding the king of his pawn protection; our Chapter 13 is devoted to this hazard.

The paradox is easily resolved. A player can afford to denude his own king if the opponent's chances of counterattack, especially by a breakthrough in the center, are slight. The first player must, in other words, already enjoy a considerable positional superiority. Specifically, he must have *control of the center* (or *greater space* behind stopped center pawns) and *superior development*, consisting in the ability to bring a larger or more effective force to bear upon a relatively small sector than his opponent can muster to its defense.

A Typical Morphy Attack

These conditions are met by White in No. 47A. His two bishops already rake the Black king-side. His two knights can quickly reach the battlefront, and so can his queen and king rook after the opening of lines. Black, on the other hand, has only four pieces in the vicinity of his king. The White king-side pawns are mobile: they are unobstructed, and no Black piece even guards the fourth-rank squares before them.

Morphy *v.* Meek 1857

NO. 47A. *White to move*

The White advanced chain cannot be destroyed (as by P – QB4 and P – KB3), so that Black has no prospect of breaking through the center.

| 1 P – KB4 | P – KB4 |

Necessary to delay White's P – B5 and to open the second rank for Black's defense. In some instances, White does best to answer P – KB4 with PxP e.p., then mass against the backward Black king pawn (as in No. 55)—but this is not one of them.

| 2 P – KR3 | N – Q2 |
| 3 K – R2 | |

Vacating the file for the benefit of the rook. An important part of the process is to dispose the pieces to best advantage behind the pawns before making the break.

| 3 . . . . | P – B4 |

Striving for counterplay. White of course wants to leave the center blocked.

| 4 P – B3 | P – B5 |
| 5 B – QB2 | P – QR3? |

The logical continuation is P – QN4, P – QR4 and P – QN5. However, this counterattack is too slow to stem the tide of events on the king-side.

6 N – B3   P – R3

NO. 47B. *White to move*

As so often happens, the defending party is compelled to make a strategically weakening move to parry a tactical threat (N – N5).

7 P – KN4	K – R2
8 R – KN1	R – KN1
9 Q – K1	N – QB3?
10 N – R4	Q – KB1

NO. 47C. *White to move*

The only chance was N – KB1. White can now capitalize his great advantage by a combination.

11 NxNP and wins

(*11* . . . KxN; *12* PxPch, K – B2; *13* PxPch, KxP; *14* P – B5ch, K – K2; *15* Q – R4ch, K – K1; *16* P – B6, BxP; *17* PxB, RxR; *18* RxR, NxBP; *19* B – N6ch, K – Q2; *20* B – B5ch, K – K1; *21* BxP, Q – R1; *22* R – N7, N – KN1 and White mates in three.)

The Cramped Position

A cramped position in itself invites a pawn storm since it is likely to confer on the opponent the two points prerequisite for success.

Reshevsky *v.* Persitz   1958

NO. 48A. *White to move*

In No. 48A, Black is cramped in the center by his own queen pawn. If he plays P – Q3 and P – K4 his king bishop becomes even more obstructed than it already is. The only solution appears to be to move P – Q4 on the principle that if the move is no good then Black's game is no good. Instead:

1 N – K1	Q – B2
2 P – B4	QR – Q1
3 P – KN4	N – Q5

Black wastes time in preparing the thrust he could have made at once by 1 . . . N – Q5; 2 P – B4, P – Q4—and now never gets time to make it at all. Observe, incidentally, that White gives Black the outpost station freely, for the knight contributes little to either defense or offense. In fact, the only value of its move is to clear the line for the queen bishop to support a center thrust.

4 P – N5	N – K1
5 P – B5	P – N3

Black rightly fears Q – R5. If 5 . . . P – B3; 6 P – N6, P – KR3; 7 Q – R5, and there is no defense to 8 BxP. But the text move is likewise inadequate.

5	B – B4	Q – B1
6	P – B6	B – Q3
7	BxB	NxB
8	Q – N4 and wins	

NO. 48B. *Black to move*

The White queen goes to KR6, compelling the Black knight to stay on K1. Then White brings a rook to KR3 or KR4, and Black can avert mate only at frightful cost of material.

Expansion on "General Principles"

Assault upon the enemy king is not the only legitimate motive for advancing a pawn wing. The mere gain of space for maneuver often brings wide benefits.

In No. 49A, Black's "hedgehog" development invites White to expand, particularly on the queen-side, since the king bishop already points in that direction.

Tartakover *v.* Saunders   1924

NO. 49A. *White to move*

1	P – Q4	P – KB4
2	N – B3	P – B3
3	P – QN4	N – B3
4	P – QR4	

White need not trouble to calculate what he is going to do with his tremendous quadruple phalanx. Against such a backward Black formation one can push pawns on general principles, trusting that specific threats will issue in due time.

4		R – N1
5 P – N5		B – Q2

Black dare not play PxP, for after RPxP his queen rook pawn would soon go lost.

6 Q – Q3		Q – K1
7 P – K4		

Even this! Now Black is threatened by P – K5. His next move is the only hope, but for lack of adequate preparation it merely opens lines for White's benefit.

7		P – K4
8 QPxP		QPxP
9 Q – Q6		PxKP
10 N – N5		N – B4
11 Q – B7		

NO. 49B. *Black to move*

The queen is safe. White will plant a knight solidly on his K4 and then resume the massacre of Black's queen-side.

The Potential Passed Pawn

Another purpose in advancing a pawn wing may be to establish an actual or potential passed pawn. (See also Chapter 21.) This operation is of course the soul of the endgame but is by no means limited to that phase.

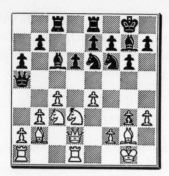

Blau *v*. Golombek   1955

NO. 50A. *White to move*

In No. 50A, the excellent placement of the White pieces enables him to sweep forward on the queen-side.

1	P – QN4	Q – N3
2	N – Q5	BxN
3	KPxB	N – B1

Thus White not only increases the range of his king bishop but also gains a pawn majority on the queen-side.

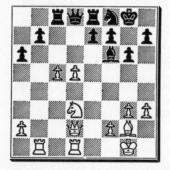

4	P – B5	PxP
5	PxP	Q – Q1
6	BxN!	BxB
7	QR – N1	

NO. 50B. *Black to move*

Here is an isolated phalanx that does not hang! It can be backed up by all five White pieces. Its further advance threatens to establish (and did) a passed pawn, costing Black a piece.

Restraint of a Pawn Wing

Of the celebrated game cited in our example No. 51, one analyst remarked, "Nimzovich has demonstrated that a pawn wing which cannot advance if it wants to is a fatal weakness in itself!" Perhaps this assertion is extreme, but certainly if your pawn mobility falls markedly below that of your opponent you stand in danger of strangulation.

Once a pawn storm against you gets under way, you must formulate a plan either (a) to break the force of the assault or (b) to counterattack through the center or on the other wing. Most desirable, however—and also most difficult—is to restrain the adverse pawn wing from advancing at all.

Johner *v.* Nimzovich 1926

NO. 51A. *Black to move*

In No. 51A, the White king-side pawns are highly mobile. The king bishop pawn is already at the fourth. With a few moves (P – KN4, P – KN5, P – KB5) White can launch a classic attack. How is Black to defend himself? Counterattack through the blocked center is impossible, while a general advance on the queen-side would surely be too slow. In this precarious position, Black finds an extraordinary resource:

  1 . . . .   **Q – Q2!!**

With the purpose, above all, of preventing the immediate P – KN4. But this looks like a feeble resource in view of White's obvious reply.

  2 P – KR3   **N – K2**

The idea is to meet 3 P – N4 with P – KR4, then if 4 P – N5, QxP and, if White captures the knight, Black has at least perpetual check; he might even try for more with N – B4.

  3 Q – K1   **P – KR4!**

Black seizes the opportunity to prevent P – N4 forever.

4 B – Q2   Q – B4!

5 K – R2   Q – R2!

NO. 51B. *White to move*

What a change from diagram 51A! White can no longer hope to play P – N4 or P – KB5. Black threatens to get a crippling bind by N – B4, P – R5, N – N6. White is thrown on the defensive, and in fact it is now *Black* who has a mobile king-side pawn wing. After due preparation Black smashed through with P – KN4 – N5. (*6* P – QR4, N – B4; *7* P – N3, P – R4; *8* R – KN1, N – R3; *9* B – KB1, B – Q2; *10* B – B1, QR – B1; *11* P – Q5, K – R1; *12* N – Q2, R – KN1; *13* B – KN2, P – KN4; *14* N – B1, R – N2; *15* R – R2, N – B4; *16* B – R1, QR – KN1; *17* Q – Q1, PxP; *18* KPxP, B – B1; *19* Q – N3, B – R3; *20* R – K2, N – R5; *21* R – K3, B – B1; *22* Q – B2, BxP; *23* BxP, B – B4; *24* BxB, NxB; *25* R – K2, P – R5; *26* R(1) – N2, PxPch; *27* K – N1, Q – R6; *28* N – K3, N – R5; *29* K – B1, R – K1; *30* Resigns.)

SUMMARY

Regard a pawn wing as truly mobile if it can actually move forward with (a) intrinsic safety and (b) tangible gain. If the gain is solely in space to maneuver, do not count an extra point for the mobile wing in addition to a point credited for greater space. However, the extra point is countable in extreme cases, as when the adverse pieces are held back in a long-lasting cramp. Also, count the mobile wing as an extra point when you already hold the two key advantages: center superiority (if not full control) and superior development.

7.   *The Backward Pawn*

IN this chapter and the next four we study certain minus points—pawn formations that are regarded as intrinsically weak. But to this characterization we must make some realistic reservations.

The theoretical weakness of a backward pawn, doubled pawn, etc., almost invariably becomes a reality in endplay. But, as Dr. Tarrasch remarked, "before the endgame the gods have placed the midgame!" Before enough heavy pieces have been swapped off so that the kings can sally into the center, a backward pawn (for example) may be

A] tolerable, for the greater gain achieved at cost of the weakness, or

B] neutral, because its weakness cannot be capitalized, or

c] irrelevant, because the issue is going to be decided by the battle of pieces, or

D] strong, through peculiarities (usually transient) of the position, or

E] weak, for the reasons expected in endplay—or even weaker!

The system advises you to count each of these pawn formations as a minus point. But you naturally must look at it dynamically. Ask yourself: Is the formation permanent or transient? Can it be capitalized by any foreseeable process in the midgame? What are the chances that pieces can be swapped off to bring about an endgame?

The Crippled Majority

By definition, a backward pawn cannot be advanced without loss, and it is subject to attack on the file. The first aspect is likely to be decisive in endplay, as is illustrated schematically in No. 52. White's single pawn on the queen-side holds back two Black pawns, owing to the backwardness of the queen knight pawn. White's majority on the other side, not being crippled,

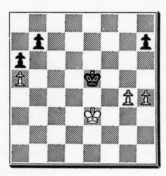

NO. 52. *White wins*

threatens to generate a passed pawn. The Black king cannot leave this side until the pawns have been entirely dissolved, so that the White king, unimpeded, can march to the queen-side and capture both Black pawns there. White need only time his play so that the Black king cannot get over to the queen-side soon enough to draw against the queen rook pawn. For example: *1* K – B3, K – B3; *2* K – B4, K – K3; *3* P – N5, K – B2; *4* K – B5, K – N2; *5* P – R5, K – B2; *6* P – R6, K – K2; *7* P – N6, PxPch; *8* KxP, K – B1; *9* K – B6 and goes to the queen-side. Or, if Black moves first in No. 52: *1* . . . K – B3; *2* K – K4, K – K3; *3* P – N5, K – B2; *4* K – Q5 and queens the queen rook pawn in time to stop the Black king rook pawn.

The Queen Bishop Pawn in the Queen's Gambit

In the midgame, the weakness of a backward pawn is most likely to arise from frontal attack.

A major variation of the Queen's Gambit is

1 P – Q4	P – Q4	5 P – K3	B – K2
2 P – QB4	P – K3	6 N – B3	O – O
3 N – QB3	N – KB3	7 R – B1	
4 B – N5	QN – Q2		

As in many variations of the queen pawn opening, Black is faced with the problem of how to get his queen bishop into play. One attempt, in the Orthodox Defense, is the immediate fianchetto:

7 . . . .   P – QN3

NO. 53A. *White to move*

White's best continuation is

8 PxP   PxP

The swap looks paradoxical, because it gives the Black queen bishop an avenue to the king-side. But 7 . . . P – QN3 has left the queen bishop pawn backward; by opening the queen bishop file for his rook (for complete discussion of half-open and open files, consult Chapters 18 and 19), White obtains powerful play against it. One of the definitive games, Capablanca *v.* Teichmann, 1913, continued:

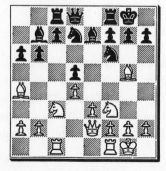

Capablanca *v.* Teichmann   1913

9 B – N5	B – N2
10 O – O	P – QR3
11 B – QR4	R – B1
12 Q – K2	

NO. 53B. *Black to move*

Black is faced with the typical dilemma. If he leaves his queen bishop pawn at home, it is weak and also cramps his own center; if he advances it, he acquires either a "hanging phalanx" or an isolated queen pawn. Yet there is no real choice; the backward pawn is too easy a target.

12	P – B4
13 PxP	NxP
14 KR – Q1	

Black has chosen the isolated queen pawn, and White immediately trains his guns on it. The same move would be a powerful reply to *13* . . . PxP.

Another instance of the dilemma of the queen bishop pawn is No. 54, which arose from a King's Indian Defense in Alekhine *v.* Reti, 1924. Black has solved the problem of the queen bishop: by enforcing P – K4 he has gotten the bishop out and swapped it for the White king knight. But White has established a strong advanced pawn, which cramps the Black center. It deprives the Black queen knight of its natural post at B3, but both players regarded its effect on the queen bishop pawn as paramount. Says

Alekhine *v.* Reti   1924

NO. 54. *Black to move*

Alekhine in his notes, "Black has to make a choice between three distinct evils: I. Weakness on QB2, in case he should allow the pawn position to remain intact. II. Weakness on QB3, in case, after P – B4, PxP e.p., he should recapture with the pawn and later on be forced to play P – Q4. III. And, finally, the line actu-

ally selected by him [1 . . . P – B4; 2 PxP e.p., NxP] through
which he obtains an isolated QP . . ."

The King Pawn in a Classical King-Side Attack

Against a king-side attack, the defender is often compelled
to move P – KB4, either to block the adverse king bishop pawn or
to intercept the adverse king bishop. But if the defender's king
pawn has not reached the fourth or been swapped off, P – KB4
leaves it backward, a possibly fatal weakness.

Capablanca *v.* Blanco   1913

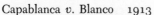

NO. 55A. *White to move*

In No. 55A, White seizes the opportunity to force a weakening
pawn move on the Black king-side.

1 Q – R3   P – KB4

Best; P – KN3 leaves a hole at KN2, and P – KR3 allows the
winning sacrifice BxP. Now the Black king is safe, but the backward king pawn is a new target.

2 BxB	QxB	5 R – K2	B – Q2
3 O – O	R – B3	6 QR – K1	R – K1
4 KR – K1	N – Q3	7 P – QB4	N – B2

Already White could win a pawn by 8 NxB, QxN; 9 BxP, but
Black would then get counterplay by QxP. So White increases the
pressure.

8 P – Q5   NxN

Not *8* . . . BPxP; *9* PxP, PxP?; *10* NxB, QxN; *11* RxRch.

9 RxN   P – KN3
10 Q – R4   K – N2

Else White could play *11* P – Q6. But now the king stands on a line of potential pin.

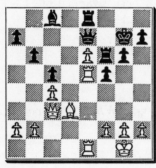

11 Q – Q4   P – B4
12 Q – B3   P – N3
13 PxP   B – B1

NO. 55B. *White to move*

Now White has won the weakling. Though Black can win the pawn back, he thereby gets into a deadly pin.

14 B – K2   BxP
15 B – B3   K – B2
16 B – Q5 and wins

(*16* . . . Q – Q3; *17* Q – K3, R – K2; *18* Q – R6, K – N1; *19* P – KR4, P – R3; *20* P – R5, P – B5; *21* PxP, PxP; *22* RxB, Resigns.)

The Acceptable Backward Pawn

A backward pawn is bearable in certain circumstances, as when

A] it can safely be advanced before it becomes fixed, or
B] the opponent cannot open the file to attack it frontally, or
C] it can be sheltered by an outpost ahead of it on the file.

A regular posit·on of the Ruy Lopez is shown in No. 56. White usually continues P – B3 (before or after castling) both to provide

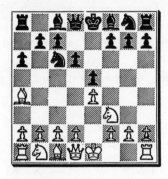

NO. 56. *White to move*

a haven for the king bishop and to support the later P – Q4. White aims for a fourth-rank phalanx. A different idea is the Duras move of 5 P – B4. This holds back the White queen pawn and temporarily makes it backward while White makes preparation to bring a rook to the queen file and then open it by P – Q4 and PxP. The move is clearly playable, since both foregoing conditions [A] and [B] obtain. For example: 5 P – B4, B – Q2; 6 N – B3, P – KN3; 7 P – Q4. A more active effort to prevent this move is 5 . . . B – N5; 6 N – B3, N – K2; 7 P – KR3, BxN; 8 QxB, N – N3; 9 N – Q5, R – QN1; 10 N – N4, N – K2; 11 N – B2 (Keres *v.* Reshevsky), and White can enforce P – Q4 just the same.

The condition [C] is illustrated in Nos. 30 and 90. The situation is epitomized in No. 57. With P – K5 White leaves his queen pawn

NO. 57. *White to move*

backward, but he also prepares an outpost station for his knight, and on arrival at Q6 the knight will shield the queen pawn from frontal attack. An added feature of many such positions is that Black is virtually compelled to post a minor piece on the square abandoned by the advancing pawn (N – Q4), if only to avoid a cramp by its retreat elsewhere. Then the backward pawn is shielded from frontal attack so long as the outpost maintains its position.

The Queen Pawn in the Sicilian Defense

After the opening moves

1 P – K4	P – QB4	4 NxP	N – B3
2 N – KB3	N – QB3	5 N – QB3	
3 P – Q4	PxP		

we reach No. 58A, a frequent position of the Sicilian Defense. Black has a half-open queen bishop file, the logical complement

NO. 58A. *Black to move*

to which is a bishop at KN2. If Black moves at once 5 . . . P – KN3, White can play 6 NxN and if QPxN, away goes the half-open file, or if NPxN, then 7 P – K5 and Black has to "undevelop" his knight. Usual, therefore, is the preparatory move

5 . . . .   P – Q3

Now White can forestall the fianchetto by

6 B – KN5

for 6 ... P – KN3?; 7 BxN would leave Black with a wretched isolated queen pawn. Hence

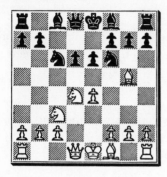

6 ....   P – K3

NO. 58B. *White to move*

Black reconciles himself to a backward queen pawn. That the frontal attack upon it is a real threat is attested by such a variation as

7	Q – Q2	B – K2	9 N(4) – N5
8	O – O – O	O – O?	

and something has to give. Naturally, this variation is not the final word. But if Black is to avoid some such outcome, he must sooner or later move P – QR3 to forestall N – N5; the formation necessary to protect the queen pawn while preparing its advance is: bishop at K2, queen at B2, rook at Q1. In a variation now fashionable, Black omits N – QB3 in order to play P – QR3 early, leading to No. 59.

NO. 59. *White to move*

Since the logical plan for White is a king-side attack to offset Black's queen-side operations, a natural continuation is

> 7 P – B4

This move prepares for P – B5 or P – K5, according to circumstances. Various continuations have been tried by Black. One is

> 7 . . . .   Q – N3
>
> 8 Q – Q2

Owing to his large lead in development, White can let his queen knight pawn go, as is seen in No. 129.

Another try from position No. 59 is

> 7 . . . .   B – K2
>
> 8 Q – B3   P – KR3
>
> 9 B – R4   P – KN4

and the subsequent triple catastrophe to Argentina is recounted in No. 119.

In the position of No. 58A, a modern variation begins 5 . . . P – K4 (No. 60). A generation ago, this move would have been roundly condemned—"A backward pawn on the open file! Unthinkable!" Yet it has a logic that is borne out by experience. The queen pawn is going to become backward anyhow, unless Black is allowed to fianchetto his king bishop in peace, and so can leave his king pawn at home. On K3, it is true, the pawn supports P – Q4 when and if that advance can be made. Meanwhile, the

NO. 60. *White to move*

third-rank phalanx inflicts Black with a case of central congestion. By P – K4, Black opens the square K3 to his queen bishop, whence it supports P – Q4 as well as would a pawn there. But the central congestion is less. And the gain of a tempo by the attack on White's knight is not trivial; as we have seen in some of the examples, Black is in continual danger of falling too far behind in development. (If White seeks to save the tempo by 6 NxN instead of retreating, then NPxN and Black can soon move P – Q4. Cf. *Chess Review*, February 1959, p. 51.)

It is not our purpose to pronounce the Sicilian a weak or a strong defense. Many thousands of games have been played without producing a final verdict! Our purpose has been to show how, even in the opening, the future of a backward pawn may be the dominating factor.

SUMMARY

Generally count a backward pawn as a minus point, but not if you can clearly foresee that

A] it can be advanced soon, or
B] it is safe from attack and is not obstructive, or
C] it is irrelevant to a crucial battle in another area.

8.   *The Doubled Pawn*

OF all theoretical pawn weaknesses, the doubled pawn is the most variable in actual value. In endplay, it is usually bad but sometimes neutral. In the midgame, it can likewise be bad or neutral but sometimes advantageous.

Endgame Weakness

A doubled pawn may be weak for any or all of three reasons:

A] The pawn is in jeopardy, having to be guarded by pieces.
B] The doubling opens a hole through which the enemy king can penetrate.
C] The doubling cripples what would otherwise be a pawn majority capable of generating a passed pawn.

The last is illustrated schematically in No. 61. White's two-to-one on the queen-side is crippled by the doubling, whereas Black's majority on the other side can produce a passed pawn. The White king is therefore tied to the king-side, while the

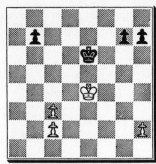

NO. 61. *Black wins*

Black king is free to roam. For example: *1* . . . P – KN4; *2* K – B3, K – B4; *3* K – N3; P – R4; *4* K – B3, P – N4; *5* K – N3, K – K5; *6* K – B2, K – Q4. Black captures the doubled pawns, then queens his queen knight pawn in plenty of time.

Cohn *v.* Rubinstein   1909

NO. 62A. *White to move*

The factor [B] above is illustrated by No. 62A. White has the inferior game, owing to the impairment of his king-side pawns, but probably can draw easily so long as the rooks remain on the board. For example, *1* R – KN1, P – KN3; *2* R – N4, R – B1; *3* P – KR4 and threatens to swap off his isolated pawn. Instead, White makes a colossal strategic blunder:

1 R – QB1??	RxR!
2 KxR	K – B3

The Black king heads for KR6 to menace the isolated pawn. The White king must hurry to KN1 to protect it, else Black will queen his king rook pawn. With the White king confined to the first rank, Black then advances all his king-side pawns to force complete liquidation, whereupon his king can cross over and capture the queen-side pawns. A later stage of the process is shown in No. 62B. From here the game continues

NO. 62B. *Black to move*

1	P – N5
2 P – K4	BPxP
3 PxKP	P – R5
4 K – N1	P – N6
5 RPxP	PxP
Resigns	

The Doubled Queen Bishop Pawn in the Queen Pawn Opening

In the midgame, the doubling of a pawn by capture *toward the center* may strengthen the command of the center and so represent a net gain.

A variation of the queen pawn opening (Nimzovich Defense):

1 P – Q4	N – KB3
2 N – KB3	P – K3
3 P – B4	B – N5ch
4 N – B3	O – O
5 P – QR3	BxNch
6 PxB	

NO. 63. *Black to move*

The White queen-side in No. 63 resembles the king-side in No. 62A. The rook pawn is isolated, and there is a hole on the knight file. Is this formation in No. 63 fatally weak? No categorical answer can be given—Nimzovich, for one, won games with both colors from this position—but it can be said that the strengthening of the White center often outweighs the hole and the isolated pawn. White threatens to establish a triple phalanx by Q – B2 and P – K4. Black cannot hold back the king pawn by fianchetto of his queen bishop, for White can play P – K3, B – Q3, and then P – K4. If Black disputes the key square by P – Q4, then White can swap off his doubled pawn and can, as has been said, "play the Queen's Gambit twice." The ideal formation for Black is P – Q3, P – QB4, P – K4. Then if White plays PxP, he is left with doubled *and isolated* queen bishop pawns. Or if White moves P – Q5, his QB3 is a "dead square." However, the maintenance of this ideal position proves so difficult that it is not often attempted. White can usually ignore the threat of multiple captures on his Q4, thanks to his extra pawn at QB3; he prepares the thrust P – KB4 in order to smash up the Black reverse salient.

The "Ruy Lopez Question"

In the much-played Morphy Defense to the Ruy Lopez— *1* P – K4, P – K4; *2* N – KB3, N – QB3; *3* B – N5, P – QR3—White can double the queen bishop pawn by *4* BxN. In compensation for his doubled pawn, Black has two bishops (against one). Which point is of greater weight? This is what we have called "the Ruy Lopez question." The question is discussed at length in Chapter 17. We mention it here merely to remind you that a doubled pawn may be entirely acceptable because the price paid for imposing it is as great as or greater than the theoretical weakness.

File-Opening

Actually, you pay a certain price almost every time you double an adverse pawn—by opening a file for your opponent (see also Chapters 18 and 19). It is easy to overlook that the value of the file to him must be weighed in the transaction, for many times it is negligible. In connection with No. 63 we mentioned several future possibilities bearing on the question of whether the doubled queen bishop pawn is weak or strong. No mention was made of the queen knight file opened for White. In No. 63 it "looks" as though the file is of little moment, and the judgment is borne out by experience. Black moves P – QN3 in any event, to support P – QB4 and also let out his queen bishop. A White rook on the file "bites on granite" unless White can engineer a full-scale queen-side attack—in contravention of his natural king-side attack based on P – K4.

Kostic *v.* Capablanca   1919

NO. 64. *Black to move*

At the other extreme lie such positions as No. 64. Here the queens glare at each other, but neither will take the dare. If either player initiates the exchange, he half-opens the queen rook file for his opponent, and this factor clearly outweighs the slight weakness of the doubled queen knight pawn. The rook presses uncomfortably on the adverse queen rook pawn and may be able to take a post at R4 or R5 to bear on the center.

Between the extremes lie many cases that cannot be judged so easily. An important case is the doubling of the king bishop pawn.

The Pinned King Knight

The pinning of the adverse knight at its KB3 by B – KN5 has double effect. First, it nullifies the knight's guard of central squares. Second, it threatens, in case the queen moves off the diagonal of the pin, to double the king bishop pawn by BxN. If the king has castled on that side, the disruption of the sheltering pawns may seriously endanger the king.

NO. 65. *Black to move*

No. 65 is a crucial position of the Giuoco Piano. White threatens N – Q5, followed by a capture on KB6 to double the pawn. This can lead to a winning attack on well-known lines: N – KR4, Q – R5, N – B5, sometimes K – R1 and P – KB4. Black cannot forestall the attack by 1 . . . P – KR3; 2 B – R4, P – KN4, for the sacrifice 3 NxP has been analyzed to a White win. A possibility is 1 . . . N – K2 allowing 2 BxN, PxB, for the knight gets to KN3 and defends actively, but the defense is still arduous. Best is 1 . . . B – K3, in order to pluck off the White knight if 2 N – Q5. The exchange 2 BxB doubles the Black king pawn— but this doubling is distinctly advantageous. It shuts out White pieces from Black's Q4 and KB4 and opens the file for the rook so that the Black queen can step out of the pin. Another defense, more frequently played, is to move P – KR3 before O – O, so as to prevent No. 65 from coming about.

Once the king bishop pawn is doubled (after O – O), successful defense usually depends on the achievement of two objectives: (a) the posting of a knight on KN3 and (b) the advance of *both* king bishop pawns to clear the second rank for lateral defense of KN2 and KR2.

Capablanca *v.* Dus-Chotimirsky   1913

NO. 66. *White to move*

In No. 66, White could avoid the disruption of his king-side by *1* B – K2. Instead, Capablanca played *1* B – K3. He does not fear the doubling of his king bishop pawn, because his pieces are poised to achieve both the defensive objectives: N – N3 and P – B4. Further, he would emerge from the transaction NxNch with more than a standoff—a merely defensible position. Owing to his more advanced center and better development (note the "bad" Black king bishop and refer to the section on the "bad" bishop in Chapter 17), he would have every prospect of being able to use the opened king knight file for an attack of his own.

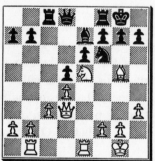

Maroczy *v.* Capablanca   1926

NO. 67. *White to move*

In No. 67, White played *1* BxN, an understandable decision, since his bishop is rather bad. Now Black could go for an easy draw by BxB. But PxB! (again Capablanca) is the move to win. The open king knight file certainly looks strong; Black can occupy it in two moves, while White does not have enough pieces left for a quick attack on the exposed king. Further, the doubled pawn is strong for a while, at least, since it repels the outpost knight.

Doubling Away from the Center

When you can recapture with either of two pawns, the rule of thumb is to capture *toward the center*. This is a good rule; yet there are exceptions. The chief motive in the exceptions is to clear lines for piece play. Consider the "Ruy Lopez question" (page 95). After 4 BxN the almost invariable reply is QPxB. This prepares to meet 5 NxP with Q – Q5, regaining the pawn. But it is not actually necessary for that purpose. After 4 . . . NPxB; 5 NxP, Black can regain the pawn by Q – K2 (3 P – Q4, P – B3; 4 Q – R5ch?? P – N3; 5 NxNP, QxPch and then wins the knight). No, the real purpose in Black's recapture with the queen pawn is to open lines at once for the queen bishop and queen: he must find compensation for the doubled pawn in piece play.

Another reason for submitting to the displacement of a center pawn away from the center is that the pawn still guards a central square from the subcenter. Its new position may be more active

NO. 68. *Black to move*

than the old. An instance is No. 68, a regular position of the Vienna Opening. Black might retreat B – N3, so as to open the queen rook file if NxB. The "book" play, however, is to let the bishop be captured on B4; the pawn that replaces it holds back the White queen pawn, and so helps to delay dissolution of the center, which would increase the range of White's king bishop. In compensation for losing a bishop for a knight, Black obtains some pressure on the queen file. He threatens to plant a knight solidly at Q5, and if White repels it by P – QB3, the White queen pawn remains backward on the open file.

The question of when or whether to allow a center pawn to become doubled upon the bishop file is not easily answered. Even a world champion can go astray here! The following two examples shed some light on the subject.

Alekhine v. Dr. Lasker   1924

NO. 69. *White to move*

1 B – Q3	NxB
2 PxN	B – Q3
3 P – KN3	O – O
4 O – O	R – K1
5 Q – B2	N – B1
6 N – Q1	P – B3

Black has posted his knight to defend his weak light squares and has shut White out of his natural outpost station by P – B3. Now he can go to work on the White weaknesses—the isolated queen pawn and the weak light squares on the king-side. Dr. Lasker evolved and executed a remarkable long-range plan, the focus of which was to force his way through to White's KR2! Perhaps White could have found a defense, but in any event could never hope for more than a draw.

Rubinstein v. Canal   1929

NO. 70. *White to move*

1	O – O	NxB
2	PxN	N – Q4
3	P – N3	NxN
4	QxN	Q – Q3
5	QR – B1	B – Q2
6	N – K5	

White subsequently expanded on both wings: P – KR4 – R5 to be swapped off, opening the rook file (Black had been forced to play P – KN3); P – KN4 – N5 to secure the outpost; P – QR3 and P – QN4 to stifle counterplay. Black never got into the game, and the king rook file eventually proved his undoing.

How is it that the doubling of the king bishop pawn and isolation of the queen pawn are weakening or fatal in No. 69 but tolerable or even strong in No. 70?

The only significant difference between the two positions is in the Black king pawn—but that is enough!

In No. 69, the king pawn has disappeared (by recapture on Q4). The queen bishop is thus free to emerge and to menace the weak squares of the White king-side that are created by the forced P – KN3. As a further consequence, the Black king bishop pawn can be moved to B3, to nullify the outpost station, without weakening the Black pawn structure.

In No. 70, the king pawn is still on K3 and is forever barred from advancing by the doubled pawn. In consequence, the queen bishop is locked in, unless it can be brought out on the queen-side, but White is able also to prevent the liberating move P – QB4. Thus the White king-side is relatively safe from assault, while Black suffers a central cramp that leaves him unable to oppose effectively a White expansion to put his doubled king bishop pawn to work. Finally, if Black repels the outpost knight by P – KB3, the selfsame king pawn is left backward on an open file.

In No. 70 the White queen pawn seems less safe than in No. 69, since here it can be attacked frontally. Actually, it is in no danger; White can defend it sufficiently with pieces that are also active in other directions (rook on Q1 that goes to KR1 with mating threat after the king rook file is opened). Black lacks central space to mass enough heavy pieces against the isolated pawn.

The foregoing analysis sheds light on why Rubinstein (the great artist of the bishop-pair!) let his queen bishop go, and why he did *not* make certain moves thereafter. Thus, with 3 NxN he could have plugged the square in front of his isolated pawn, but that is just what he did *not* want to do, for *3* . . . KPxN would reproduce, in all essentials, No. 69. Again, by *4* PxN he could have de-isolated the queen pawn, but then Black could have made the very move that White's machinations were designed to prevent—P – QB4, with subsequent liberation of the queen bishop.

SUMMARY

In general, count a doubled pawn as a minus point, remembering also to count a plus point for any immediate benefit conferred by the doubling, such as a half-open file or an extra guard to an important square. (Thus the doubling is in many cases neutral.)

Also bear in mind that even when a doubled pawn is a clear weakness, the capitalization thereof is usually remote.

9.   *The Isolated Pawn*

THE intrinsic weakness of the isolated pawn (or *isolani*) is that it cannot be guarded by another pawn: it has to be guarded by pieces. Under concentrated attack it may go lost or may tie up so many pieces for its defense that another sector of the board is fatally weakened.

In endplay, the isolani is apt to be weak without compensation. In No. 62 we saw how the isolated king rook pawn betrays White, compelling the king to defend it and so take up a miserable post on the back rank. The Black king is thus able to reach the sixth rank and eventually to capture the undefendable queen-side pawns.

Yet, even in endplay, the isolani may be neutral. In No. 62, picture the Black king rook pawn standing on R6. Then the isolani would be of no consequence, since the Black king would lack an avenue to attack it. The real weakness of the White position is not so much in the isolani as in the holes left by doubling of the king bishop pawn. In most examples of endgame isolani we likewise find the pawn to be weak or neutral according to other features: the holes, the king positions, etc.

Similar considerations affect the isolani in the midgame, but here we find an added factor: the pawn "fights back" exactly as would a supported pawn on the same square. Especially when it is a center pawn, it contributes to large-scale operations that keep the opponent too busy to concentrate on the lowly pawn.

The Isolated Queen Pawn

The pawn that most frequently becomes isolated in the opening is the queen pawn. The evaluation of this isolani in various circumstances goes through the whole gamut of relevant factors, and we accordingly base this whole chapter upon it. The reader is to understand that the same factors should be weighed as to an isolated king pawn, bishop pawn, etc., but here the judgment is usually easier.

A variation of the Queen's Gambit is

Rubinstein *v.* Marshall   1912

1	P – Q4	P – Q4
2	N – KB3	P – QB4
3	P – B4	P – K3

NO. 71A. *White to move*

White now isolates the Black queen pawn.

	4 PxQP	PxP

4 . . . QxP would let White gain ground rapidly by 5 N – B3 and 6 P – K4.

	5 N – B3	N – QB3
	6 P – KN3	

White fianchettoes his king bishop to hit at the isolani.

	6	N – B3
	7 B – N2	

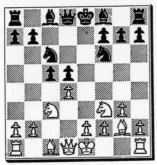

NO. 71B. *Black to move*

The usual continuation by Black is 7 . . . B – K2, the idea being that if White gains a tempo by 8 PxP, BxP he has to face the immediate threat of P – Q5. The isolani here stands strong and chases the queen knight. Later, White can scarcely avoid playing P – K3, whereupon Black can get rid of his isolani if he pleases.

The present player decided, however, to avoid the loss of a tempo:

7	PxP
8 KNxP	B – QB4
9 N – N3	B – QN5

Now Black threatens to give White an isolated queen bishop pawn. There is no good way to guard QB3 a second time, hence:

10 O – O	BxN
11 PxB	O – O

NO. 71C. *White to move*

Whose isolani is weaker? Apparently White's, for it exerts less influence on the center. Seeing this, White changes the picture by a pawn sacrifice.

12 B – N5	B – K3
13 N – B5	Q – K2
14 NxB	PxN
15 P – QB4	PxP
16 KBxN	PxB
17 Q – Q4	

NO. 71D. *Black to move*

Now the sacrifice is seen to be temporary, since White will quickly win the pawn on his QB4. But more, he has inflicted no less than three isolated pawns on his opponent, and surely he will be able to annex at least one of them, thus finally emerging at least a pawn ahead.

Blockade, Attack, Destroy!

The isolani is perhaps weakest in a queenless midgame—that is, a position in which disappearance of the queens largely eliminates direct attack on either king, but in which enough pieces remain for heavy attack on the isolani *together with collateral maneuvers.*

Typical is No. 72A. Here we see the working out of the formula put succinctly by Nimzovich—"Blockade, attack, destroy!"

Kan *v.* Bondarevsky 1937

NO. 72A. *White to move*

1 N – QN3	B – N3
2 QN – Q4	

The point of the blockade is to squelch counterplay that might be generated by advance of the pawn.

2	KN – B3
3 B – N5	O – O
4 O – O – O	

The massing of pieces against the victim begins.

4	N – N5

To take the outpost station (N – K5) would be useless. White replies B – K3, then ousts the knight by P – B3. His weakness of K3 would then be sufficiently covered by B – B2.

5 B – R4	B – Q1
6 B – N3	B – B3
7 N – KB3	

NO. 72B. *Black to move*

Now that the isolani is prevented from advancing, White can remove his blockader to open a frontal attack.

7	N – N3
8 P – KR3	N – R3
9 N – B4	KR – Q1
10 R – Q3	R – Q2
11 KR – Q1	QR – Q1
12 B – R2	

Black's bishop and king knight have gotten into awkward positions. Now White's threat of P – KN4 – N5 necessitates rescue operations that impair the Black king-side. In eight more moves White won a pawn.

In almost all successful operations against an isolani we see the attack on the pawn combined with *collateral threats* based on such a tie-up of the defending pieces. A striking instance is No. 73. One might expect White to play Q – Q2 or P – QR3 to prevent B – N5ch, which would disrupt the classic process B – K2, O – O, Q – Q2, R – Q1, etc. Instead,

Denker *v.* Pinkus   1940

NO. 73. *White to move*

1 B – Q3!

launching a blitz against the Black king, not with expectation of a mate but to draw the defenders away from the isolani. The success of this stratagem was spectacular:

| *1* . . . . | B – N5ch | 3 N – N5 | P – B4 |
| 2 K – B1! | N – B3 | 4 P – KR4 | Q – K1 |

Black has to stop the terrible threat of Q – R5. Already the isolani is forsaken.

5 Q – N3	Q – Q2
6 R – Q1	K – R1
7 B – N5	

and the isolani dies in its tracks. (Black blundered and lost a piece to boot: 7 . . . Q – K2; 8 QxP, R – Q1??; 9 QxRch.)

For further remarks on operations against a weak isolani, see No. 95.

The Mobile Isolani

We turn now to the conditions under which an isolated pawn may be strong. First of all, its fighting power is greatly enhanced if it is able to advance; by the same token, its jeopardy is less because it can choose the square on which to fight for its life.

In No. 74, the White queen pawn is seen to be safe, for defenders can be mobilized more quickly than can attackers. But more, White can get rid of it, if he pleases, by P – Q5. On examining the consequences of this advance, we discover that the pawn is actually a fighting power of considerable magnitude, hence—

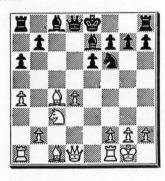

Rubinstein *v.* Tartakover   1925

NO. 74. *White to move*

1 P – Q5!	PxP
2 NxP	NxN
3 BxN	O – O
4 Q – B3	

White has gained a magnificent central post for his king bishop, whence it cramps the Black queen-side and also eyes the king bishop pawn. Despite ingenious tactical maneuvers, Black could not escape the eventual loss of a pawn and the game.

In No. 75, White threatens to win a pawn by PxP, for after a Black recapture comes BxPch, regaining the piece on QB5. So—

Denker *v.* Siff   1933

NO. 75. *Black to move*

1	PxP
2 PxP!	

The tame recapture with the knight holds no winning prospects. In fact, White would face a Black majority of pawns on the queen-side. The recapture with the pawn, on the contrary, confronts Black with a passed pawn; even though it be isolated, Black will have to move dexterously to paralyze it. Meanwhile, White has two open files and an outpost station on his K5 with which to generate collateral threats. He is warranted in believing that even if his queen pawn is stopped and eventually lost, he will gain at least a pawn elsewhere.

As so often happens, the collateral threats brought a decision before the isolani could even be attacked.

2	N – B3
3 KR – K1	Q – Q3
4 N – K5	P – QN4

Not *4* . . . QxP; *5* NxP, RxN??; *6* R – K7.

5 B – N3	B – N2?

Intent on blockading the pawn, Black overlooks the king-side danger.

6 NxP	RxN
7 BxRch	KxB
8 Q – B7ch	Q – Q2
9 QxQch	NxQ
10 R – B7	B – B1
11 KR – QB1	

White wins the bishop and remains the exchange ahead.

The Role of the Initiative

The intrinsic weakness of the isolani is often inconsequential with the queens still on the board, because the opponent has no time to attack it—he is busy with other affairs. In No. 76, the White queen pawn is not even once attacked and could not be effectively attacked at all without extensive regrouping of the Black pieces. But Black has to occupy himself with bolstering his broken king-side. Further, he has a weak third-rank phalanx, neither pawn being able to advance without obvious disadvantage. As was demonstrated by the further course of the game, these pawns are in actual jeopardy, though they are mightily protected at the moment, because White can draw some defenders away and swap off others.

No. 76 and No. 72A serve to illustrate the general principle: the isolani is likely to be strong or weak according as the owner has or has not the initiative—the superior development that lets

Capablanca *v.* Fine   1937

Eliskases *v.* Landau   1938

NO. 76. *White to move*   NO. 77. *White to move*

him pick his own battleground and initiate the tactical threats. A further example is No. 77. Here White's initiative is so strong that he can afford to swap queens, even though an isolani usually becomes more vulnerable as the board is cleared. With *1* Q – QB5! White practically forces the swap. Then he gets his rook to QB7, menacing everything in sight. Black cannot oppose rooks on the file without losing something. (*1* . . . QxQ; *2* RxQ, KR – QB1; *3* KR – QB1 threatens to win a piece by NxB. If *3* . . . RxR; *4* RxR, then *4* . . . R – QB1 is again no good because of *5* NxB, RxR; *6* NxNch and *7* PxR.) Without going into tactical details, White can estimate that Black could win the isolani only at cost of giving up his queen knight pawn—a transaction much in White's favor, since it would give him a queen-side majority.

Inviting the Isolani

The conditions that bring about an isolani often contribute to its compensations. This fact is the key to some otherwise mysterious opening moves.

The fashionable retort to the Caro-Kann Defense is the Panov Attack:

1 P – K4	P – QB3
2 P – Q4	P – Q4
3 PxP	PxP
4 P – QB4	

NO. 78. *Black to move*

With this move White seems to saddle himself with an isolated queen pawn merely to see if he can get away with it. Actually, he proposes to accept this remote weakness for an immediate gain in center control and in development. After 4 . . . PxP; 5 BxP, White's pieces come out to excellent posts with great rapidity; he has open files for both rooks; the Black king pawn is held back, and at the same time Black must continually reckon with P – Q5 (see No. 74).

The examples in this chapter might seem to indicate that an isolani is weak if it is Black and strong if it is White. Don't rely on that as a rule! Yet, there is a measure of truth in it, for White, by virtue of his first move, is the more likely to establish those points of advantage which outweigh the weakness of the isolani.

An example on the other side—and a remarkable one—is No. 79, from a consultation game, 1914, with Capablanca and Reti on the Black side. The symmetrical pawn formations augur a routine draw if Black continues a solid development. In an effort

Faehndrich v. Capablanca
Kaufmann   Reti   1914

NO. 79. *Black to move*

to gain winning chances, Black played *1* . . . P – QB4, conceding an isolated queen pawn but getting an open diagonal for the king bishop. The subsequent proceedings, in which Capablanca worked out an unlikely looking queen-side attack to reach a won endgame, are eulogized by Reti in his book. Indeed, Reti regarded this game as a trail-blazer toward "hypermodernism," one tenet of which is to regard "routine moves" with suspicion.

SUMMARY

Count an isolated pawn as a minus point if it is actually under attack, or if it can be quickly attacked. Even if it can be adequately defended, saving the pawn is not enough—it is still a debit if its defense ties up a number of pieces or endows the opponent with a long-lasting initiative.

In the endgame, reckon the isolani as weak unless you can definitely see that it is neutral (not in jeopardy).

In early play, reckon the isolani as neutral unless you can definitely see that it is weak or strong. Remember that the conditions that brought about the isolation may carry some compensation—an open file, center control, a mobile pawn, etc. The fate of the pawn almost always hinges on which side has the net plus in the major points: center control, greater space, superior development and the like.

BY "hanging pawns" is usually meant a fourth-rank phalanx isolated from other pawns and under frontal attack.

The most frequent case is a phalanx on the queen and queen bishop files, resulting from a queen pawn opening.

1 P – Q4	P – Q4	7 R – B1	P – B4
2 P – QB4	P – K3	8 PxQP	KPxP
3 N – QB3	N – KB3	9 PxP	PxP
4 B – N5	B – K2	10 B – N5ch	QN – Q2
5 N – B3	P – QN3	11 O – O	O – O
6 P – K3	B – N2		

Zukertort *v.* Taubenhaus   1887

NO. 80A. *Hanging Pawns*
White to move

The Black phalanx is obviously precariously placed. The queen
pawn is twice attacked; it is twice defended, but the defenders
are bothered by the White bishops. White can add to the pressure
with both rooks, while Black will have a problem clearing the
queen file for a rook and at the same time maintaining the guard
duties of his minor pieces. Can the phalanx form a chain for self-
defense? At the moment, P – Q5 would lose a pawn, while P – B5
would cede White the splendid station Q4 and also leave the
Black queen bishop bad.

We must rate the hanging pawns a clear minus point.

NO. 80B. *White to move*

A later position of the same game is shown in No. 80B. White
has won the queen bishop pawn in return for his king pawn.
The Black weakness persists in the form of a weak isolani. After
22 N – B5, Q – K2; 23 B – N5, B – B3; 24 Q – Q4, "White controls
the whole board" (Euwe).

A Connected Phalanx Can Hang

The sense in which an isolated phalanx "hangs" is that both
pawns are backward, having to be guarded by pieces alone, and
that neither can advance without serious disadvantage.

Thus a phalanx can hang though not wholly isolated. For example, in No. 81 the White phalanx is connected to the king bishop
pawn, which amply guards the king pawn. But the queen pawn
is backward and cannot be immediately advanced because the

White bishop is unprotected. To form a defensive chain by
P – K5 is objectionable on several grounds. For all practical
purposes, the phalanx hangs just as though there were no pawn
at KB3.

Patay *v.* Reti   1923

NO. 81. *White to move*

The state of suspension need not be of long duration to allow
the opponent decisive tactical opportunity. In No. 81, the tying of
two White pieces to the defense of the queen pawn permits Black
to seize the queen bishop file and get a rook to the seventh rank.
If *1* R – Q2, R – QB1; 2 P – Q5, B – R3; 3 R – K2, R(Q2) – B2
and R – B7 next. The actual play was similar:

1 R – Q3	R – QB1	4 P – QR3	B – R3
2 KR – Q1	R – B7	5 RxR	RxR
3 R(1) – Q2	R(2) – B2	**and Black wins**	

Another instance of a connected but hanging phalanx is No.
82A. Pictorially, the Black phalanx looks imposing. It seems quite
safe, since the only pawn open to attack on the file is guarded by
the queen pawn. But now look at it dynamically. Neither the
king pawn nor the king bishop pawn can advance and live. White
has the means to attack the pawns, notably P – B4. Black cannot
reply P – K5 without losing the pawn, while PxP would leave
his king bishop pawn isolated on an open file. Hence Black can
but try to maintain his phalanx intact, and White can prepare to
strike again, say by a timely PxP, followed by P – Q4, while Black

must continually reckon with the protection of his king bishop pawn when White opens the king bishop file.

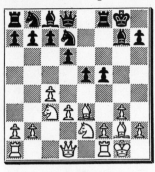

Pachmann *v.* Donner   1955

NO. 82A. *Black to move*

1	N – KB3
2 Q – Q2	P – B3
3 P – KR3	

White has time to indulge in the luxury of stopping N – N5. The move also prepares for P – KN4 in certain eventualities.

3	N – R4
4 P – B4	Q – K1
5 K – R2	Q – N3
6 Q – K1	N – Q2
7 R – Q1	K – R1
8 P – Q4	

NO. 82B. *Black to move*

Voilà! White threatens a double swap to leave the Black king bishop pawn isolated, also to open the center for infiltration by his excellently posted pieces. If 8 . . . P – K5, then 9 P – KN4, PxP; 10 BxP, etc.

8	R – KN1
9 Q – B2	B – B3

Black tries to prevent the center swaps by preparing a counter-attack against White's KN3. But White is not deterred.

10 QPxP	PxP	12 NxP
11 R – Q6	PxP	

Even this! The intended counter fizzles out after *12 . . .* QxPch; *13* QxQ, NxQ; *14* KR – Q1, and Black loses material before he can extricate his pieces.

12 . . . .   **NxN**

13 BxN and wins

(*13* . . . Q – B2; *14* R – K1, B – N2; *15* R(6) – K6, N – B1; *16* R – K7, QxP; *17* RxB, RxR; *18* R – K8, K – N1; *19* B – Q6, R – KB2; *20* Q – K3, P – B5; *21* Q – K5, R – B4; *22* RxNch, RxR; *23* Q – N5ch, Resigns.)

Shaky Center Pawns

The foregoing examples emphasize what we have said previously: the mere occupation of the center by pawns does not spell control of the center. So long as the opponent has center or wing pawns "yet to be heard from," the center control remains in abeyance.

Overextension can lead to a shaky center, which we may as well call "hanging pawns" when they have the characteristic disability to advance safely in the face of attack.

A spectacular instance of overextension is No. 83. White observes that if Black plays PxP the White king knight gets a good

Kevitz *v.* Kotov   1955

NO. 83. *White to move*

post and threatens a fork at K6. White therefore seizes the opportunity to broaden his imposing phalanx with

1 P – N4

But he has failed to reckon with the logical thrust

1 . . . .   P – KB4!

Now the White queen pawn is doubly attacked. There is no time for PxBP, for then PxQP wins a pawn. If PxKP, then QNxP and all the Black pieces reach good posts in a hurry. So White tried

2 P – Q5   PxQP
3 BPxP

Unfortunately, White cannot play 3 NxQP to keep the file open against the backward queen pawn, for then PxP would win a pawn.

3 . . . .   QN – B3
4 PxP   PxP

Black emerges with a strong central phalanx; White with an isolated and useless queen pawn. The moral of all this is that in the initial position, No. 83, the White phalanx already hangs. White must immediately seek as favorable a dissolution of the center tension as he can get. Plausible is 1 P – Q5, so that if PxP he can keep the file open by NxQP. The move P – KB4 is less to be feared if it merely attacks the White king pawn, since White can then bring guards to its defense (B – Q3, R – K1).

Inviting Pawn Advances

The main line of Alekhine's Defense begins

1 P – K4   N – KB3
2 P – K5   N – Q4
3 P – QB4   N – N3
4 P – Q4

NO. 84A. *Black to move*

In olden times, this defense would have been condemned as against all principle. Black has nothing developed except his king knight, which has been chased to QN3, usually a post far inferior to KB3. White has three pawns in the center, one of them already on the fifth. What does Black have to show for his eccentric play?

The answer is that the White pawns hang. Black has gained targets for attack. He will gain time by hitting them with simple developing moves. White must move dexterously to parry the threats of winning a pawn, or isolating a pawn, or forcing the pawns into a dead formation. For example:

Jackson *v.* Denker   1935

4	P – Q3
5 N – KB3?	B – N5
6 P – KR3?	BxN
7 QxB	N – B3

NO. 84B. *White to move*

Already White is in serious trouble. Both his king pawn and queen pawn are threatened. If 8 PxP, then NxQP; 9 Q – Q3, QxP. If 8 Q – K4, then PxP; 9 PxP, Q – Q5 with much the better position.

Another game continued from No. 84A:

Lessing *v.* Denker   1938

4	P – Q3
5 PxP	BPxP
6 N – QB3	P – N3
7 B – K3	B – N2
8 R – B1	O – O
9 B – Q3	N – B3
10 QN – K2	

NO. 84C. *Black to move*

White wants to keep his pawn on Q4 to guard K5 and also to support an eventual P – QB5. But he is too ambitious; he should have made a concession to safety by 10 P – Q5, N – K4; 11 P – QN3.

10 . . . .   P – Q4!

Thus Black forces either the isolation of the queen pawn or the premature advance P – B5.

11 P – B5	N – B5	13 Q – Q2
12 BxN	PxB	

If 13 RxP, then Q – Q4, winning the king knight pawn and so wrecking the king-side.

13 . . . .   B – B4

14 RxP

Faced with B – Q6, White has to hurl himself on the sword after all.

14 . . . .   Q – Q4

15 R – R4   QxNP

and Black wins

Criteria

When do pawns hang and when don't they? This question can be perplexing, depending as it often does on the survey of many tactical possibilities. In general, the same criteria can be applied to each pawn of a phalanx, separately, as are applied to an isolated or a backward pawn. The pawn is weak if it is or can be attacked, especially through the file, and if its defense will tie up several pieces. It is also weak if, when attacked by an enemy pawn, it can neither push on nor swap itself off without serious disadvantage. There is a difference, however, in favor of the phalanx over the single pawn. The phalanx is apt to offer wider choice of defensive measures, e.g., an advance to form either of two chains.

Szabo *v.* Bisguier   1955

NO. 85. *White to move*

Let us apply the criteria to an example, No. 85. The backward queen pawn on the open file looks shaky. But it is defended by knight and queen, and one or both rooks can be brought to the queen file. Clearly this is enough for mere defense, since Black can scarcely bring even three pieces to the attack. In fact, in two moves (B – N3, R – Q1) White could actually threaten P – Q5.

Now examine the Black pawn attacks. At the moment, neither P – K4 nor P – QB4 is playable. What pieces can Black bring up to threaten either advance? Surely White can stop P – K4 by O – O and R – K1, then N – K5 if need be. Against such a process as P – QN3, Q – B2, P – QB4, he can post his queen on K3 and then play PxP, thus saddling Black with an isolated queen bishop pawn. Finally, in some contingencies he might even play P – B5, leaving his queen pawn permanently backward but nailing down Q6 as an outpost station for his knight.

White is so far ahead in both the defense and offense that the verdict must be that the phalanx does *not* hang; on the contrary, it is strong. It holds back the king pawn and queen bishop pawn, one of which Black *must advance* if his queen bishop is ever to get into the game.

The actual continuation was

1 N – K5

To hold back the queen knight pawn.

1	Q – B2
2 O – O – O	P – B4
3 Q – K3	

White would be happy with 3 . . . PxP; 4 RxP.

3	P – QN3
4 PxP	PxP
5 P – KN4 and wins	

SUMMARY

Count a minus point for a phalanx that hangs according to the foregoing criteria. Remember that isolation of the phalanx from other pawns increases the danger, but connection on one side does not guarantee the safety of the pawn on the other side.

11. *Holes*

IN a narrow sense, a hole is a square on the third rank, in front of a pawn on the second, no longer capable of being guarded by a pawn (because the adjacent pawns have advanced or disappeared). An example is Black's KN3 in No. 9. The endgame weakness of a hole may be that it is an avenue for penetration by the enemy king, e.g., White's KR3 in No. 62A.

Now, when the pawns become depleted by exchange, holes arise necessarily. Also, it is virtually impossible to advance the pawn front without leaving holes, if only momentarily. Therefore, a more particularized definition is needed:

A hole is a square that

A] lies in a sensitive area;

B] is not guarded by a pawn, though such guard would normally be expected (or did, in fact, exist previously);

C] can probably be exploited by the opponent as an avenue or a post for pieces.

Under [c] we dismiss all those inconsequential holes incidental to strong pawn advances. We have just seen an instance in our study of No. 85. White's move 5 P – KN4 leaves holes—in the narrow sense—at KR3 and KB3. But Black is far from having the means to exploit them. In fact, he must defend against the general advance of the White king-side wing whereby the "holes" become transformed into "greater space behind the front line."

The areas that are, in general, always "sensitive" are (a) in front of the castled king and (b) the center.

The Holes after P – N3

In fianchettoing a bishop, you create a hole at R3, and also at B3 if you advance the adjacent center pawn. The bishop supplants the pawn in guard duty, so that the potential weakness is covered. And of course your bishop gains a post from which it exerts powerful influence on the center and sometimes on the enemy flank also.

But if your bishop is swapped off, the hole stands out in nudity. It is often a pronounced weakness when you have castled on that side.

In No. 86A, Black feels uncomfortable in the face of the White threat to post a knight on Q5. To exclude the knight by 1 . . . P – K3 would leave the queen pawn backward on an open file. So Black goes in for a remedy that is worse than the disease:

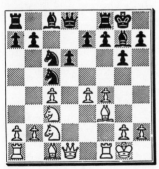

Darga v. Toran   1955

NO. 86A. *Black to move*

1	BxN?
2 PxB	Q – R4
3 P – B5	

It is certainly worth a pawn to White to open the diagonal for his queen bishop, stop P – KB4, and so get started on exploitation of the compromised Black king-side. Black takes the proffered pawn, else he has nothing to show for his last two moves.

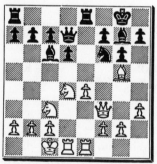

3	QxBP
4 B – R6	R – K1
5 N – K3	Q – Q5
6 Q – K1	N – Q2
7 R – Q1	Q – N3
8 K – R1	N – B3
9 B – N5	N – K4
10 Q – R4	

NO. 86B. *Black to move*

The White threat is of course more serious than merely to win a pawn on KB6. Once White gains this square for occupation by his pieces, the Black king must speedily succumb to the attack.

10	K – N2	12 N – Q5	NxN
11 B – K2	N(4) – Q2	13 PxP!	Resigns

For if either PxP, *14* R – B7ch (or RxPch), KxR; *15* Q – R7ch (or QxPch), K – K3; *16* B – N4ch, K – K4; *17* RxNch, KxP; *18* B – B3 mate.

Another instance is No. 87A. White threatens to advance his king-side pawns, backed by rooks. Black wishes to ease his position by exchanges.

Alekhine *v.* Brinckermann 1927

NO. 87A. *Black to move*

1	N – R4
2 P – KN4	BxN
3 RxB	N – N2
4 B – B6	

Black has no time for queen-side counterplay, for White threatens to vacate Q4, then move B – Q4 and Q – B6. Black must bolster up the dark squares of his king-side as best he can.

4	R – K3	7 R – K3	N – N2
5 QR – Q1	N – K1	8 Q – B4	Q – R5!
6 B – Q4	Q – K2		

Black defends well. Here he stops the deadly move Q – R6.

| 9 QR – K1 | QR – K1 |

NO. 87B. *White to move*

Black has escaped an immediate debacle. But there is no parry to the White threat of P – KB4 – B5. The weakness of the dark squares in the Black camp is incurable.

Exploiting Holes Despite the Bishop

Although the fianchettoed bishop guards the holes, it is not quite so efficacious as the pawn in interdicting their occupation. If a hole is guarded only by the bishop, the opponent need only bring up two pieces to ensconce one of them in the hole.

Pachmann v. Najdorf 1955

NO. 88. *White to move*

In No. 88, Black's last move (B – N5) was a routine procedure. After the forced 1 P – KB3, the bishop retreats, and Black thinks he gains a tempo in forcing the White king bishop pawn to take two moves instead of one to reach B4 (where obviously it wants to go). But the routine move has an unexpected outcome:

1 KN – K2?   N – Q5!

Naturally! Now the bishop cannot be repelled by P – KB3. Imperative is *2* P – KR3, e.g., B – B6; *2* BxB, NxBch; *3* K – B1 and then "castles by hand" with K – N2.

2 O – O?   N – B6ch

3 K – R1   P – KR4

What a sorry spectacle for White! To play BxN would leave his light squares desperately weak. To move the king knight so as to attack the Black knight again with the queen would allow NxRP, when P – KB3 is no good because of NxR. White cannot shake loose from the bind without long regrouping; meanwhile Black threatens to open the king rook file and hit with his rook. (White was smashed quickly, resigning 11 moves later.)

Holes in the Center

It is just possible to guard all four center squares by pawns, i.e., pawns on K4, Q4, KB3, QB3. But even if you can establish this formation, you cannot expect to maintain it. Your opponent will attack it and force the exchange or advance of some pawns. Further, you will often change the formation voluntarily to open lines for your own pieces.

Thus you are sooner or later compelled to take a stand: you must judge which squares should be kept pawn-guarded and which you can afford to abandon to adverse occupation. The question of central holes is a matter of *relative values*.

In Nos. 30 and 31, White moves P – K5 to oust the defending knight from Black's KB3. At the same time he opens the post Q4 to occupation by the knight. This is a typical example (and the most frequent case) of a give-and-take move. In these examples, White gets more than he gives, for his king-side attack is stronger than any counterplay based on the outpost knight.

That this is not always true is illustrated in No. 89. After *1*
P – K5, N – Q4, White is by no means prepared to launch a
king-side attack. His king bishop is not yet on the diagonal
opened; Black's KR2 is already guarded by the other knight. If
2 BxB to make way for N – KN5, then RxB and the rook stands on
the second rank for guard duty. In any event, the Black position
is solid enough to afford P – KR3 to hold the White knight at bay.
Finally, White's queen knight pawn is loose, and Black is well
developed to launch a center counterattack by P – QB4. In short,
1 P – K5 would be premature. White should patiently continue
his development, as by *1* Q – K2.

Dr. Lasker *v.* Capablanca   1914

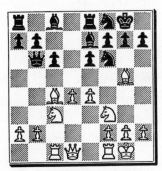
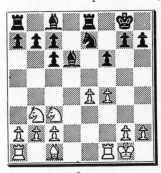

NO. 89. *White to move*   NO. 90. *White to move*

A notable example of giving to get is No. 90. (Again the Ruy
Lopez question!) The desirable advance for White appears to
be P – K5, to oust the king bishop from its fine post. But with
N – N3 Black can bring two additional pieces to the guard of
its K4; to bring up three attackers besides his king bishop pawn,
White would have to double rooks on the king file and maneuver
a knight to KB3 or his bishop to QB3. Meanwhile, the king
bishop pawn would need additional protection by P – KN3. Then
the light squares of the White king-side would be very weak,
and the Black knight and queen bishop could probably exploit
these squares strongly. All in all, the advance P – K5 is a pipe
dream.

1 P – B5!

As has been said, this is the move of a tyro or of a grandmaster! White renounces P – K5 and gives Black that square as an unassailable outpost station. But look at what he gets! Black's queen bishop is shut in, and White nails down K6 as a potential outpost station, on which a knight will settle if the bishop is developed at QN2 or QR3. Can Black afford to keep his queen bishop at home merely to guard his K3? (Capablanca did not think so; he let the White knight settle at his K3 as the lesser evil.) Also, White vacates the square KB4 for his next move, whereby he swaps off Black's most active piece, his king bishop.

1	. . . .	P – QN3
2	B – B4	B – N2
3	BxB	PxB
4	N – Q4	

White has even undoubled Black's pawn for him, restoring the possibility of central counterattack by P – Q4, but the outpost at K6 outweighs these concessions.

The Hole at Q3

A famous tragicomic example of the hole at Q3 is No. 91

Paulsen *v.* Morphy   1857

NO. 91. *White to move*

from "the good old days." White naturally wants to play P – Q4 to shut off the menacing bishop. But he needs an additional guard for Q4, so

1 P – B3?	Q – Q6!

Her majesty is not too proud to dedicate herself to the restraint of the lowly pawn! In struggling to oust the intruder, Black falls victim to one of Morphy's brilliant combinations.

2 P – QN4	B – N3	4 QxP	B – Q2
3 P – QR4	PxP	5 R – R2?	

Missing his chance to break loose by 5 Q – R6.

5	QR – K1	7 PxQ	R – N3ch
6 Q – R6	QxB!	8 K – R1	B – R6
		and Black wins	

(Black threatens mate in two by B – N7 and B – B6. The rook must move, but R – N1 allows mate by 9 B – N7ch, RxB *10* R – K8ch. Hence 9 R – Q1. Then Black can play BxP, and the only way to stop mate is Q – B1, giving back the queen for a bishop. The remaining Black pieces are still able to weave a mating net.)

Guard of the third-rank central squares must often be entrusted to pieces, for the center pawns must go forward sooner or later. Natural development usually keeps these squares so well protected and shielded that one doesn't give them a thought. Yet, vigilance

Capablanca *v.* Janowski   1918

NO. 92. *Black to move*

must never be relaxed. No. 92 shows how even the momentary opening of a hole at Q3 can have serious consequences.

The position arises from the Queen's Gambit, in some lines of which Capablanca's freeing maneuver, . . . N – Q4, is good. So Black plays

1 . . . .   N – Q4?

But White (happening to be Capablanca!) perceives that this move, good when the White queen knight stands on QB3, is here bad. The momentary pin of Black's king bishop leaves his Q3 a momentary hole.

2 N – Q6!   B – QB3

If 2 . . . BxB; 3 NxQB, Q – K2; 4 NxB, QxN; 5 PxP and White wins a pawn.

3 N – K4

Black is in a mess. White threatens, among other things, to pick off the queen bishop pawn. Black cannot play PxP, because his queen bishop is loose. If 3 . . . BxB; 4 N(3)xB, P – KR3; 5 N – KB3, Q – K2; 6 PxP and at the least Black will have an isolated pawn on the open file. Black tried the heroic measure

3 . . . .   P – B4

but could not save himself from the consequences of his backward king pawn and the hole at his K4.

The Weak-Square Complex

A whole series of squares of one color may become holes through the disappearance of the bishop tied to squares of that color. Such a situation is often called a "weak-square complex."

A beautiful example of creating such holes and then exploiting them was given by Teichmann in a famous game, No. 93A. At first glance, the positions seem to be equal, or perhaps slightly in Black's favor because of the bishop. But when we note the inferior position of the Black queen as compared with the White, we realize that Black is in some difficulty. White proceeds to aggravate it by forcing the following exchanges:

Teichmann *v.* Allies   1902

NO. 93A. *White to move*

NO. 93B. *Black to move*

1	N – Q4	NxN
2	RxN	RxR
3	QxR	

Now the Black queen-side pawns are under fire; they have to move into a chain to save themselves, since the Black queen cannot get across to their defense.

| 3 | . . . . | P – QN3 |
| 4 | Q – K5 | P – QB4 |

White has achieved his first object: Black's Q3 as well as his K2 and QB2 are open to invasion because the heavy pieces are not in the vicinity and his bishop is of the wrong color.

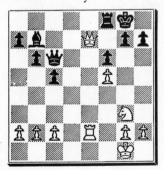

5	P – KB4	B – B1
6	P – B5	B – N2
7	Q – K7	Q – QB3
8	R – K2	P – B3

NO. 93C. *White to move*

The White queen dominates the Black camp, and the Black pieces cannot co-ordinate to repel the intruder.

9 N – K4   Q – Q4

The attempt to draw by 9 . . . R – B2; (*10* Q – Q8ch, R – B1;
11 Q – K7, R – B2) is futile, for after *10* Q – K6 (threat N – Q6),
QxQ; *11* PxQ the passed pawn is too strong.

10 N – Q6   B – B3

Even a rook move on the rank is impossible, for then Q – B7ch
and N – K8 would decide. Black can only await White's pleas-
ure. But how is White to deliver the knockout blow? At the moment, the Black defense is adequate. The answer comes:

11 P – KR3   P – B5

12 P – B3   P – KR3

13 K – R2!

The White king threatens to trek up the dark squares to KN6,
when QxNP mate will impend. Black is powerless to halt the journey—his wretched bishop betrays him in the end!

Many master games have demonstrated that, in the Queen's
Gambit, Black must tread warily to avoid falling into a "weak-
square complex" on his queen-side. One of the classics is Capablanca *v.* Mieses, 1928, No. 94A.

Capablanca *v.* Mieses   1928

NO. 94A. *Black to move*

The "book" move in this position is now *1* . . . P – B3. Instead,
Mieses tried

1	P – QR3
2 PxP!	

The idea behind this unexpected exchange is: Black will be forced to move P – QB3 sooner or later. His king bishop will disappear in a swap with White's queen bishop. Thus all the dark squares on the Black queen-side will be left irretrievably weak.

2	PxP
3 Q – N3	P – B3
4 B – Q3	N – R4
5 BxB	QxB
6 O – O	N(4) – B3
7 N – QR4	

NO. 94B. *Black to move*

The process of nailing down the weaknesses begins.

7	N – K5
8 BxN!	QxB
9 Q – N4 and so on	

The "and so on" means that White continues with the regular procedure against a retarded and immobilized pawn chain. He brings up his own pawns, P – QN4 and P – QR4, and disposes his pieces behind them (R – QB5 after an exchange of knights) to enforce P – QN5. (See "The Minority Attack," p. 215.)

SUMMARY

Count a minus point for a third-rank hole in front of the castled king or a hole at any vital central square, if the opponent has the means and time to use it.

Remember that a hole left by the advance of a center pawn is sometimes far outweighed by the plus accruing from the advance.

Count a minus point for a "weak-square complex" in the form of an immobilized pawn chain against which the opponent can launch a general invasion of pieces and/or pawns.

12.   *The Outpost Station*

BY an *outpost* is commonly understood a knight planted in the enemy half of the board and guarded by a pawn.

This chapter is concerned with the pawn play that creates *stations* for outposts, regardless of what pieces are to occupy them. Of course, since the short-stepping knight is peculiarly dependent on such stations to get at the enemy, they are mainly occupied by knights. But the station may serve a bishop or rook, or each of several pieces in turn. (The word *outpost* may mean either the piece or the square on which it stands. To avoid ambiguity, we will invariably use *station* for the latter sense.)

In our broadened definition, a pawn guard is essential to constitute a square an outpost station, but remote location is not— a player may be said to have a station in his own territory when he normally would be denied use of the square by an adverse pawn. (The term *strong square* has sometimes been used for this near-home station.)

It will be seen that outpost stations are much akin to holes, discussed in the preceding chapter. There is some overlap, but it is not total. A hole may provide an avenue of infiltration but not (for lack of a pawn guard) a tenable station. A station may be created through no fault in the adverse pawn formation but because the pawns cannot guard every important square on the board.

Station in Front of an Isolani

The square ahead of an isolated pawn is the ideal outpost station: the pawn masks the piece from frontal attack, and by definition it is immune from pawn attack. In No. 72 (among others) we have seen the utilization of such a station as an incident in the campaign against the isolani. Here we must point out that even when the ultimate objective is solely to capture the weakling, and even when occupation of the station is intended merely as a preliminary blockade, the outpost often proves essential to those collateral threats on which the campaign hinges.

To emphasize this point we append a further example, which also clarifies what is a station and what is not.

Tarrasch v. Teichmann   1910

NO. 95A. *Black to move*

In No. 95A, if we apply the Point Count we cannot credit either side with an outpost station. It is true that Black can move N – K4 and White can move N – Q5. But neither outpost is secure, since it can be ousted by a pawn. For White, P – B4 is a safe move, and it is aggressive; in fact, White will assuredly make it, with threat of P – B5 – B6 if given the opportunity. For Black, P – QB3 is dubious, since the queen pawn is thereby left backward on an open file. Still, it may prove playable, and in any event the White bishop will have to retreat before White can play N – Q5.

White has a point for pawn on fourth *v.* pawn on third, which here looms large because he also has mobile king-side pawns

(P – B4 etc.), whereas Black's prospect of enforcing P – Q4 is dim. Black can do no better than lash out with *1 . . .* P – KB4, though White keeps the whip hand with *2* B – B4ch and *3* P – B4. Instead, Black commits a tactical error that makes his plight worse:

1	. . . .		B – Q2?
2	BxB!		QxB
3	P – K5		

White seizes the chance to isolate the Black queen pawn. Of course *3 . . .* NxP is no good because of *4* QxN.

3	. . . .		KR – Q1
4	PxP		PxP

NO. 95B. *Outpost Station*
        White to move

Now comes the siege of the weakling.

5 R – Q2	Q – K3	*7* R – K2	Q – B5
6 KR – Q1	N – K4	*8* P – N3	

Before resuming active operations, White wants to dispose his queen-side pawns to be safe and to squelch counterplay.

8	. . . .		Q – B3
9	P – QR4		R – K1
10	N – Q5		

The primary purpose of this move is to get the knight out of the way of the queen bishop pawn. But incidentally the outpost threatens N – B6ch and also eyes the weak pawn at QN3.

10	N – N3
11 R(2) – Q2	R – K3
12 P – QB4	

NO. 95C. *Outpost Knight*
Black to move

Black can delay but cannot prevent the maneuver N – K3 – B5.

12	QR – K1	16 R – Q5	Q – R6
13 P – R3	Q – B4	17 N – B5	R – N3
14 K – R2	P – R3	18 Q – QB3	Q – R7
15 N – K3	N – K4		

The queen was threatened with capture by R – QR1.

| 19 R(5) – Q2 | Q – R6 |
| 20 RxP and wins | |

The Fourth-Rank Outpost

On first glance at No. 96, we see that Black has a bad bishop, while White has a strong, if modest, station for his knight, Q4. White seems to lead by two points. On second look, we see that White must reckon with Black counterplay based on the half-open queen bishop file and the possible post for his knight at QB5. The White queen bishop pawn is weak and will be even weaker if P – QN3 is played to repel the Black knight. The actual play is a homily on the importance of the White station Q4.

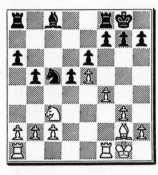

Tarrasch *v.* Teichmann   1912

NO. 96. *White to move*

1	N – K2	B – Q2
2	N – Q4	

Though the knight reaches out into enemy territory, that fact is here negligible. The strength of the knight is that it guards QB2 and so permits White to regroup his pieces without loss of time.

2	. . . .	QR – B1
3	K – B2	R – B2
4	K – K3	R – K1

Black prepares against the possibility of P – KN4 and P – B5. This is not yet a serious threat—still, what is Black to do? Attack along the queen bishop file is stalled by White's refusal to compromise himself there—as by P – QB3, which would create a target for attack by P – N5.

5	R – B2

Not to guard the rank but to open the way for the king bishop to reach the center.

5	. . . .	N – N2
6	B – B1	N – R4
7	P – N3	

This move is of course vitally necessary. Nothing is to be feared from unguarding QB3—e.g., 7 . . . R – B6ch; 8 K – Q2, KR – QB1; 9 B – Q3 and now the threat of a White king-side advance becomes real.

7		P – R3
8 B – Q3		N – B3
9 NxN		

The outpost has served his purpose. He can now disappear to make way for the king. With his queen-side secured, and his king beautifully centralized, White can launch the king-side break-through. The score is now: Black, −1 for bad bishop; White +2 for better king position (see Chapter 22) and mobile pawn wing.

The Station at K5

When Black sets up a chain by P – Q4, P – K3 (as in the French Defense, Queen's Gambit, etc.), his K4 beckons to the White king knight. This square becomes a full-fledged outpost station if Black also moves P – KB4, as in the Stonewall Defense. But even when the king bishop pawn is unmoved, the White outpost is often immune, either because (a) tactical urgencies forbid the removal of the Black knight from KB3 to permit P – KB3 or because (b) Black cannot afford to weaken his K3 by this move.

The difference between pictorial and dynamic stations is seen in No. 97. If we look at the pawn formations alone, we count possible stations at each player's K5 and QB5. But the White pieces prevent Black from occupying his K5. Likewise, a White knight tour to reach QB5 would be futile; the station can be killed by P – QN3, and this move does not appreciably weaken Black's QB3, since he has the open file there and White has not. Black can conceivably lash down his QB5 as a station by bringing a rook to the file and moving N – QR4 – B5, since White can never move P – QN3 without serious weakening of his QB3. Some preparation is required for this maneuver, else it might lead simply to forced recapture on QB5 with the queen pawn and consequent plugging of the square. But White's K5 is a real station, since he can occupy it at once and can bring up enough pieces to avoid plugging. The White knight at K5 will be a greater menace than would a Black knight at QB5, since the former bears on the already compromised Black king-side.

In short, there is only one real outpost station, and it belongs to White. The game continued:

Milner-Barry *v.* Znosko-Borovsky   1928

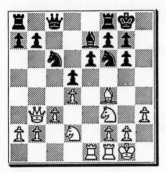

NO. 97. *White to move*

1 N – K5   N – Q2

Black seeks salvation in exchanges.

2	QN – B3	QNxN
3	NxN	NxN
4	BxN	

Black has rid himself of the knights, but White still has use of the station for his bishop and rook. Black cannot hope to save his king pawn if he ever plays P – KB3. If he plays B – KB3, or Q – Q1 and B – Q3, White can submit to the swap of bishops, since his rook on K5 will be equally menacing. In any event, the outpost will contribute to an attack on the king engineered by king-side pawn advances to open lines.

The advantages that may accrue from a strong outpost are many and various; we need not enumerate them. You can often occupy a station on general principles without troubling to calculate the future. However, calculation is called for when your outpost can be attacked by pieces and exchanged, particularly when you will have to recapture with a pawn and so plug the station. We have already discussed this question in Chapter 4. An instance of premature occupation of the station is No. 35. In No. 34, on the contrary, the pawn that replaces the knight after NxN is equally or more menacing.

An important case arises in the Pillsbury Attack (Queen's Gambit). Here White's N – K5 is the prelude to a king-side attack by which White counters the Black pawn-majority attack on the queen-side. The strength of White's operation rests, *inter alia*, on the fact that Black dare not swap off the outpost.

Pillsbury *v.* Tarrasch   1895

NO. 98. *White to move*

No. 98 is from the definitive game on this question.

1 **N – K5**   **P – N4**

If *1* . . . NxN; *2* PxN, N – Q2; *3* BxB, QxB; *4* P – B4, and Black has a weak queen pawn, while White has strong king-side pawns plus a superb post for his knight at Q4. Consequently, Black has nothing better than to continue his queen-side advance, and White has time to reinforce his outpost.

2 **P – B4**

This move gives Black his K5 as a station, but White can capture the outpost when it arrives, without detriment to his attack.

2	R – K1	5 BxB	RxB
3 Q – B3	N – B1	6 BxN	PxB
4 N – K2	N – K5	7 Q – N3	P – B3

This move is inevitable sooner or later to stop P – B5 – B6.

8	N – N4	K – R1
9	P – B5	

Thus White lashes down his K6 and opens KB4 for use of his pieces. He has won the skirmish of the outposts. Though his own knight has been ousted from K5, it has found another strong post on the king-side. The Black outpost has been captured, and the pawn that replaces it helps rather than hinders White, since it masks his backward king pawn.

The Station at Q5

The king pawn openings engender an outpost station at Q5. An instance is No. 99, from a Ruy Lopez.

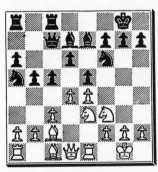

Ivkov *v.* Letelier   1955

NO. 99. *White to move*

1	PxKP	PxP
2	N – Q5	Q – Q3

If 2 . . . NxN; 3 PxN, the pawn is passed, and though it can be supported only by pieces it is very strong.

3 NxNch

White seizes the tactical opportunity to double the Black king bishop pawn; Black cannot recapture with either the queen or bishop. Here we see one of the advantages often enjoyed by an outpost: the power to sell its life dearly.

3	. . . .	PxN
4	Q – K2	P – N5
5	N – R4	

White's maneuver has created a new outpost station, KB5, and now the knight heads for it.

| 5 . . . . | K – R1 | 7 N – B5 | BxN |
| 6 Q – R5 | R – KN1 | 8 PxB and wins | |

The "outpost pawn" is just as bad for Black as the knight. It prevents R – N3 and keeps the king bishop pawns bottled up so that Black cannot bring pieces to the defense of his king. White threatens R – K3 – R3, and then Black cannot defend his KR2 by R – N2 because of B – R6, R – N1; B – B8.

Stations on the Sixth Rank

In Nos. 90 and 93 we saw the devastating power of a knight entrenched on K6 or Q6. Naturally, such stations are not easily achieved, but once your opponent has created a hole in the heart of his camp its occupation is worth some trouble and sacrifice.

Furman *v.* Smyslov   1949

NO. 100. *Black to move*

In No. 100 Black is threatened with loss of a pawn on his QR4 by BxN. Black seeks revenge in the center, where the White chain seems shaky.

1 . . . .   P – B4

Against the supine 2 P – B3 Black would now get a lively attack by PxP; 3 PxP, Q – KB3; 4 B – K3, Q – N7. Yet how else is White to avoid the smash-up of his center and loss of a pawn?

2 B – Q7!

White puts his finger on the flaw—the hole that Black has

created at his K3. If now 2 . . . PxP, then 3 B – K6ch, K – R1;
4 QxP and the White center is impregnable. Black therefore plays
to win a pawn.

2	Q – K4	5 BxBch	KxB
3 B – B3	QxKP	6 Q – R3	
4 B – K6ch	K – R1		

Black has his pawn, but the White outpost is more than compensation. The Black king is in trouble. (Black has to meet the
threat QxPch; he has no time for QxN or BxP.)

Plugging the Outpost Station

The possession of a strong outpost station, like undisputed control of the center, is almost sure to generate additional
advantages. You should therefore try to neutralize an adverse
station promptly, as

A] by guarding it with enough pieces to prevent its effective occupation, or to swap off all dangerous pieces, or

B] by disposing your own pieces so as to render the outpost harmless.

A third resource is occasionally available:

C] compelling your opponent to recapture with a (harmless) pawn and so plug his own station.

The last outcome can usually be avoided by judicious retreat
of the outpost, or by timing the initial occupation of the station
correctly. In the following example, it was forced by ingenious
tactics.

Jacobs *v.* Evans   1955

NO. 101. *Black to move*

In No. 101, Black has a backward queen pawn on an open file. White has play against it, and he also has use of the strong station in front of it. However, if he plants his knight there he wants to be sure that he can retake with pieces should there be a series of exchanges on the square: should he recapture with a pawn, his attack on the backward queen pawn would be blocked. Black, conversely, wants to force this outcome.

1	N – N3	3 N – K1	R – B1
2 B – N3	B – N5	4 Q – Q3	

Observe that White is compelled to defend himself against one-move threats. Against the next one he has no alternative.

4	B – K3	6 N – Q5	NxN
5 BxN	BxB	7 KPxN	

Q.E.D.!

The Battle of Outposts

Once an outpost station is created, it is likely to be the focus of battle so long as pieces remain on the board that might occupy it advantageously. Two examples follow.

Denker *v.* Kashdan 1932

NO. 102A. *Black to move*

In No. 102A, White threatens P – K5, wherefore—

1	P – K4
2 BPxP	PxP
3 P – Q5	

White stabilizes the center, since he wants to post a knight on the station opened up at his KB5. Though this outpost can be ousted, it will have done its duty if it induces P – KN3.

3	N – N3
4 N – K3	Q – B4
5 K – N2	QR – B1
6 P – KR4	

The attack on his queen bishop pawn holds White's knight on K3 for the moment. But Black cannot prevent N – B5 in the long run. He therefore seeks counterplay on the queen-side.

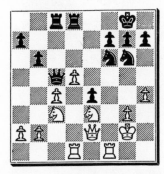

6	P – B3
7 QR – Q1	PxP
8 KPxP	P – K5

NO. 102B. *White to move*

Black advances the king pawn to give himself an outpost station on K4. White has permitted this move, by 8 KPxP, because the Black king pawn is weak, and its advance gives White access to his Q4.

9 P – N3	R – K1
10 N – B5	R – K4
11 N – N5	

Now this knight, too, will reach an outpost station, QB6, via Q4 or R7.

11	P – QR3
12 N – R7	R – B2
13 N – B6	R – K1
14 Q – N2 and wins	

The threat of NxKNP and QxN costs Black some material.

In No. 103A, each side would like to install a knight at his QB5. Then a capture of his outpost would give him either a queen-side majority of pawns or the first opportunity to double rooks on the open file. Of course, the outpost could be expelled by P – QN3, but only if QR3 were guarded by a piece or if the knight's move to that square were harmless. On the other hand, each player would like to gain space by advancing his queen-side pawns rather than holding his queen knight pawn back to guard his QB4.

The consequence of these positional desiderata is a sharp skirmish.

Tarrasch *v.* Noa   1885

NO. 103A. *White to move*

1	P – QN3	N – N5
2	P – QR3	

White does not trouble to save his bishop by B – N1, for, with the center blocked, knights are more useful than bishops. For the same reason, Black does not play NxB.

2	. . . .	N(5) – B3
3	P – QN4	P – R3
4	P – KR4	N – N1

Since QR4 is no longer available as a route to B5, the knight embarks on a tour via Q2 and N3.

                    5 K – K3

And White vacates Q2 to allow N – Q2 – N3 – B5. The knight tours are interrupted by a skirmish over control of the open file.

5	R – B2
6 R – B2	KR – QB1
7 KR – QB1	K – B1
8 P – N4	B – K1

Now back to the knights.

9 N – Q2	N – Q2
10 N – N3	N – QN3
11 N – B5	N – B5ch
12 BxN	PxB

NO. 103B. *White to move*

White has won the first skirmish: his outpost is ensconced, while the Black outpost has been swapped off. However, Black has obtained a station in the center, and White must keep his knight on QB3 to play NxN in answer to N – Q4. Thereby the Black queen bishop pawn will gain protection, and White's outpost will be in danger of capture by R – R1 and P – QN3.

It behooves White to remove his outpost promptly to the better station Q6 before its avenue (K4) is closed.

13 N(5) – K4!	P – QN4
14 N – Q6	R – N1
15 P – B5 and wins

White opens a file on the king-side and goes to work on the Black king with his rooks. (15 . . . B – Q2; 16 R – B2, N – Q4ch; 17 NxN, PxN; 18 P – N5, P – KR4; 19 R(1) – B1, K – N1; 20 P – N6, P – B3; 21 R – K2, B – B3; 22 R(1) – K1, R – Q1; 23 K – B4, PxPch; 24 RxP, K – B1; 25 N – B7, R – K1; 26 N – N5, R(2) – K2; 27 N – R7ch, Resigns.)

SUMMARY

Count a plus point for an outpost station when there is any reasonable prospect that it can be occupied by a piece with enhancement of its influence.

If the station is in front of a backward or isolated pawn, you are usually entitled to count a plus point for the station besides a minus point to the opponent for his weak pawn. Exception arises when occupation of the station would permit exchanges that would plug it with a pawn.

As a general rule, a square is not countable as an outpost station if it can be attacked by an adverse pawn; however, there are many exceptions, arising from the circumstances that the pawn advance to attack the post would incur a minus point for a hole, backward pawn, etc.

13.   *The Compromised King-Side*

THE three pawns in front of the castled king put up the strongest defense if they are left unmoved. The triple phalanx exerts maximum guard of the third rank. The pawns themselves are guarded by the king and are as remote as they can be from the reach of enemy pieces.

The wing is said to be *compromised* when one or more of the pawns has advanced *unfavorably*.

The danger of such advances may lie in either or both of two circumstances:

A]   holes are opened through which enemy pieces may infiltrate;

B]   the advanced pawns become targets of attack, if only by way of pawn exchanges to open files.

Nevertheless, king-side pawn advances are often compulsory to strengthen certain aspects of the defense, e.g., P – KB3 or B4 to allow guard of N2 by a rook on the second rank; P – KN3 to shield R2 from the adverse king bishop; P – KR3 to exclude a knight or a bishop from its KN5. And for offensive purposes, we often see the king denuded entirely of his infantry, as in the classical attack spearheaded by P – KB4, P – KN4. (See Nos. 15, 18, 47, 48. In No. 51 both sides struggle to advance their king-side pawns.)

Thus it is not possible to formulate a simple generality such as interdicting the advance of any pawn in front of the castled king as weakening. That is possibly true in a remote theoretical sense, but the practical questions are: Is the weakening serious? Can it ever be capitalized? How far is it outweighed by the immediate gain in defensive or offensive power?

One principle that has been proposed is that the advances are weakening when they are made under attack. While this is often true, it is by no means universal.

The question whether a king-side is compromised or not must be judged from the position as a whole—the solidity of the pawn formation, the posting and mobility of the pieces.

The Doubled King Bishop Pawn

The doubling of the king knight pawn upon the king bishop file has been discussed in Chapter 8. Nos. 66 and 67 show cases in which the doubling is actually advantageous, since the king can be defended from attack and the player can use the opened king knight file for an attack of his own. But these cases are the exception; as a rule, the doubling of the king bishop pawn seriously exposes the king, as remarked in connection with No. 65. An instructive instance is No. 104.

Tarrasch *v.* Janowski   1907

NO. 104A. *Black to move*

In No. 104A, Black need not yet fear the doubling of his king bishop pawn by BxN. His other knight is poised to go to KN3 at need, and also supports P – KB4. The natural continuation is to shut out the White king bishop by *1 . . . P – Q4.* Instead Black plays

1	B – N5?
2 P – B3	B – K3

This move seems good by analogy with No. 65—but mark well the difference!

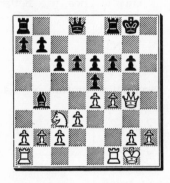

3 BxN	PxB
4 BxB	PxB
5 P – B4	N – N3
6 NxN	PxN
7 Q – N4	

NO. 104B. *Black to move*

The Black triple phalanx has moved picturesquely from the second rank to the third—where it hangs. The Black king is fatally compromised.

The Holes after P – KN3

In Chapter 11 we discussed the danger of leaving holes around the castled king by P – KN3. Nos. 86 and 87 show the voluntary swapping off of the fianchettoed king bishop to parry a tactical threat—a remedy worse than the ill. No. 105 demonstrates the elimination of the fianchettoed bishop by refined tactics.

White threatens *2 N – Q5, Q moves; 3 NxP, QxN; 4 BxN* winning the exchange besides the pawn. If *1 . . . QR – Q1,* then *2 N – Q5, Q – Q2; 3 N – B6ch* achieves White's object. Neverthe-

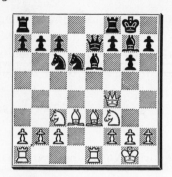

Matanovich *v*. Kieniger   1955

NO. 105A. *White to move*

1   B – QB5

less, this line, or Q – B3, giving up a pawn at once, was better than Black's actual choice.

1	P – N3
2 B – R3	

The first threat is renewed, and a second now appears, N – K4. Black is compelled to part with his king bishop.

2	BxN	*4* QR – Q1	N – R4
3 PxB	Q – Q2	*5* Q – R6	

NO. 105B.
*Compromised King-Side
Black to move*

White threatens N – N5. To guard his KR2, Black is forced to compromise his king still more by advancing the king bishop pawn.

5	P – KB3	8 BxN	PxB
6 BxP	PxB	9 RxB	QxR
7 QxPch	K – R1	10 R – Q4 and wins	

The mate threat costs Black his queen (Q – B5). The Black pieces are no match for the White queen, knight, and pawns. Thus, *10* . . . Q – B5; *11.* Q – R5ch, K – N2; *12* RxQ, NxR; *13* Q – N4ch, followed by *14* QxN.

File-Opening after P – KN3

Another hazard of P – KN3 is that it may enable the opponent to open the king rook file by P – KR4 – R5. This danger is acute if he has castled on the other side and his king rook still stands on its home square. Thus, in No. 106,

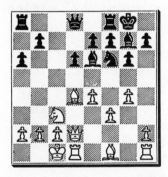

Katetov *v.* Golombek   1946

NO. 106. *White to move*

1 P – KR4!

Black normally has choice of two moves to oppose the file-opening: mechanical blockade by P – KR4, or P – KR3 so as to answer P – R5 by P – KN4. Here, both courses lose a pawn: *1* . . . P – KR4; *2* BxN, BxB; *3* PxP, PxP; *4* Q – R6. Or *1* . . . P – KR3; *2* BxN, BxB; *3* QxRP; if *2* . . . PxB; *3* QxQP. Black can but try counterattack.

1	P – QN4	5 PxP	BPxP
2 N – Q5	BxN	6 B – Q3	R – B2
3 PxB	Q – B2	7 Q – N5 and wins	
4 P – R5	QR – B1		

(7 . . . N – K1; 8 RxP, KxR; 9 QxPch, K – N1; 10 R – R1, N –
B3; 11 BxN, Resigns in view of 11 . . . RxB; 12 R – R8ch, KxR;
13 Q – R7 mate.)

Loosening Up KN3

The exchange of the rook pawn for a pawn on the adverse
KN3 not only opens the king rook file but also loosens up the
enemy square, KN3. Thus, in the final position of No. 106, White
threatens in certain contingencies (as 7 . . . Q – N2) to play
BxKNP, sacrificing his bishop for the two remaining king-side
pawns.

A remarkable demonstration of the peril in such loosening up
was given by Alekhine in No. 107. White's queen-side minority
attack is in full swing. He threatens to isolate and then win a
pawn there. How is Black to be saved? His actual move looks like
a futile gesture.

Reti *v.* Alekhine   1925

NO. 107. *Black to move*

1 . . .	P – KR4
2 P – N4	P – R3
3 R – QB1	P – R5
4 P – R4	PxP
5 RPxP	

What has Black accomplished? He is in no position to utilize
the opened king rook file.

| 5 . . . . | Q – B2 | 7 PxP | R – K6!! |
| 6 P – N5 | RPxP | | |

The saving counterattack. PxR loses at once to QxPch, and
Black himself threatens RxNPch. Later analysis decided that
White might have drawn with B – B3; instead he played for a
win by N – B3—and lost to an "immortal" combination.

Inducing P – KN3

The tyro chess player looks for a way to checkmate at every turn; the master is satisfied with more modest aims. The difference is, of course, that the master knows how to utilize small advantages.

One of the "modest aims" that may turn into a major triumph is to induce the opponent to move a pawn in front of his castled king.

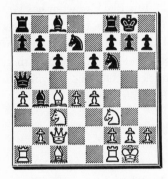

Denker v. Schwartz   1930

NO. 108. *White to move*

In No. 108, the preliminary maneuver is brief and simple.

1	P – K5	N – Q4
2	N – KN5	P – KN3

Mission accomplished. That the Black king is seriously compromised may be judged from the following circumstances: (a) The hole at KB3 is an outpost station, due to White's king pawn. Its occupation by knight (or pawn) would be murderous. (b) White's queen bishop is available to exploit the holes. (c) White has four minor pieces and the queen readily available to assault the king-side. (The king bishop serves where it stands, by threat of removing the defensive knight at Q4.) Black has only three minor pieces for defense. (The king rook is more hindrance than help, since KB1 could better be occupied by the queen knight or king bishop.)

                  3 QN – K4   B – K2
                  4 Q – Q3

The threat is 5 Q – KR3, P – R4; 6 P – KN4. There is no adequate defense.

                  4 . . . .   P – KR3
                  5 NxKP!   PxN
                  6 BxP and wins

In No. 109, White counts points for the half-open king bishop file and the broken Black queen-side. But Black's queen has good scope, and his half-open queen knight file is not to be despised. If all heavy pieces were swapped off, the bishops of opposite colors would probably assure Black an easy draw. White therefore bends his energies to direct attack on the king, in which the first step is to force an impairment of his pawns.

Tarrasch v. Bird   1898

NO. 109. *White to move*

1 Q – R4	QR – Q1
2 R – B3	Q – B5
3 Q – B2	Q – KN5
4 P – KR3	Q – N3
5 R – N3	Q – R4
6 Q – B6!	R – Q8ch
7 K – R2	P – N3

The game is still full of fight, but White has the upper hand. The bishops of opposite color are now a detriment to Black, for he cannot adequately defend the king-side holes.

P – KR3: Pro and Con

A whole book might be written about the move P – KR3. The question of when this move is weak and when it is strong is one of the most difficult in chess. All that we can do here is to indicate the factors to be weighed.

First let us examine the dangers to the pawn itself. It is under fire of the adverse queen bishop; if it is or can be attacked a second time, the sacrifice of the bishop for two pawns—plus exposure of the king—may be a good investment.

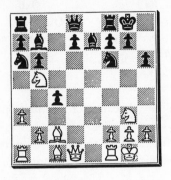

Bronstein *v.* Keres   1955

NO. 110. *White to move*

No. 110 shows the sort of thing that has happened in a thousand guises. White has let go of two pawns to set the stage for

1	**BxP!**	**PxB**
2	**Q – Q2**	**N – R2**

The pawn cannot be held; if K – N2, then N – B5ch.

3	**QxRP**	**P – B4**
4	**NxBP**	**RxN**
5	**BxR**	

Black has had to return more than the sacrificed piece to avoid mate, and his king is still in trouble.

A pawn at KR3 is under fire of an outpost knight at its KB5. The outpost is all the harder to dislodge after P – KR3 because P – KN3 leaves the rook pawn loose, unless time has been taken to guard it by K – R2 or B – KB1. Even if the knight can be repelled in this way, the rook pawn becomes dangerously weak because deprived of pawn protection. A classical demonstration of these facts was given by Capablanca in No. 111.

Capablanca *v.* O. Bernstein 1911

NO. 111. *Black to move*

1	P – KR3
2 B – R4	N – R2
3 BxB	QxB
4 Q – Q3	QR – N1
5 P – QN3	N – N4
6 QR – Q1	Q – K4
7 Q – K3	

Black seems to have a good game, because of the half-open files and the centralization of his queen. The fact is, however, that he lacks effective posts for his minor pieces and his queen will be chased away. White threatens 8 P – KB4; this move can be delayed but not prevented.

7	N – K3
8 N(3) – K2	Q – QR4

Since Black can no longer prevent P – KB4, he goes on a looting expedition.

9 N – B5!	N – B4
10 N(2) – Q4	

The outpost is secure and constantly menaces the king, besides exerting collateral threats such as *11* N – K7ch and *12* NxQBP. White won by a combined attack of queen and knight on Black's KN2.

The Pin of the King Knight

In the days of Anderssen, Morphy et al., it was quite the custom to move P – KR3 early so that the opponent could not—Heaven forbid!—move B – KN5, pinning the king knight. The later view of this custom is expressed by the two queries in this quotation from a book of Morphy's games (No. 112):

Anderssen *v.* Morphy   1858

NO. 112. *White to move*

9 P – KR3?	O – O
10 O – O	P – KR3?

These queries are not interpolated from hindsight: neither move, in fact, had detrimental consequences. (White lost through the weakness of his backward queen pawn, which became an isolani after P – Q4 and soon was captured.) But the pendulum has swung back a little way. We now regard it as rather arbitrary to query the moves in this position. Chess is not so easy! White takes a calculated risk in a good cause: he must move P – Q4 sooner or later but cannot well do so if his king knight can be pinned and destroyed. The Black P – KR3 seems less purposeful, and in fact Black had to take defensive measures against a possible sacrifice BxKRP. Yet, had the game taken a different course, it might have turned out to be useful preparation for a general king-side pawn advance.

The case is clearer in No. 113A, which resulted from these opening moves:

Journoud *v.* Morphy   (1858?)

1 P – K4	P – K4
2 N – KB3	N – QB3
3 B – B4	B – B4
4 N – B3	P – Q3

NO. 113A. *White to move*

5 P – KR3?

The query appended by all the editors is here fully deserved. At this juncture, 5 . . . B – KN5 would be a poor move. White answers 6 P – KR3, and if B – R4; 7 P – KN4. This unpinning procedure is dangerous after White has moved O – O, but not before, for then he can move O – O – O and continue his pawn storm of the king-side.

5	B – K3
6 B – N3	N – B3
7 P – Q3	Q – Q2
8 O – O	O – O
9 K – R1	P – KR3

NO. 113B. *White to move*

This move looks risky and *is* risky. White is about to open the king bishop file, after which the rook's attack on the king knight combined with the bishop's attack on the king rook pawn will threaten at least the win of a pawn. We can only conclude that Morphy had calculated the ensuing play to move 20—evidently the editors thought so in omitting the traditional query at move 9!

10 N – R2	P – Q4

This center break is what saves Black's king-side. Intent on his wing attack, White sacrifices a pawn to avoid wholesale exchanges.

11 P – B4	QPxP
12 BPxP	NxP
13 N – R4	B – N3
14 NxB	RPxN
15 P – O4	N – B3

NO. 113C. *White to move*

White wants to prove that 9 . . . P – KR3 was a mistake. In-sufficient is *16* BxP, e.g., BxB; *17* BPxB, QxQP; *18* QxQ, NxQ; *19* RxN, PxB; *20* RxRP, K – N2; *21* R – R5, P – KB4. Hence:

16	RxN	PxR
17	BxP	KR – Q1
18	Q – K1	N – K2
19	Q – R4	N – N3
20	QxBP	QxP

and Black wins

P – KR3 by the Book

The move P – KR3 is often made merely to parry an im-mediate threat. But it can have solid positional value, as is at-tested by the fact that it is accepted in a number of opening varia-tions.

For example, if from No. 113A we continue *5* P – Q3, N – KB3, we reach the standard symmetrical position of the Giuoco Piano. The best continuation is no doubt *6* B – K3, but *6* P – KR3 is also a "book" line.

In No. 114, a common position of the Ruy Lopez, White wants to play P – Q4. But it has been found that the reply B – N5, with the immediate threat of doubling the king bishop pawn, gives

Black adequate counterplay. The "book" move is therefore
P – KR3, preventing the pin in preparation for P – Q4.

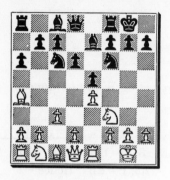

NO. 114. *White to move*

The "book" does not guarantee you against trouble: you still
have a game to play! You must try to direct the course of the
game so that the "remote theoretical weakness" of P – KR3 does
not become an actuality. No. 115 is a position that arose after
the Ruy Lopez P – KR3. White has failed in his task. Black has
obtained the strong station KB5 for his knight, in consequence
of both P – KR3 and the disappearance of White's queen bishop.
Black, too, has moved P – KR3, but this move has turned out to
be strong, for it has induced White to play BxN (at KB3), and
White has no king-side attack.

Blau *v.* Van Scheltinga   1947

NO. 115. *White to move*

1 B – B1

White dreams of repelling the outpost by P – KN3.

1	N – B5
2 K – R2	P – KN4
3 N – N1	

Directed against P – N5.

3	P – N5!
4 P – KN3	NxP
5 NxN	PxN
6 Q – Q2	Q – N3
and Black wins	

White cannot remove the advanced pawn (7 BxP? Q – R4).

SUMMARY

Count a point minus for compromised pawns in front of the castled king. Regard the compromise as serious if the opponent has a lead in development and can quickly work up a king-side attack.

Most perilous is likely to be a doubled king bishop pawn; P – KN3 is less so, but still leaves dangerous holes; P – KR3 is often innocuous or strengthening, but needs watching. The advance of the king bishop pawn is often essential to strengthen center-command or to spearhead an attack, but is compromising if the king pawn is thereby left backward.

As explained in Chapter 6, the king-side pawns may often be advanced away from the castled king to spearhead an attack; the king is not thereby compromised if (a) you have enough pieces in the vicinity to prosecute the attack; these pieces also guard the king; (b) the center is blocked and the opponent cannot break through to get behind your front line.

14. *The King in the Center*

THE king is usually tucked away in a corner, by castling, for two purposes:

A] to remove the king from the open central lines, where he could be more readily attacked, and

B] to connect the rooks and clear the center for occupation by the fighting pieces.

Forfeiture of the right to castle, by an early move of the king, can have disastrous consequences to the king's safety or the rook's development or both.

The Check at R5

The commonest cause of a forced early king move is a queen check at KR5 after the king bishop pawn has advanced, at a time when the interposition P – KN3 is not feasible. Every beginner has to learn once and for all that after *1* P – K4, P – K4; *2* N – KB3 the move P – KB3 is no good—*3* NxP, PxN; *4* Q – R5ch, P – N3; *5* QxKPch and wins the rook, or *4* . . . K – K2; *5* QxKPch, K – B2; *6* B – B4ch.

A similar error is sometimes committed by beginners in essaying the King's Gambit: *1* P–K4, P–K4; *2* P–KB4, PxP; *3* N–KB3, P–KN4; *4* P–Q4? P–N5; *5* N–K5, Q–R5ch and the king takes a trip.

Even the masters sometimes err by opening the diagonal prematurely, as witness No. 116. Black has laid himself open to Q–R5ch, which will be embarrassing because then P–N3 fails to NxP. He can do no better than play P–N3 at once, though manifestly his king-side pawns are then very wobbly. But at least he would retain the opportunity to develop naturally by N–K2 and B–N2. Instead, he tries to develop while keeping his pawns intact.

Spassky *v.* Taimanov   1955

NO. 116. *Black to move*

1	N – K2?
2 PxP	QPxP
3 Q – B3	Q – Q2
4 R – Q1	Q – K3
5 B – K3	P – N4??

Black loses patience and tries to batter his way out of the bind. But now White hurls a thunderbolt:

6 NxP!	PxN
7 Q – R5ch	Q – B2
8 RxRch	BxR
9 R – Q8ch and wins	

Black will have three pieces for his lost queen, but White gains five pawns, and the Black king has no haven of safety.

Sacrificing to Hold the King

It is generally worth a pawn, if not more, to hold the enemy king in the center and subject to attack. This consideration enters into certain "book" variations. For example, No. 117 is a regular position of the Queen's Gambit Accepted. Black threatens PxP,

Giplis *v.* Klasup   1954

NO. 117. *White to move*

and then White must choose between NxP, leaving the pawns balanced and so diminishing his chances for a win, and PxP, affording Black play against the isolani. The "book" move (since Reshevsky *v.* Vidmar, 1936) is

1	P – Q5!	PxP
2	P – K4!	P – Q5

The "book" move is to refuse the sacrifice by O – O – O. Fatal is *2* . . . PxP; *3* NxKP. The text move proves to be insufficient; Black never gets a chance to castle out of trouble.

3	N – Q5	NxN
4	PxNch	N – K2
5	P – QR4	P – B5
6	NxP!	BxP
7	PxP	PxB
8	N – B5	R – Q1
9	PxP and wins	

The passed pawn soon costs Black a piece.

In No. 118, White has already sacrificed a pawn to gain a large lead in development. He must strike quickly before Black has time to consolidate his dangling center.

Najdorf *v.* Ilivitsky   1955

NO. 118. *White to move*

| 1 N – K4 | P – Q4 |
| 2 BxN! | |

Not 2 NxNch, PxN; 3 BxP, B – K2; 4 BxR? B – N4.

| 2 . . . . | PxB |
| 3 NxPch | K – K2 |

Now White has his pawn back. The Black center pawns are strong, but the exposure of his king lets White make further inroads.

| 4 Q – N4ch! | P – B4 |

If KxN, then Q – R4ch wins the queen. If Q – Q3, the same move sets up a deadly battery.

| 5 QxPch | Q – Q3 |

If KxN, Q – Q4ch wins the rook (since P – K4 loses to Q – R4ch).

6 Q – Q4	B – KN2
7 NxPch	K – B1
8 Q – N6! and wins	

The subject of sacrifice to keep the king in the center brings to mind the triple catastrophe to Argentina at Gothenburg, 1955. The tale is oft-told but will bear repetition. Three Russian players sat on the White side against three Argentine players, all of whom uncorked a prepared variation of the Sicilian Defense. All three games reached the position No. 119. All three Blacks made the key moves:

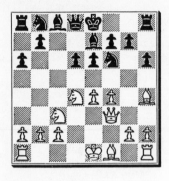

Spassky *v.* Pilnik   1955
Keres *v.* Najdorf   1955
Geller *v.* Panno   1955

NO. 119. *Black to move*

| 1 . . . . | P – KN4 |
| 2 PxP | KN – Q2 |

All three Russians made the enticing sacrifice to open the dangerous diagonal:

| 3 NxP! | PxN |
| 4 Q – R5ch | K – B1 |

Next on the program for White is to move the king bishop so as to follow with the rook check at KB1. The Argentine contingent had analyzed the White sacrifice and had concluded that there was a sufficient defense in 5 . . . N – K4 (on 5 B – B4); 6 B – KN3, QN – Q2 whereby Black maintains the knight guard of his tender spot, KB2. But all three Russians found the refutation of this defense with

5 B – N5!!

There is no time to capture this bishop, which therefore stands ready to pluck off the reinforcing queen knight. All three Russians won.

Cramping of the Rook

The plight of a rook locked in the corner by its own king is usually overshadowed by the plight of the king. But here is a simon-pure case in which the rook alone was the sufferer.

In No. 120, Edward Lasker (Black) had just played R(R1) – B1, thinking to seize the file with the gain of a tempo. He could scarcely have anticipated the jolt

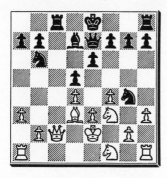

Janowski *v.* Ed. Lasker   1924

NO. 120. *White to move*

1 QxRch!?

Janowski (White) was not a routine player! He decides that his own compromised position will be relieved from immediate assault if he gives up the queen for rook and knight. The opening of the king rook file will prevent Black from castling, wherefore he will.go for some time without the active services of his rook, while White can prepare to penetrate on the queen bishop file. The fact is that Black kept the upper hand throughout the long game, which eventually came down to the extraordinary situation of lone queen against a knight and three pawns. After overlooking several chances to clinch the win, White blundered into a perpetual check.

Voluntary Forfeiture of Castling

The possibility of a mating attack is much lessened if the queens are swapped off. The king then often stands better on K2 or Q2, ready to march into the center, than in the corner. It is not too much to say that, if the queens are exchanged early, you should view castling with suspicion. The king should stay in the center unless it can be driven away by the adverse bishops.

No. 121 is a regular position of the Queen's Gambit. Strong is Alekhine's Attack:

NO. 121. *White to move*

1 N – K4

threatening to go to N5 or N3 and R5. The point is that

1	Q – N5ch
2 Q – Q2	QxQch
3 KxQ	

is good for White. His king is centralized, while the Black king is not.

Even with queens still on the board, the king may stand better in the center (or subcenter) than at the side. In some positions the rook is wanted at the side rather than in the center. An instance is No. 122. Black might move O – O – O preparatory to advancing his king-side pawns. But he would first have to prepare against BxQRP and would also have to reckon on a counterattack by queen-side pawn advances. Yet he must get his king out of the way quickly to bring a rook to K1, since his knight will soon need additional protection. The solution is

Corzo *v.* Capablanca   1913

NO. 122. *Black to move*

1 . . . .   K – B1!

Here the king is perfectly safe and also guards the king rook, an important factor in the later play. In contrast, the position of the White king is miserable. He bottles up the king rook, and thus deprives himself of a much-needed flight square.

The voluntary forfeiture of castling is anticipated in certain regular openings. An example is the Bishop's Gambit:

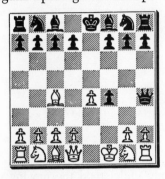

NO. 123. *Black to move*

1 P – K4	P – K4
2 P – KB4	PxP
3 B – B4	Q – R5ch
4 K – B1	

White will gain a tempo by N – KB3, and eventually will castle "by hand" (as by K – B2, KR – B1, K – N1). The object of the pawn sacrifice and bishop move is to gain a large lead in development, plus eventually the half-open king bishop file.

SUMMARY

Count a point minus for the king held in the center against his will. Do not debit forfeiture of castling made voluntarily for sound purpose, or made after queens are exchanged and no mating attack is to be feared.

15. *Development*

BY *development* is commonly understood the moving of one's pieces off the first rank at the beginning of a game. The normal process is to advance two or more pawns to let out the bishops and queen, advance these pieces together with the knights, then castle. The development is regarded as complete when the rooks are connected—that is, "attack" each other on the first rank.

This criterion is used for convenience. It is not intended to imply that you must connect your rooks before embarking on maneuvers typical of the midgame. Indeed, you are often forced into a front-line skirmish that leaves you no opportunity, for many moves, to clear your back row.

Nevertheless, it is vital to bring your pieces into action as quickly as possible. To put it precisely, you must not let your opponent gain too large a *lead* in development. The possible consequences are illustrated by the following two examples.

The Numerical Lead

After sixteen moves, the "Immortal Partie" of Anderssen *v.* Kieseritzky (1851) reached the position of No. 124.

NO. 124.

Superior Development
Black to move

White has three minor pieces and the queen in action, plus mobile pawns in the center and king-side. Even the king rook is active. Against this colossal force Black has only one piece off the back row—a queen that is in trouble. Among White's many threats are several that would compel Black to waste further time in saving the queen (N – Q5, P – K5, etc.). It is no wonder that White can afford a liberal expenditure (two rooks and a queen!) to break into the Black camp.

$$1 \ldots \ldots \qquad \mathbf{B – B4}$$

There is nothing better. Above all, the king needs room.

2	N – Q5	QxP	6	NxPch	K – Q1
3	B – Q6	BxR	7	Q – B6ch	NxQ
4	P – K5	QxRch	8	B – Q7 mate	
5	K – K2	N – QR3			

It is no derogation of this brilliant combination to point out that White could have won the game in many ways from the diagrammed position. The hard work was behind him—the achievement of his enormous lead in development.

This is but an extreme example of a general truth: winning combinations arise of themselves when one player has a considerably greater number of pieces· developed than does his opponent.

The Qualitative Lead

No. 125A is, pictorially, at the other extreme from No. 124. Here there is no mating attack in prospect, nor remotely conceivable. All the pieces and pawns left on the board stand at home, with the sole exception of the White knight. White seems to have a one-piece lead in development—yet, we may say, he always has that by virtue of his first move.

Actually, the White lead in time is a little greater. For, if the knight also stood on its home square (KN1), we would have to give White two moves in succession to reproduce the present position. Thus White has actually gained one tempo over his initial one.

Further, and even more important, the knight at Q4 is singularly powerful. By the threat of going to N5 and thence to B7, it compels Black to lose further time in (piece) development, and from Q4 it hampers the normal development of the Black queen-side.

Keres *v.* R. Byrne   1955

NO. 125A. *Black to move*

1	P – QR3
2 B – K3	P – K4
3 N – N3	B – KB4
4 O – O – O	N – Q2

The knight has to go here because Black cannot well allow N – B5. Besides, he wants to bring his king to the defense of the queen-side.

5 B – Q3	BxB
6 RxB	

The exchange is another gain of tempo for White—a bishop that has moved twice disappears for one that has moved once.

    6 . . . .   O – O – O
    7 N – R5!

The threatened attack on the queen knight pawn (by R – B3ch and R – N3) is difficult to meet. If 7 . . . B – N5; 8 NxP, KxN; 9 R – N3.

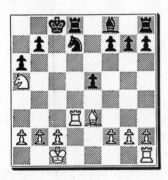

NO. 125B. *Black to move*

    7 . . . .   P – QN3
    8 R – B3ch   B – B4
    9 N – N3

White wins a pawn.

This example illustrates the principle that we must not compare the development of the two sides by the number of pieces alone: we must also examine the effectiveness of the posts taken by the pieces. The single White knight of No. 125A represents a considerable *qualitative* lead.

Counting Tempos

A way of comparing the development of the two sides, during the very early stage of a game, is to count the number of moves each would have to make to reach the present position. If the two totals are the same, with White to move, or if White is one ahead when Black is to move, then White has merely retained his initial tempo. In other circumstances, one side has gained in time.

Colle System   Nimzovich *v*. Fluess   1906

NO. 126. *Black to move*   NO. 127. *White to move*

For example, in No. 126, each side can reach its present position in eight moves. But it is Black's turn; therefore White has
lost a tempo along the way. (This he did by taking two moves
to get his king pawn to the fourth.)

Again, in No. 127, the White position is reached in two (pawn)
moves; the Black, in three. It is White's turn; he has lost his
initial tempo. (This occurred by the capture KPxQP, answered
by QxP.)

The method has its uses—it detects past losses of tempo. But it
does not render a verdict on the merits of the present position.
In No. 126, the fact that Black has gained a tempo does not
mean that White has lost the initiative; on the contrary, White's
delayed P – K4 is very powerful (see No. 43). Furthermore, when
counted by this method, the tempos change rapidly. Continue
with the forced moves from No. 126: *1* . . . PxKP; *2* NxP, NxN;
3 BxN, N – B3; *4* B – B2. The new White position can be reached
in seven moves; the Black, in six; the turn is Black's: therefore
White has regained his initial tempo.

In No. 127 the method reports that Black has gained a tempo.
Here the count appears to represent something tangible, for Black
has one piece off the back row while White has none.

The Tally of Developed Pieces

A better method of estimating the relative development is to count the number of pieces of each color off the back row, plus any developing moves on the first rank itself (castling; a rook move to a central file).

We concede at once that this method ignores all pawn moves; also the qualitative aspect of development. But it is a good point of departure. The mere number of pieces developed is certainly important. Suppose that White has four pieces in action and Black one. Unless the White pieces have taken poor posts, Black's game is precarious, and if all the White pieces stand on good posts, Black is probably lost.

In many of the regular openings, one side or the other gains a lead of one unit in development—and this is often transient. The critical point is reached when one side has a lead of two units. For example, suppose that White has three pieces developed, Black has one, and it is White's turn to move. His lead may not produce a mating attack, but it will often produce *lasting advantages*.

Consider No. 128. White has established the advanced salient of the French Defense and so has greater central space. He has also expanded on the queen-side. Black's queen bishop is "bad"

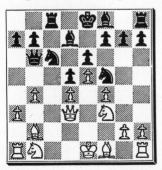

McConnell *v.* Morphy   1850

NO. 128. *Black to move*

and at the moment is immobilized by its own friends. The king bishop is restrained by the White pawns on both wings and can take only the modest post K2. From these considerations, we might conclude that White has the better game.

But, look at the development. White has three pieces developed; Black has five; and it is *Black's turn to move.* Black has a lead of three units: can he not capitalize it in some way before White catches up? Morphy found the answer:

1	BxPch!	4 Q – Q1	N – K6
2 PxB	NxNP	Resigns	
3 Q – Q2	R – B7		

How Tempos Are Lost

During the opening, as we have noted, the lead in piece development is likely to change frequently, within the narrow limits of one unit either way. The causes of change are:

A] pawn moves;
B] multiple moves by the same piece;
C] exchanges.

Every pawn move is a lost tempo as concerns piece development. This very fact points out that you need not "view with alarm" every tempo loss. Pawn moves are indispensable, both to let your pieces out and to dispute control of the center. Some brevities have been won by pawn moves alone! But a thousand times more games are lost by superfluous or premature pawn moves.

Multiple Moves by the Same Piece

Among the maxims sometimes propounded to beginners is: Never move the same piece twice until you have moved each piece once. Of course, this counsel of perfection is not a practical program. After *1* P – K4, P – K4; *2* N – KB3, N – QB3; *3* B – N5, P – QR3, White has got to move his bishop a second time. He loses a tempo but not his lead, since Black has previously given up a tempo by the rook pawn move.

A second move by an already developed piece is a net loss of time only when the opponent's intervening move is developing. Thus, after *1* P – K4, P – Q4; *2* PxP, QxP, White has momentarily lost his initial tempo—Black has a piece off the back row and White has none. White at once regains it by *3* N – QB3, and the developed queen has to move a second time. (If *3* . . . Q – Q1, White stands two units ahead. The only good alternative is *3* . . . Q – QR4, but then White stands to gain a tempo later, for the queen almost always has to retreat in the face of White developing moves.)

We are here concerned with the mechanics of the tempo, not with the tactical question of when a loss of tempo is unavoidable or acceptable. However, excessive loss of time becomes a strategical matter, by conferring on the opponent a point for superior development. This is the general case against "pawn-grabbing." A queen raid into enemy territory usually costs two or three tempos, the queen being chased back by developing moves. The time thus gained is often worth more than the pawn.

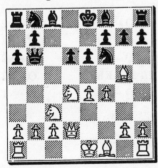

Keres *v.* Fuderer 1955

NO. 129. *Black to move*

No. 129 is a position arising from the Sicilian Defense. The present view is that Black might as well take the proffered pawn, to justify his previous move (Q – N3). We venture to predict that the whole variation will be discarded for Black. One of the definitive games continued:

| 1 . . . . | QxP | 3 P – K5 | KN – Q2 |
| 2 QR – N1 | Q – R6 | | |

The White tempo gains show starkly in the variation *3 . . .* N – Q4; *4* NxN, PxN; *5* R – N3, QxP; *6* R – K3.

4 P – B5	NxP	7 NxN	PxN
5 PxP	PxP	8 N – K4	P – Q4
6 B – K2	QN – B3	9 O – O	

Now White has all his pieces in action, while Black has only queen and knight out—both badly exposed. Black's next move may be regarded as a blunder, but his game is hopeless in any event.

9	Q – R5
10 B – R5ch	K – Q2
11 RxB and wins	

One well-posted piece may be worth two pieces indifferently placed. Moving the same piece twice in the opening may be worthwhile to reach a strong post. A celebrated instance is the game Alekhine *v.* Wolf, 1922:

1 P – Q4	P – Q4	7 Q – R4ch	B – Q2
2 N – KB3	P – QB4	8 Q – N3	N – B4
3 P – B4	BPxP	9 Q – K3	P – KN3
4 PxP	N – KB3	10 N – KB3	Q – B2
5 NxP	P – QR3?	11 Q – B3	R – N1
6 P – K4	NxKP		

Alekhine *v.* Wolf   1922

NO. 130. *White to move*

In eleven turns, White has moved his queen four times and his knight thrice—and he has a won game!

Naturally, such maneuvers can succeed only in exceptional circumstances. First of all, the opponent must set the stage by a bad mistake (P – QR3). Second, there must be a modicum of strategical advantage: by giving up his king pawn, White is able to maintain the more important queen pawn, which exerts a cramp on the Black development. Third, precise tactics must be found to prevent the opponent from repelling the lighthorse attack by simple and good developing moves.

On the queen check (Q – R4), Black cannot play Q – Q2 because of B – QN5, while P – N4 fails upon BxPch or NxP. The forced 7 . . . B – Q2 both masks the Black queen's attack on the queen pawn and leaves the Black queen knight pawn loose. The protection of this pawn after 8 Q – N3 is awkward; after Q – B1 or B2 the queen would later be chased by a White rook on the open queen bishop file. If 8 . . . N – Q3, then 9 B – KB4 and again the queen knight pawn is in jeopardy. Since the Black knight can be chased with a gain of tempo anyhow (by B – Q3), 8 . . . N – B4 seems natural. The White queen is attacked with gain of a tempo, yet White regains the tempo two moves later, when he attacks the unprotected knight. After 9 Q – K3 Black is at a loss how to develop. The desirable 9 . . . P – K3 is too compromising. Hence 9 . . . P – KN3, with its consequent forfeiture of king-side castling. Observe that in No. 130, despite his repeated moves of the same pieces, White is not behind in the tally of developed pieces—two each. But he has an enormous qualitative lead.

Exchanges

When two pieces are exchanged, the moves they have previously made disappear from the reckoning. If one piece has moved more often than the other, its disappearance represents a loss of one or more tempos.

Tartakover *v.* Capablanca   1924

NO. 131. *White to move*

In No. 131, the development is even: each side has two pieces off the back row, and it is White's turn.

1 BxN?

White was under the misapprehension that he wins a piece (*1 . . . RxB?; 2 Q – R4ch*). He overlooks

1 . . . .   N – Q4!

Guards the bishop and also threatens the fork at K6. White has no time to save the bishop.

2 K – B2   RxB

Now tally the development. It is again White's turn; he has one piece developed, while Black has three pieces. (The move of the rook to QN1 is actual development, as Black soon demonstrated by P – QN4, hitting the White bishop at QB4 and opening his own QN2 for his queen bishop.) This would also have been the count had *1 . . . RxB* been tactically feasible. Thus White has lost two tempos in the transaction. Where did they go? The answer is that the White queen bishop moved twice to exchange itself for a Black knight that had not moved at all.

The moral is *not* to avoid early swaps: you can no more do so than you can avoid pawn moves. The moral is to embark on exchanges with your eyes open to their effect on the status of development.

In No. 132A (Nimzovich *v.* Capablanca), White evidently aimed to reach a draw by "woodchopping."

Nimzovich *v.* Capablanca 1927

NO. 132A. *White to move*

1	PxP?	NxP
2	N – N3	B – N2
3	NxN	BxN
4	Q – R4	Q – B3
5	B – R6	BxB
6	QxB	N – N5
7	Q – K2	KR – Q1

Compare the two diagrams. In No. 132A, the tally of developed pieces is 3 – 3, with White to move. In No. 132B, the tally is 4 – 2 in Black's favor. The Black gain has been even greater when we

NO. 132B. *White to move*

consider that the knight has had to move three times to reach QN5. White has lost the tempos by his own hand—the ill-advised exchanges. Nor is the loss purely formal, for now Black controls the queen file and threatens to plant his knight at Q6.

Superior Development

As used in this book, "development" refers not only to the early process of bringing out one's pieces but also to their disposition at any stage of the game. In the second sense, a player may have "superior development" in endplay. We deliberately refrain from distinguishing the two senses by two different words, because the two aspects should always be considered together.

Further, any present disposition of pieces should be weighed not only for what it *is* but also for what it may *become*.

There is no simple yardstick for determining which side, if either, has the better development, nor whether the difference amounts to a countable point under the system. We have indicated factors to be considered. One is the lead in the number of pieces brought out, during the opening or early game. A lead of more than two units is likely to be decisive (No. 124). Tempos are of necessity handed back and forth in the opening; undue weight must not be placed on a transient lead (No. 126). Another factor is the effectiveness of the posts to which the pieces are brought. A single strongly posted piece can bring accumulating advantage (No. 125A). A third consideration is the future of the pieces. A player who can develop quickly and naturally has a countable (even decisive) advantage if his opponent is cramped or has to overcome special difficulties (No. 130).

The evaluation process cannot be adequately illustrated with a few examples. The reader is urged to study the many positions in this book (over a hundred) in which one side is credited with a point for superior development.

Every Little Move Has a Meaning All Its Own

A lag in development without corresponding gain elsewhere implies faulty management. The fault may be twofold in nature: the occasional mental lapse and its consequent meaningless move and/or the inattentiveness to the play of the opponent. This holds true not only for the opening but for every phase of the game.

It is abundantly clear that every White and Black move adds a net plus or minus to the position. It is equally clear that the fine distinction is lost on you, unless you understand the meaning of the move or can ascribe some purpose to it. Even when you stall or your opponent bides his time, you must know or ascertain exactly what is going on. In this way, if his play bodes ill (to you), it can be stopped dead in its tracks, diverted or countered.

If it bodes well, by all means it must be ignored or encouraged.

Be positive about your own moves in the sense that you feel that they contribute to your general welfare.

SUMMARY

Count a point plus for superior development, consisting in a significant lead in time, or in better-posted pieces, or in better prospects of future deployment.

16. *Space*

THE player who controls the greater space on the board is better able (a) to post his pieces effectively, (b) to transfer pieces from one wing to the other, and (c) to concentrate pieces quickly for defense or attack in one sector.

It is not always easy to determine which side, if either, controls the greater space. The difficulty arises from trying to appraise the squares in the no-man's-land between the two armies. However, in the Point Count System, these squares are sufficiently treated under other topics: center control, superior development, open files, etc. We will therefore restrict our consideration to *the space behind one's own front lines.* This is in accordance with practical experience. Space as such is significant when there is a definite front line. When the front line is liquidated and the movement of pieces is relatively untrammeled, any spatial advantage must necessarily take the guise of superior development.

The Cramped Position

If one player enjoys greater interior space to a degree which is countable as a point under the system, his opponent's position is more or less *cramped.* Thus we may regard the point as a plus for greater space or a minus for a cramped position, as we please. There is only one point at issue, except in extreme cases.

Let us dispose of the extreme case first. In No. 133, White has

Capablanca *v.* Treybal   1929

NO. 133. *White to move*

all the space in the world, while the Black pieces are locked into ten squares behind their own pawns. No Black piece can even break out of the prison, while White has an avenue into the Black camp, the queen rook file. (Black cannot challenge control of the file, for if he ever captures a White piece at his QR2, the resulting White passed pawn, plus the opening of the file on Black's backward queen knight pawn, is murderous.)

In this extreme case we must credit White with two points, a plus for his space and a Black minus for the cramp. White may count another plus for his absolute command of the open file, and debit Black another for his wretched bishop (which in truth impairs Black's defense by obstructing his major pieces). White, with a four-point edge, has a "won game," though the process of winning it may be (and was) protracted.

The more usual picture of a cramp is presented by No. 134, which arises from the Hanham Variation of Philidor's Defense.

NO. 134. *White to move*

Having chain *v.* phalanx, Black necessarily has a little less central space, which is further reduced (deliberately) by keeping the king bishop locked in by P – Q3.

However, mark well that Black has reasonable prospect of finding good posts for his pieces and then of dissolving the center. One possibility is N – QN3 and B – K3, perhaps with P – QR4 to secure the position of the knight. Another is R – K1, N – KB1, then N – K3 or N – N3, the queen bishop being brought out at K3 or N5. Finally, since the center is still elastic, White will constantly have to reckon with KPxQP and with P – Q4. White has the better game, with a point for greater space, since he can move quickly to meet and minimize each Black maneuver— but that is all.

Bastrikov *v.* Panov   1938

NO. 135.
Cramped Position
Black to move

More serious is the Black cramp in No. 135, for the reason that the center is blocked. To increase his space, Black would have to enforce P – QN4 or P – KB4. If we shut our eyes to all the White pieces except those which prevent these breaks, we see that it does not much matter how the rest of the White army is disposed. Black suffers from inability to find posts for his pieces from which they can bear on enemy territory. Perhaps he can move N – Q2 – KB3; then what? Where is he to place his other knight, two bishops and queen?

Nevertheless, Black's plight is not so bad as to warrant crediting White with two points for it.

White does have a second point, however, in his mobile king-side pawns, which threaten a classical storm (P – KN4 – N5). A third point is in prospect, for superior development, by a massing of pieces on the king-side (e.g., O – O – O and QR – KN1). Black must bolster his king-side in a hurry.

The Strategy of Restraint

In the opening, one desideratum is to bring out one's pieces quickly and effectively. Another is to hamper the development of the adverse pieces, when opportunity offers. Restraint of the adverse army builds up a spatial advantage and on occasion can turn into complete strangulation (see No. 4).

The primary force of restraint is exerted by the front-line pawns. In Chapter 4 we saw how a single advanced pawn (Q5) may seriously hamper the opponent's entire development. Faulty tactics can lead to strangulation in the opening, as has been demonstrated in games of Tarrasch, Nimzovich and others. A famous instance is Taubenhaus *v.* Tarrasch, 1885:

1 P – QB4	P – K3	3 P – K3	P – QB4
2 N – QB3	P – Q4	4 N – B3?	P – Q5!

This advance, usually interdicted for Black by his tempo behind, is possible here because of White's restricted development.

5 N – K2	N – QB3	10 P – R3	B – Q2
6 N – N3	P – KR4	11 P – K4	P – B3
7 P – QR3?	P – R5	12 N – R2	P – KN4
8 N – K2	P – K4	13 B – Q2	P – R5
9 P – Q3	P – R4		

Of Black's thirteen moves, eleven have been pawn advances—and he now has a won game! His pawns have staked out the major space and have imposed a permanent cramp on the White forces. Under the system, he scores a double point, with a third

Taubenhaus *v.* Tarrasch   1885

NO. 136. *White to move*

to come (for superior development) when he mobilizes his pieces to smash up the helpless enemy.

Expansion

In Chapter 6 we discussed the desirability of expansion as a means of attack. No. 136 and other examples remind us that expansion also has its defensive aspect. To keep one's army too compact courts suffocation.

In Chapter 5 we mentioned the danger of delaying the central pawn advances too long. Some delay is imposed on Black by White's initial tempo; in close openings particularly, Black must not falter in the constant effort to gain his fair share of space. A signal triumph of expansion was achieved by Black in No. 137A.

A King's Indian Defense has produced No. 137A. Black has moved P – K4 after due preparation, and now we have the familiar situation that whoever initiates a swap of center pawns

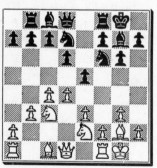

Spanjaard *v.* Van den Berg

NO. 137A. *Black to move*

gives an advantage to his opponent. To let the pawns dangle is a greater strain on Black than on White. White can continue with P – KB4, and perhaps, after due preparation, P – K4 and P – B5. Black can play R – K1; then what? He does not like to move his queen knight so long as White can play P – Q5, to which the riposte is N – B4 and then P – QR4 to maintain the outpost.

$$1 \ldots \ldots \qquad \text{P – KR4}$$
$$2 \ \text{P – KR3}$$

To keep the file closed by P – KN4 in case of P – R5.

$$2 \ldots \ldots \qquad \text{P – R3}$$

These two moves by Black seem to say naïvely, "Since I can't expand in the center, I will expand on the extreme wings!" Well, there are worse reasons for pawn shoves! But Black is actually implementing a subtle plot.

$$3 \ \text{P – QR4}$$

To prevent P – QN4.

$$3 \ldots \ldots \qquad \text{R – K1}$$
$$4 \ \text{B – R3} \qquad \text{P – K5!}$$

Now he shows his fangs. This move is usually hazardous in such positions, but Black has calculated well.

$$5 \ \text{Q – B2} \qquad \text{N – B1!}$$

Now if White takes the king pawn, Black gets the king rook pawn and freedom for his queen bishop.

$$6 \ \text{K – R2} \qquad \text{B – B4}$$

Now the real purpose of 1 . . . P – KR4 is revealed.

$$7 \ \text{P – Q5} \qquad \text{N(3) – R2}$$

Directed against N – Q4.

8 N – Q4?	BxN
9 PxB	N – N4
10 N – K2	N – B6ch
11 K – R1	N – R2

NO. 137B. *White to move*

What a transformation! Now Black has the major space, plus better development and a mobile king-side pawn wing. He won in a romp.

(*12* N – B4, N(2) – N4; *13* P – R4, NxRP; *14* B – B1, N(5) – B6; *15* B – K3, P – R5; *16* Q – B1, Q – B3; *17* BxN, NxB; *18* K – N2, K – N2; *19* R – R1, R – KR1; *20* Q – B3, B – N5; *21* QR – QB1, PxP; *22* PxP, P – KN4; *23* N – R3, RxN; *24* RxR, BxRch; *25* KxB, R – R1ch; *26* K – N2, N – K8ch; *27* Resigns.)

The Open Board

The question of which player commands the greater space on an open board—and what advantage it is to him—can be very intricate. The relative value of squares controlled becomes much more important than their mere number. That is why, in the Point Count System, we restrict our consideration to space behind the front lines, whenever these exist. The spatial advantages on the open board are to be estimated under specific heads: center control, open files, etc.

Nevertheless, positions are seen occasionally in which one player's quantitative command is so great as to merit a point in itself, in addition to whatever is due for specific center control, etc. In No. 138 we trace the rise of such a position.

In No. 138A, Black has had the queen-side trouble that is his usual lot in the queen pawn openings. His queen bishop pawn is backward on an open file, and its advance to QB4 will result in a hanging phalanx. However, he can make a defensive stand after B – N2, R – B1 and R – K1. White strikes while the iron is hot—that is, while the queen bishop pawn is unprotected:

Kramer *v.* Busek   1955

NO. 138A. *White to move*

1 P – K4	PxP
2 NxP	NxN

If 2 . . . N – Q4, then 3 QR – B1 and protection of the pawn is very awkward.

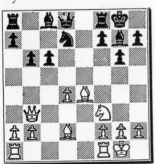

3 BxN

NO. 138B. *Black to move*

White's queen pawn is now isolated, but his attack on the queen bishop pawn hits first. If 3 . . . B – N2; 4 QR – B1, R – B1; 5 Q – R4. Black is practically forced to "undevelop"—

3	N – N1
4 P – Q5	

Now White can afford to let both weak pawns disappear, for then his pieces will reach strong central posts.

4	B – N2	7 KR – Q1	Q – N2
5 B – N5	Q – Q2	8 B – Q5!	
6 PxP	BxP		

Gaining a tempo as against BxB.

8 . . . .   **BxB**

9 **RxB**

NO. 138C. *Black to move*

Now White has a clear lead in development. With one more move his queen rook will get into action, whereas Black has to bring out his knight again and then find places for his rooks. But more: the extraordinary command over all the central squares entitles White to an additional point for space alone. To appreciate how great is that command, examine the various tries for Black development—e.g., ·9 . . . N – Q2; *10* QR – Q1, N – B4?; *11* RxN.

SUMMARY

Count one point plus for significantly greater space behind your own front lines, or one point minus to opponent if his pieces are markedly cramped. Do not count both points, except in extreme cases.

On an open board (center pawns dissolved), estimate spatial advantage in terms of other, specific points, except that control of an extraordinary number of important (especially central) squares rates an extra point.

17. *Minor Pieces*

THE bishop and knight are rated approximately equal. However, the particular position may favor one or the other. Bishops are usually superior on an open board; knights, on a crowded board. The positions that favor the bishop are more frequent; hence the bishop is regarded as the generally superior piece.

The differences in favor of the bishop are:

A] The bishop can operate at long range. It can attack squares on both wings simultaneously.

B] The bishop can maintain its guard over a square even when compelled to retreat for its own safety.

c] The bishop counterattacks a pawn that attacks it.

The differences in favor of the knight are:

A] The knight can reach squares of both colors.

B] The knight's mobility is not obstructed by adjacent pieces.

In an ending of king, bishop and pawns *v.* king, knight and pawns, the pieces fight equally well when the pawns are all on one wing (or center). The crucial cases arise when there are pawns on both wings, so that the long-range power of the bishop is significant.

The Triumph of the Bishop

No. 139, an ending from actual play, poses the question of bishop *v.* knight in about its simplest conceivable form. The game continued:

Stoltz *v.* Kashdan   1928

NO. 139. *Black to move*

1	K – B1
2 K – B1	K – K2
3 K – K2	K – Q3
4 K – Q3	K – Q4
5 P – R4	

White must put his king-side pawns on dark squares to save them, for the bishop can soon reach KB8 via B1 and QR3. An alternative try, keeping the pawns as they are to prevent the approach of the Black king, is K – B3, N – B2 – K3. But then the bishop takes the long diagonal to bear on the king knight pawn, and Black moves P – B4 – B5, ousting the knight. To secure the knight's position by P – N3 abandons the whole idea, since it opens an avenue of light squares to the Black king.

5	B – B1
6 N – B3	B – R3ch
7 K – B3	

The king must stay near the queen knight pawn to save it.

7	P – R3
8 N – Q4	P – N3

The Black pawns defend themselves by preventing the approach of the knight. This possibility underlines the inferiority of the knight: its short range.

9 N – B2	K – K5	13 N – B6ch	K – B4
10 N – K3	P – B4	14 N – Q7	B – B1
11 K – Q2	P – B5	15 N – B8	
12 N – N4	P – R4		

If White does not attack the knight pawn, the Black king will go to N5 and annex the rook pawn. But now the knight must look to its own safety.

15	P – N4
16 P – N3	

If PxP, then KxP and the knight is trapped.

16	PxRP	19 N – K7	B – K3
17 PxRP	K – N5	20 P – N4	KxP
18 N – N6	B – B4	Black wins	

This beautiful ending raises the question: Is the possession of bishop *v.* knight (the pawns being divided) sufficient in itself to win, or is an additional advantage required? For we must note that in No. 139 the Black king reaches the center ahead of the White king, and so can take the fourth rank. Perhaps there would be no win without this lead.

Without attempting to answer the question, we can safely conclude that bishop *v.* knight can be turned into a win by the help of minimal added advantage.

The Triumph of the Knight

The foregoing pronouncement becomes significant when we study the endings in which a knight wins over a bishop. Here we invariably find that the knight is supported by very marked collateral advantage, usually two points under our system.

In No. 140, the game continued:

Mitchell *v.* Van Scheltinga   1937

NO. 140. *Black to move*

1		P – N5
2 PxP		PxP
3 B – R6		

To play B – N7 and BxN loses by the "outside passed pawn" (discussed in Chapter 21).

3		K – Q4
4 K – B2		K – K5
5 K – N3		

Passive defense is useless, e.g., 5 K – K2, N – B6; 6 B – B4, P – B3, followed by P – KR4 – R5, after which Black will actually threaten NxP. White must then give up his bishop for the two king-side pawns, after which the Black king can capture all three remaining White pawns.

5	P – B4	8 B – Q4	N – B6
6 B – B8	P – B5	9 P – KR3	
7 B – B5	K – B4		

If White merely makes waiting moves with his bishop, Black moves P – KR4 – R5 and wins as in the previous note.

9	P – KR4	14 K – N3	N – Q8
10 PxPch	PxP	15 P – R3	K – K5
11 B – N6	N – N4	16 KxP	NxPch
12 B – Q4	N – K5ch	Black wins	
13 K – R4	N – B7		

(17 K – N5, N – B7; 18 B – B5, K – Q6; 19 K – B5, KxP; 20 K – K4, K – N6; 21 K – Q5, P – B6; 22 K – K4, NxP; 23 K – Q3, N – B5; 24 B – B8, P – R4; 25 B – N7, N – N7ch; 26 K – K2, P – R5; 27 Resigns.)

From the subsequent play, we see that in the initial position of No. 140 Black has two weighty points: an outside passed pawn on the king-side and better king position (discussed in Chapter 22). After the White king bishop pawn is forced off, all the light squares of the center are open to invasion. The pawn structure is such as to devalue the bishop and enhance the knight. The bishop is of the wrong color to defend the invasion squares, whereas the knight can drive the Black king from light squares and also attack the pawns on the dark squares.

The "Bad" Bishop

A bishop is called "bad" when it moves on squares of the same color as those on which most of its pawns are fixed, especially center pawns. The badness may consist in either or both of two consequences:

A] The bishop is blocked or actually locked in by its own pawns.

B] The duplication by bishops and pawns leaves squares of the opposite color insufficiently guarded.

Locked-in bishops can be seen in many diagrams in this book. It is not by chance that most of them are Black queen bishops, for Black's difficulty common to many queen pawn and Queen's Gambit variations is how to get the queen bishop into action. (See "The Queen Bishop Pawn in the Queen's Gambit," Chapter 7.) Many games are lost by failure to solve this problem.

In the French Defense (*1* P – K4, P – K3) Black voluntarily obstructs his queen bishop, and in Philidor's Defense (*1* P – K4, P – K4; *2* N – KB3, P – Q3) he voluntarily blocks his king bishop. These bishops are not usually called "bad," however, for the reason that their obstruction is expected to be temporary. Both defenses, after due preparation, aim at a partial or total dissolution of the center pawns.

In applying the system, we must therefore take the dynamic rather than the pictorial view of a blocked bishop. It is "bad" only to the extent that the blocking pawns are fixed. Further, a bishop may function strongly in backing up a pawn. For example: bishop at QN2, pawn at Q4, knight at K5; the bishop reinforces the outpost.

In contrast with the locked-in bishop, the wrong-color bishop is often a more serious weakness than the pictorial view might indicate. We have seen an instance in No. 140. The fact that White's bishop moves on dark squares, and that the king pawn and queen bishop pawn are fixed on dark squares, does not "look" catastrophic. Yet it proves fatal.

Another instance is No. 141A. The position looks drawish and *is* drawish. The bishop is held at bay by the White pawns and cannot attack their bases. The knight is excellently posted for defense but cannot penetrate farther into the Black camp. What ensued might be entitled, "How Not to Play Chess":

Auerbach *v.* Lilienthal   1949

NO. 141A. *Black to move*

1	P – QB4?	4 N – K2	B – K3
2 PxP e.p.	PxP	5 K – B2	P – Q4?
3 R – Q2	K – K2	6 P – B5!	

Black has gratuitously given himself a hanging phalanx, to secure which he has been more or less forced to put the pawns on light squares, thus making his bishop bad. The damage may not look serious, since the bishop still has an outlet in one direction, but in fact it was enough to lose the game.

The Bishop-Pair

The wrong-color danger of a single bishop is ameliorated or nonexistent when the player has two bishops. The bishop-pair proves in practice to be somewhat stronger than bishop plus knight and markedly stronger than two knights. The superiority is primarily due to the long range of the bishops and their faster pace in maneuvers, as can be seen by the examples in the next section and elsewhere.

A contributory cause is the bishop-pair's greater option of exchange. The owner is better able to avoid minor-piece swaps, if he pleases, or force them to his advantage.

Consider No. 142. The Black bishops prevent penetration by the White king, as well as restricting somewhat the activity of the knight. The Black king threatens to come forward to QN4 or Q4, according as White disposes his knight. Even if White could

NO. 142. *White to move*

oppose and swap bishops, the transaction would not be inviting, for Black would be left with bishop *v.* knight and pawns on both wings. White tried to get his knight to Q4:

1 N – B2

But this overlooks that the swap of a bishop for his knight is also damaging, in view of the pawn structure.

1	B – N3ch!
2 K – Q2	BxN
3 KxB	

White is left with a bad bishop against a good bishop. The Black king comes forward to Q4; Black forces an exchange of pawns on his king-side. White is unable to defend penetration on either wing.

The value of the bishop-pair is affected by collateral factors, above all by space and mobility—factors arising from the pawn structure. Two extreme examples are cited below.

In No. 143 White has the bishop-pair against bishop and knight. Is this point purely pictorial? His king bishop is locked behind his own pawns. However, his monopoly of space enables him to get the bishop into action by a maneuver that Black, for lack of space, cannot oppose:

Tarrasch *v.* Teichmann 1905

NO. 143. *White to move*

1 B – QB4!	K – N1
2 P – N3	K – B1
3 P – R4	N – Q2
4 B – B1	K – K1
5 B – R3	

Thus the bishop encroaches on what little space Black has behind his own lines. Black was eventually suffocated. But one hesi-

tates to ascribe any major share of the victory to the bishop-pair.
The lowly pawns did most of the work! (It is probable that White
can win from position No. 143 if a knight is substituted for his
king bishop.)

In No. 144, White surprisingly plays

Nimzovich *v.* Levenfish 1911

NO. 144. *White to move*

1 BxN!

leaving himself two knights against two bishops. Part of the ex-
planation lies in the immediate sequel:

1	QxB
2 Q – R5ch	P – N3
3 Q – K2	

Thus the Black king-side, already compromised, is further impaired. The rest of the story is, of course, that the knights have
fine squares available—one is already strongly entrenched. The
Black queen bishop is bad, and the effort to free it by an eventual
P – QB4 (which was tried) will weaken the Black center and
facilitate invasion past it directed at the king. (The immediate
3 . . . B – Q3; 4 P – KB4, BxN; 5 PxB would plug the outpost
station, but the pawn there plus White's grip on the king bishop
file would be even more uncomfortable.) A few more moves are
given to show the working of White's plan.

3	R – Q1	6 K – R1	B – Q3
4 N – Q2	O – O	7 P – KB4	
5 QR – K1	KR – K1		

The Ruy Lopez Question

After the opening moves

1 P – K4	P – K4
2 N – KB3	N – QB3
3 B – N5	P – QR3
4 BxN	QPxN

NO. 145. *White to move*

Black has a doubled queen bishop pawn, which, as we know, can turn out to be a serious weakness. In compensation, he has the bishop-pair. Which has the better game?

This is what we call "the Ruy Lopez question," since it can arise, and has arisen, in every variation of that opening.

Masters partial to knights, such as Tchigorin, prefer the White side. But "two-bishop masters," such as Tarrasch, Janowski and Rubinstein, have given convincing quantitative evidence that Black has the better prospects.

Here is one of the definitive games.

Taubenhaus *v.* Tarrasch   1903

1 P – K4	P – K4
2 N – KB3	N – QB3
3 B – N5	N – B3
4 O – O	NxP
5 P – Q4	N – Q3
6 BxN	QPxB
7 PxP	N – B4

NO. 146A. *White to move*

For discussion of the position after 8 QxQch, KxQ, see No. 166 in Chapter 19.

| 8 Q – K2 | N – Q5! | 10 N – B3 | B – KN5! |
| 9 NxN | QxN | | |

To force the exchange of queens, after which the bishop-pair will be the major fighting force.

11 Q – K3	QxQ
12 BxQ	B – N5
13 N – K4	B – KB4
14 P – QB3	B – K2
15 N – N3	B – Q6

NO. 146B. *White to move*

Observe that White could not well avoid opening the hole that the bishop now occupies. To leave the pawn at QB2 would have tied down a rook to its protection.

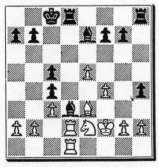

16 KR – Q1	O – O –O
17 R – Q2	P – QB4
18 P – KB4	P – KR4
19 QR – Q1	P – B5
20 K – B2	P – R5
21 N – K2	P – QB4

NO. 146C. *White to move*

The first stage of a classic process is completed. The knight has been deprived of useful posts, and for lack of its help the bishop, too, has been hemmed in. The second stage was to swap off all the rooks, to allow the Black king to enter the fray. The third stage was to bring forward the king and the queen-side pawns to obtain a passed pawn. When a Black pawn arrived at QN5, White was compelled to exchange and so undouble the Black pawns, else the Black king would have invaded via the light squares and captured a pawn for nothing. (An important preliminary was B – QN8, to force P – QR3 and so open the light squares to invasion.) The fourth stage was—resignation. The passed pawn cost White a piece. He could never activate his own king-side majority, for the bishops held back these pawns while still raking the queen-side.

For other games bearing on the Ruy Lopez question, see Games III and IV in Chapter 25.

The Bishop-Pair in the Queen's Gambit

Positions having some resemblance to Nos. 145 and 146A often arise in the Queen's Gambit Declined. Thus:

1	P – Q4	P – Q4
2	P – QB4	P – K3
3	N – KB3	N – KB3
4	N – B3	B – N5
5	P – QR3	BxNch
6	PxB	

NO. 147. *Black to move*

Again a doubled queen bishop pawn is compensated by the bishop-pair. But the balance is more clearly in White's favor here than is the Ruy Lopez position (No. 146) in Black's favor. In the first place, White has here captured *toward*, not *away from*, the center. The extra queen bishop pawn contributes to center control. In the second place, White can immediately undouble by PxP, if he wishes, and then he can "play the Queen's Gambit twice" by P – QB4.

The sole real weakness of the White position is the isolated queen rook pawn, but much water must flow over the mill before Black can do anything about it.

The "Minor Exchange"

Such great store is set upon the bishop-pair nowadays that to capture an enemy bishop for a knight is regarded as "winning the minor exchange." Witness two examples.

Von Scheve v. Tarrasch   1892

NO. 148. *Black to move*

1	N – KR4
2 B – N3	NxB
3 RPxN	

Evans v. Larsen   1949

NO. 149. *White to move*

1 N – B5	R – K1
2 NxBch	QxN
3 O – O	P – B4
4 P – QN4	P – B5

In the "romantic" period of chess, Tarrasch's "time-wasting" maneuver to get a bishop for a knight caused some lifting of eyebrows. Yet no tempo was actually lost, since the bishop, too, had to move. In 1949, no one questioned the merit in Evans' idea of going after the Black king bishop—the only question was whether White could survive the actual gift of two tempos to Black.

SUMMARY

Count a point plus for the superior minor piece or pieces. Normally this means: bishop *v.* knight, or bishop-pair *v.* knight plus another minor piece. When exception arises, you can clearly see features that exceptionally favor the knight or devalue the bishop.

Count a point minus for a permanently bad bishop.

18.   *The Half-Open File*

A PLAYER is said to have a half-open file when his pawn has disappeared from it but the opponent's pawn has not.

Standing on a half-open file, a rook may function in any of a number of ways: attack upon the enemy pawn; attack upon enemy pieces; restraint of a pawn advance or other operations on the file; protection of an advanced piece; advance from the first rank to gain access to other files.

We will study these effects in typical positions arising from various openings.

Queen Bishop File in Queen's Gambit

In the Queen's Gambit, White can obtain a half-open queen bishop file at the cost of liberating the Black queen bishop. In the typical position, No. 150, Black's queen bishop pawn is in

Najdorf *v.* Pilnik   1955

NO. 150. *Half-Open Files*
Black to move

jeopardy. White can attack it a second time by Q – B2, and there is no good way to defend it a second time. Desirable in such positions is P – QB4, both to put the pawn under protection of the queen knight pawn and to make room for its support by rooks. At the moment, P – QB4 is not feasible, for after PxP White would win the queen pawn. In related positions where P – QB4 is playable, the result is a hanging phalanx (Chapter 10).

In the present position, Black tries to ease his problem by exchanging queens.

1	Q – N5ch	4 N – B3	B – N2
2 Q – Q2	QxQch	5 N – K5	
3 KxQ	P – QB3		

The outpost not only attacks the backward queen bishop pawn but also prevents the normal development N – Q2. If Black later ousts the knight by P – KB3, he has to reckon with a "weaksquare" complex on his king-side.

5	R – B1
6 P – QN4	P – QR4
7 P – N5	

Of course White will not open the file for Black's benefit. Now Black can get rid of his weak pawn by PxP, but the consequences are catastrophic. White will control the open queen bishop file and will penetrate to the seventh rank (see Chapter 20 for a discussion of such penetration). Therefore Black keeps the file closed:

7	P – QB4
8 P – QR4	R – K1
9 B – N4	RxN

Despair. Black cannot otherwise develop his queen knight and queen rook. But the sacrifice is insufficient and loses quickly.

That the rook on the half-open file may exert an important pin is illustrated in No. 151. Black is in process of recovering a pawn sacrificed on his K4. White seizes the tempo to make a routine positional move, which nevertheless contains a tactical sting.

Capablanca *v.* O. Bernstein   1914

NO. 151. *White to move*

1 R – B1	P – B3
2 B – N3	PxP
3 P – N4!	B – R2

If 3 . . . BxP; 4 N – Q5 (note the crucial pin), Q – Q3; 5 NxB, QxN; 6 RxP with strong penetration.

4 BxNP!

Owing to the pin, White can now win all three queen-side pawns for a bishop. Materially, this is an even exchange, but White in addition penetrates with his pieces and holds the Black king in the center.

4	RPxB	6 N – Q6ch	K – B1
5 NxNP	Q – Q1	7 RxP and wins	

The Minority Attack

A prime danger of the half-open queen bishop file in possession of the better-developed side is that it may enable that player to execute a *minority attack*. The object of the attack is to saddle the opponent with a pawn weakness—either an isolated pawn or a backward queen bishop pawn. The process is illustrated by No. 152.

Flohr *v.* Euwe   1932

NO. 152. *Minority Attack*
          White to move

Material, it will be noted, is absolutely even. Each king is relatively secure. White and Black pawn structures appear to be sound. White's control of the half-open queen bishop file seems to be counterbalanced by Black's domination of the half-open king file. Yet, despite the apparent balance of points, White practically enjoys a forced win!

To illustrate the winning plan, we append diagrams of the pawn structure.

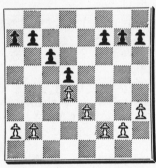

NO. 152A. *The original pawn skeleton*

NO. 152B. *White's first goal*

NO. 152C. *Black's first alternative*

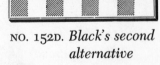

NO. 152D. *Black's second alternative*

Black's queen bishop pawn is backward and an easy target.

Black's queen-side pawns are isolated and easy prey.

Now continue the game from diagram No. 152.

1 P – N4	N – K3	5 N – R2	R(3) – K3
2 QR – N1	N – B2	6 N – B3	P – B3
3 P – QR4	P – R3	7 N – Q2	R – K1
4 N – B1	R – K2		

Black can undertake nothing; he can but wait for the break. White now indulged in some useless maneuvers before getting back on the right track. The idea is to enforce P – QN5, which can be done by posting the knight at QR3, queen at N3, and rooks on the queen knight and queen bishop files. After P – QN5, Black has to choose between allowing PxRP, isolating his rook pawn and leaving the queen bishop pawn backward, and a double exchange of pawns, leaving both his queen knight pawn and queen pawn isolated. In either case, White can soon win one of the weak pawns.

The game continued:

8 N – N3	R(3) – K2
9 N – B5	Q – B1

Here is a case in which occupation of the outpost station is purely "pictorial." The knight bothers Black a little but threatens nothing. White presently discovers that the queen bishop file must be left open for frontal attack and the knight must be posted to support the crucial P – QN5.

10 KR – QB1	R – Q1
11 N – Q3	Q – N1
12 N – B4	N – K3

Black hurls himself on the sword, not waiting for the White knight to go to QB3 or QR3.

13 NxN	RxN
14 P – N5	

This is often the culminating move of a minority attack. Black has to choose between two weaknesses, an isolated queen knight pawn or a backward queen bishop pawn. Here he chooses the former.

14	RPxP
15 PxP	PxP
16 RxP	P – QN3
17 Q – N3	Q – Q3
18 R – N1 and wins	

One of Black's two isolated pawns goes lost.

An instance in which Black obtained the minority attack is No. 153. White has created the possibility by P – QN3, leaving holes after the disappearance of his queen bishop. He should now seek to guard the holes by Q – B1, and if Q – N5, then Q – N2. Instead:

Bogolyubov *v.* Capablanca   1924

NO. 153. *White to move*

1 Q – Q2	QR – B1
2 P – B3	P – QR3
3 N – K5	B – N4
4 P – B3	

White refuses Black's offer to let him double the queen knight pawn—rightly so, for the opening of the queen rook file would far outweigh the remote weakness of the doubled pawns.

4	BxB
5 NxB	R – B2
6 QR – B1	KR – B1
7 R – QB2	N – K1
8 KR – B1	N – Q3

Possibly White can parry the attack by 9 N – B5. He actually played N – K5, and Black soon won a pawn.

Frontal Pressure on a Pawn Wing

In No. 154A, White has an endgame advantage in his queen-side pawn majority. If all the pieces were removed from the board, he would likely have a won game. If merely the heavy pieces were removed, Black would have an uphill fight to draw. Black's task is therefore to restrain the pawns with his heavy pieces. He accomplishes it in exemplary fashion.

D. Byrne *v.* Benko   1958

NO. 154A. *White to move*

1 Q – B1

The queen knight pawn needs protection. Bad would be 1 B – Q4, P – K4 with rapid counterattack in the center.

1	B – QR3

Black gets rid of his potentially bad bishop.

| 2 BxB | QxB |
| 3 B – R6 | |

White seizes the opportunity to swap off Black's good bishop.

3	KR – B1
4 BxB	KxB
5 Q – Q1	P – K3

Since Black's heavy pieces can quickly double or triple up against the pawns, White must put them into a defensive formation, pending the time when he can effect some swaps and relieve the pressure.

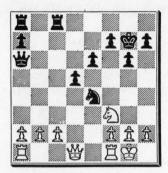

NO. 154B. *White to move*

6	P – B3	Q – N3
7	R – N1	QR – N1
8	P – KR4	P – KR3

So as to meet P – R5 with P – N4.

9	N – Q2	N – B3
10	Q – K2	Q – N4!
11	QxQ	RxQ

NO. 154C. *White to move*

Black has invited the swap of queens to avert the bind White would get if he could post his queen at K5. White now has to meet the threat of R(1) – N1, since P – N3 in defense would leave the queen bishop pawn hopelessly weak.

| 12 | KR – B1 | R – R4 |
| 13 | P – R3 | |

This move cannot be avoided, for if R – R1, Black can move R – B3 – R3. Now that the pawns are in a reverse salient, no advance under fire is possible.

| 13 | . . . . | R(4) – B4 | 15 | K – B1 | N – Q3 |
| 14 | P – KN3 | N – K1 | 16 | R – K1 | R – QN1 |

Forcing the White king rook back again by a threat to double on the queen knight pawn.

17 KR – B1   R – B2
18 K – K2   P – K4

NO. 154D. *White to move*

Having immobilized the White queen-side majority, Black can now activate his majority on the other side.

19 K – B1	K – B3	22 K – Q1	N – K5
20 K – K2	K – K3	23 K – K2	N – B4
21 K – K1	P – B4	24 P – KB4	

Else Black will play P – N4, and the steamroller will be even stronger.

```
            24 . . . .           P – K5
            25 R – B2
```

White unfortunately cannot use the posts opened up by P – K5, e.g., 25 N – B1, N – R5; 26 R – B2? RxBP.

25 . . . .   K – Q3
26 K – K3   N – K3
27 R(1) – QB1   P – QR4

NO. 154E. *White to move*

Black's plan is to double rooks on the queen bishop file, after which he will threaten P – Q5. White at the moment could parry the threat by N – N3. Black therefore advances the queen rook pawn to deprive the knight of this post. White blocks P – QR5, but then his queen rook pawn becomes a target for attack.

28	P – R4	R(1) – QB1
29	N – N3	R – B5
30	NxP	

Else he loses a pawn with nothing to show for it.

30	. . . .	P – Q5ch!
31	K – B2	RxRP
32	N – N3	P – Q6

and Black wins

In No. 154 and kindred positions, the question arises: When is a majority pawn wing an advantage (because of the potential passed pawn) and when is it a liability (because of adverse pressure through a half-open file)? The answer is to be found in the *collateral* points. In No. 154A, Black can count a point for superior development (outpost knight, strong king bishop) and another for two-to-none in center pawns. The development lead permits him to force the White pawns into a defensive formation, greatly impairing their mobility and also giving Black a spatial advantage. Then at last Black is able to capitalize his second point, the center pawns.

Half-Open Files in the Sicilian

In the Sicilian Defense, Black swaps his queen bishop pawn for the White queen pawn, thus gaining two-to-one in center pawns. He also gets a half-open queen bishop file, through which he hopes to exert pressure on the White queen-side, to reinforce which he will fianchetto his king bishop if he can. He will often try to establish an outpost station at his QB5 by P – QR3 and P – QN4, then bring his queen knight there.

Offsetting Black's two-to-one, White gets a center pawn on the fourth *v.* a pawn on the third, together with a half-open queen file. His general plan is to use this file to restrain the advance of

Black's center pawns, while building up a king-side attack based on P – KB4 and then P – B5 or P – K5.

The pawn-on-fourth is a more immediate advantage than the center two-against-one. White's prospects remain better, as a rule, until Black succeeds in playing P – Q4 without disadvantage. One difficulty in enforcing this move is that White's P – K5 may then be troublesome.

Aronin *v.* Boleslavsky   1952

NO. 155. *Black to move*

For example, in No. 155 the play went

1	**P – Q4**
2 **P – K5**	**N – K1**
3 **P – B4**	**P – B3**

If Black cannot smash up the pawn chain, his game is no good.

$$4 \ \mathbf{O - O - O}$$

Now if *4* . . . PxP; 5 PxP, BxP; *6* N – B3. If then *6* . . . B – N2; 7 NxP; White recovers his pawn and Black is left with an isolated king pawn. Or *6* . . . BxN; 7 QxB; Black holds the extra pawn but is left dangerously weak on the dark squares of his king-side. Also, his center pawns, subject to pressure on both half-open files, are weak.

Queen File in the Ruy Lopez

In some lines of the Ruy Lopez, White moves P – Q4 and obtains a half-open queen file by a central swap of pawns. Black frequently has to reckon with the pin of his queen pawn by the

White queen or rook on the file. An amusing instance is the "Tarrasch Trap":

1 P – K4	P – K4	7 B – N3	P – Q4
2 N – KB3	N – QB3	8 PxP	B – K3
3 B – N5	P – QR3	9 P – B3	B – K2
4 B – R4	N – B3	10 R – K1	O – O
5 O – O	NxP	11 N – Q4	
6 P – Q4	P – QN4		

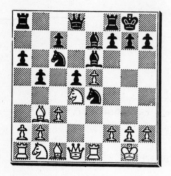

NO. 156. *Black to move*

11 . . . .　　　　　Q – Q2?

Correct is NxN.

12 NxB and wins

After either PxN or QxN, White wins a piece with RxN, the Black queen pawn being fatally pinned in either case.

The Moscow Variation develops from the same line, No. 157.

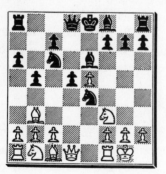

NO. 157. *White to move*

The usual move hereabouts is P – B3, to preserve the king bishop after Black retreats N – B4. Smyslov played

1	Q – K2	B – K2	3	B – K3	O – O
2	R – Q1	N – B4	4	P – B4	

forcing a swap and so weakening the Black queen-side pawns.

The queen file sometimes becomes fully opened, with White in control of it. Thus, in No. 158:

Lombardy *v.* Horowitz   1955

NO. 158. *Black to move*

1	. . . .	NxN
2	QxN	N – B4
3	N – B3	O – O
4	B – K3	NxB
5	QxN	P – Q4
6	PxP e.p.	BxP
7	QR – Q1	

The rook brings about an uncomfortable pin of the bishop. The Black queen cannot readily find a good post off the file.

King Bishop File in the King's Gambit

Many a king-side attack is based on the opening of the king bishop file, for frontal pressure on what is initially the opponent's weakest square, his KB2. The King's Gambit

1	P – K4	P – K4
2	P – KB4	PxP

attempts to lay the foundation for an attack by at once opening the file. An easy way for Black to get a bad game is to let his advanced pawn go without a struggle. For example (as played by many a beginner): 3 N – KB3, N – QB3?; 4 P – Q4, P – Q3?; 5 BxP. White now has everything he aimed for—the half-open king bishop file, two-to-one in center pawns, the fourth-rank phalanx and material equality.

The valid defenses depend upon maintaining the advanced pawn for a long time or on swapping it off advantageously. In either case, the White rook's pressure on the file is intercepted until Black can develop his king-side and castle. After 3 N – KB3, Black should move 3 . . . P – KN4 or 3 . . . P – Q4 or 3 . . . N – KB3 with the intention of following up with both of the foregoing moves.

The effect of P – Q4 is not only to open the line for the queen bishop but also to decoy the White king pawn off the file, so that it can no longer threaten to embarrass Black pieces by advancing to K5. (After 3 . . . P – Q4; 4 P – K5 is not embarrassing because Black can neatly sidestep the pawn: 4 . . . P – KN4; 5 P – KR3, N – KR3; 6 P – Q4, N – B4 with the better game.)

Even in later positions, where Black's P – Q4 loses the pawn and so restores material equality, the move is advisable if it gains a tempo essential to the preservation of the advanced king-side pawns. A wholly open king file is less of a peril to Black than a White king bishop file half-open to Black's KB2 or KB3.

Half-Open King Rook File

A half-open king rook file is sometimes a sufficient basis for a king-side attack.

No. 159A is a regular Ruy Lopez position in which the usual continuation by Black is R – K1 and N – B1. Instead, Black tries an inferior maneuver:

Bergsma v. Fischer 1955

NO. 159A. *Black to move*

1	N – N3?
2 N – K3	N – R4
3 B – B2	B – B1

Black has to make some concession in view of the positional threats N – B5 and N – N4.

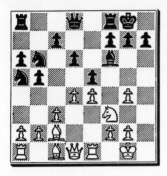

4 N – N4   BxN
5 PxB

NO. 159B. *Black to move*

Besides the half-open king rook file, White has gained a doubled pawn that is actually advantageous, since it provides an extra battering-ram on the king knight file. White utilizes the file promptly, while Black attempts to prevent P – N5.

| 5 . . . . | P – R3 | 7 K – N2 | P – B4 |
| 6 P – KN3 | N – Q2 | 8 P – Q5! | |

Naturally White blocks the center to deprive Black of counterplay.

| 8 . . . . | B – N4 | 10 N – R4 |
| 9 R – R1 | P – B3 | |

Now the Black bishop cannot be maintained on N4 (against P – KB4). After its exchange, the White steamroller is free to advance. White crashed through on the king rook file and won.

SUMMARY

Count a point plus for a half-open file if you see a clear prospect of posting a rook or queen upon it with effect. Regard it as a potential plus in any event. A doubled pawn incurred to gain a half-open file is negligible if you have a net plus over your opponent in other points, especially in the major points of development, space and center control.

19.   *The Open File*

AN open file (as distinguished from a half-open file) is one on which there are no pawns of either color.

The importance of open files in endplay is obvious: rooks need open files to get out from behind their own pawns and assail the enemy. In early play, the open file offers much the same possibilities as the half-open: support of an advanced piece, pin of an adverse piece, etc., as discussed in Chapter 18. Only the operations involving frontal attack on a pawn (such as the minority attack) are ruled out.

The completely open file, however, offers more frequent opportunity for penetration by a rook into the hostile camp. The file "beckons" to a rook as the outpost station beckons to a knight. This is its opportunity to sally forth and to exert its powers along the rank as well as the file.

The Doubled Rooks

The explosive power of two rooks doubled on an open file needs no proving. But we will give two illustrations, chosen because the preliminary maneuvers bear upon our next topic.

In No. 160A, White has the bishop-pair and also is an extra tempo (besides his initial tempo) ahead in development. It is not obvious how he can capitalize his lead. Black can reinforce his

Gligoric v. Rabar 1955

NO. 160A. *White to move*

strong defensive king knight by QN – Q2, and even by P – KR3: no king-side blitzkrieg seems feasible. After connecting his rooks, Black can bring pressure on White's backward queen bishop pawn.

1 B – KN5	Q – Q3

Evidently Black does not like his position after *1* . . . QN – Q2; 2 N – K5, Q – B2; 3 NxN, NxN; *4* Q – R5 or *4* QR – B1.

2 BxN

Heresy!

2	QxB
3 N – K5	

Now we see that White gave up his bishop merely to delay for a move the development of the Black knight.

3	Q – Q3
4 Q – R5	

The picture begins to clarify. The invaluable defensive knight is gone, and Black must make a pawn move seriously compromising his king.

4	P – N3
5 Q – R6	

Black's following moves are dictated by the threat of N – B3 – N5, when his only defense of KR2 will be to post queen or rook on the second rank and advance his king bishop pawn. This advance will leave his KN3 weak, so that he will have to reckon with a possible BxNP.

5	B – R3
6 BxB	NxB
7 QR – K1	

NO. 160B. *Black to move*

The threat is now R – K3 – R3, with a possible NxNP after the king bishop pawn moves.

7	QR – B1
8 R – K3	R – B2
9 KR – K1	

Since nothing immediate comes of 9 N – B3, P – B3, White takes the opportunity to double on the file for a possible later R – K6.

| 9 . . . . | P – B3 |
| 10 N – N4 | Q – Q1? |

Necessary to prolong the game was QR – B2.

      11 R – K8! and wins

In No. 161A, White has clear superiority because of his outpost knight, which ties down a Black heavy piece to defense of the queen pawn.

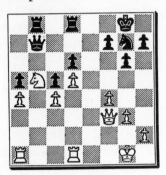

Denker *v.* Polland 1933

NO. 161A. *White to move*

The logical continuation is to seize control of the open king file. But after *1* R – K1, Q – Q2 Black is ready to move R – K1 and dispute the file. White therefore first ties down a piece to defense of the queen rook pawn.

1	Q – B3	R – R1
2	R – K1	Q – Q2
3	R – K2	

Now White can double rooks, and Black cannot challenge with R – K1 since the swaps would finally cost him a pawn.

3	. . . .	P – R4
4	QR – K1	N – B4

Black has prepared this post for the knight to prevent R – K7, which would be murderous. Next White maneuvers to dislodge the knight.

5	K – B2	QR – N1

A little pleasantry; if QxP, then R – R1 with counterplay.

6	R – K4	R – R1	*9* K – N2	N – B4
7	K – B3	QR – N1	*10* P – N4	PxP
8	P – R3	N – Q5ch	*11* PxP	N – R3

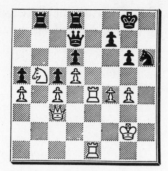

NO. 161B. *White to move*

12 P – B5!

Preventing QxPch. If *12* . . . PxP; *13* R – K7, Q – B1; *14* Q – B6. So Black makes a last desperate effort to prevent the penetration of the rook.

12	R – K1
13 NxP	RxR
14 NxR	QxRP
15 N – B6ch	K – B1
16 P – N5 and wins	

(*16* . . . NxP; *17* N – Q7ch, QxN; *18* Q – R8 mate.)

Control of an Open File

A rook standing on a half-open file can rarely be challenged by an enemy rook (which would have to maneuver its way in front of its own pawns through some other open file). You are therefore said to "have" a half-open file the moment your pawn disappears from it, provided that you have a reasonable prospect of being able to bring a rook to it.

You cannot ordinarily "have" a completely open file with such immediacy. Your rook is in general subject to challenge by an adverse rook. Control of the file may depend on the outcome of a local skirmish; in the end, it may still remain common property.

You "have" an open file only if your rook on it cannot be challenged by an adverse rook (without serious disadvantage).

All manner of tactics may enter into the skirmish. In No. 160,

White utilizes his greater space to double rooks behind an outpost. Black is hindered from doubling in opposition by his lesser space and by the collateral threats to which the outpost contributes. Then when the outpost retires, White has absolute command of the file because of the doubling.

In No. 161, White gains the tempo to begin doubling (R – K2) because the Black heavy pieces are momentarily tied down and awkwardly posted (queen on QN2 instead of Q2). After he has doubled, the "explosive force" of the rooks is too great to permit challenge.

When rooks already oppose each other on a file, the effort to double has to reckon with the simple dissolution RxR. That defense is inadequate in circumstances shown schematically by the next two diagrams.

NO. 162. *White to move*   NO. 163. *White to move*

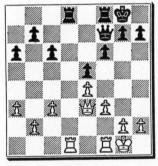

In No. 162, White may move 1 R – Q2, threatening to double. If *1* . . . RxR; 2 QxR, Black cannot yet challenge with R – Q1; but *2* . . . Q – K2 accomplishes nothing, for after 3 R – Q1 White has absolute control. Black is betrayed here by the circumstance that his queen does not guard his crucial square Q1, whereas the White queen guards his crucial square Q2.

In No. 163, White moves *1* R – B5, threatening to double. Then *1* . . . RxR; 2 QPxR alters the pawn constellation in White's favor. The guarded passed pawn is a potential winning advantage.

Since this is not a book on tactics, we will leave the subject here. Many of the illustrative positions studied in this text include instructive battles for an open file, notably Nos. 46, 77, 81, 120, 132 and 138.

The Fight to Open a File

In the classic king-side attack, the long-range purpose of the pawn onslaught is to force open a file. Some of the tactics of preventing file-opening have been discussed elsewhere, as in connection with No. 106. An instructive example on the same subject is No. 164.

Rubinstein *v.* Teichmann   1908

NO. 164. *White to move*

If White continues with *1* P – N6, Black can answer *1* . . . BPxP; 2 PxP, P – R3. Thus both files available to the White rooks are kept closed. And of course the answer to *1* P – R6 is P – N3 with the same effect.

The potential power of the rooks is here so great, however, that a sacrifice is worthwhile to open a file for them.

1 BxPch!	KxB
2 P – N6ch	K – N1

If *2* . . . PxP, then *3* PxPch would probably be sufficient. The open king rook file should triumph. But White has a stronger line, owing to Black's failure to move P – QN4 in time: *3* NxN, PxN; *4* N – N5ch, K – N1; *5* QxPch (or *4* . . . K – R1; *5* PxPch or *4* . . . K – R3; *5* N – B7ch).

3 NxN	PxN
4 P – R6!	

The threat to clear away both remaining Black pawns leaves Black no time to capture the knight—e.g., 4 . . . PxN; 5 PxPch, QxP; 6 PxP with unanswerable mate threats. Black's best chance was BPxP.

4	P – B3
5 PxP	PxN
6 R – R8ch	KxP
7 R – R7ch	K – N1
8 Q – B5	P – B6
9 RxQ	Resigns

Efforts by both sides to open lines precipitate a colorful battle in No. 165. First White tries to open the king knight file.

Pachmann *v.* Toran   1955

NO. 165. *White to move*

1 P – KN4	BPxP

Of course Black must capture to keep the file closed.

2 KBPxP	N – B5

Black offers a pawn in order to open the diagonal for his king bishop.

3 NxN	PxN
4 BxKBP	PxP
5 B – B5!	

Black cannot well refuse to exchange, for White threatens 6 BxB, QxB; 7 BxP and also 6 B – K6ch, BxB; 7 PxB and wins the queen pawn. Thus White gets his open king knight file after all.

5	BxB	9 RxR	KxR
6 PxB	RxP	10 R – N1ch	K – R1
7 B – R6	K – R1	11 N – K4 and wins	
8 BxBch	RxB		

(*11* . . . Q – KB1; *12* Q – B3ch, R – K4; *13* N – Q2, Q – B5; *14* R – B1, Q – Q5; *15* QxQ, PxQ; *16* R – B8ch, K – N2; *17* RxN, and Black continued for ten moves before resigning.)

Neutralizing an Open File

If your opponent can bring a rook to an open file, and you cannot or will not, you do not necessarily hand him a point. You may be able to neutralize the file—that is, make it of no practical use to him. This means, above all, keeping the squares on your side adequately guarded so that his rook cannot penetrate.

Consider No. 32, Zukertort's "immortal" against Blackburne. To counter White's king-side advance, Black doubles rooks on the open queen bishop file. Should White challenge his control, the disappearance of all the rooks would leave White with insufficient material for a king-side breakthrough. White therefore lets Black have the file but keeps his pieces so disposed that the Black rooks cannot penetrate. Above all, the king bishop guards the vital square QB2. When White finally lets this bishop go to get rid of the Black knight, Black gets a rook to the seventh. But now it is too late, for White launches an extraordinary combination to win on the king-side.

Porges *v.* Tarrasch   1892

NO. 166A. *White to move*

A model of patient neutralization of an open file is afforded by Tarrasch (Black) in No. 166A. The position arises from a Ruy Lopez. (See No. 146. In No. 146A, play 8 QxQch, KxQ, producing No. 166A.) White seems to "have" the open queen file, since he can move his rook to it (with check, no less), and many moves must pass before Black can bring a rook to it.

9 N – B3	P – KR3

Black wants to post his king on the queen-side. He prevents N – N5 so as to avoid having to protect the king bishop pawn with his king.

10	P – QN3	B – K3
11	B – N2	B – K2
12	QR – Q1ch	K – B1
13	KR – K1	

NO. 166B. *Black to move*

Black has had to develop slowly and modestly, to be sure. But White has found no way to increase his seeming lead. He could have gained nothing by doubling rooks on the open file; Black's pieces prevent any penetration.

13	P – KN4

Black can take time for this expansion because his position is solid. He forestalls a later P – KB4 by White.

14 N – K4	P – N3
15 N – Q4	NxN
16 RxN	K – N2
17 N – B6	

NO. 166C. *Black to move*

The outpost station is occupied, but of what value is it? The knight hampers Black not at all. The other seeming points in White's favor are likewise devalued. The open file is useless and can actually be challenged. The advanced pawn merely blocks the White bishop and protects the Black bishops from frontal attack. To make anything of this pawn, White would have to enforce P – KB4 – B5.

17	P – QR4
18 P – QR4	P – B4
19 R – Q3	P – B5

Voilà! Black rids himself of the weakness with which he has paid for his bishop-pair, the doubled pawn. His queen-side majority soon produces a passed pawn that wins the game.

SUMMARY

In the opening or midgame, count a point plus for a rook on an open file if it cannot be immediately challenged by an adverse rook, and if the file is clearly useful.

At any time, count a point plus for absolute control of the only open file.

20. *The Rook on the Seventh Rank*

THE ultimate triumph of the open file is to get a rook to the seventh rank, whence it strikes at the enemy pawn base. This "pig" (Spielmann's epithet) is the more odious when it also menaces the king.

The Confined King

In No. 167, the forces are equal. Both sides have weak pawns that cannot well be defended from depredation by the rooks. At first glance it might seem that Black has the edge, since he is about to capture the queen bishop pawn with a check, after which he can capture the queen rook pawn and emerge with two connected passed pawns on the queen-side. But the paramount factor is that the White rook not only hits the Black pawn base

Capablanca *v.* Tartakover   1924

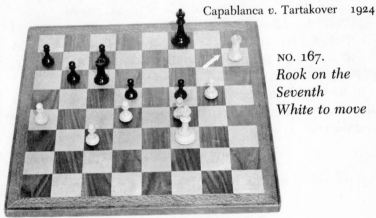

NO. 167.
*Rook on the
Seventh
White to move*

but also confines the king to the first rank. Black is lost, because he will presently be trussed up by mating threats.

1 K – N3!

Key move which paves way for king incursion and assist to advance of passed pawn.

1	RxPch
2 K – R4	R – B6

Useless is 2 . . . R – B8; 3 K – R5, R – R8ch; 4 K – N6, for Black could not swap rooks: the king knight pawn would march right down.

3 P – N6	RxPch
4 K – N5	R – K5

There is no time for RxP; the rook must prepare to defend the first rank.

5 K – B6	K – N1
6 R – N7ch	K – R1
7 RxP	R – K1

Necessary to stop mate. Now the Black pawns "fall like ripe apples" (Alekhine). After 8 KxP the king annexes the queen pawn, and Black cannot stop the tide of passed pawns.

(8 KxP, R – K5; 9 K – B6, R – B5ch; 10 K – K5, R – N5; 11 P – N7ch, K – N1; 12 RxP, R – N8; 13 KxP, R – QB8; 14 K – Q6, R – B7; 15 P – Q5, R – B8; 16 R – QB7, R – QR8; 17 K – B6, RxP; 18 P – Q6, Resigns.)

In No. 168, White's game is obviously superior because of his bishop-pair menacing the cornered king. But one would not expect the end to come so swiftly:

1 R – KB1   R – KB1

If the bishop retreats, 2 R – B7.

2 R – Q1   Resigns

Capablanca *v.* Hodges   1915

NO. 168. *White to move*

The rook reaches the seventh after all, after which the mate threat is irresistible. (The purpose of *1* R – KB1 is to compel Black to block his KB1. If at once *1* R – Q1, N – B1 gives Black a breathing spell.)

Rook-and-Pawn Endings

Rook-and-pawn endings are proverbially among the most difficult. The reason is perhaps that they require extremely accurate judgment as to when to attack and when to defend. The neophyte is apt to err by too much defending. A threatened pawn is often best abandoned in favor of a counterattack to capture an adverse pawn.

Another difficulty is that an extra pawn is not necessarily a "won game" so long as there are rooks on the board. In fact, these endings abound with pawn-down draws. Indiscriminate pawn-grabbing, even though it eventually nets a pawn, may be insufficient to win. Victory may slip away if you take a *wrong* pawn instead of a *right* one.

A typical dilemma is seen in No. 169. Shall White play *1* RxBP? Then Black may answer *1* . . . R – R7 and start his queen rook pawn on its way, supported presently by the other rook at QR1. White will have to use both his rooks to stop this pawn, wherefore Black can pick off the queen bishop pawn. (Nor will the advance of this pawn constitute an adequate counterthreat, since the Black king is near enough to aid in stopping it.) The best

Tarrasch *v.* Duras   1914

NO. 169. *White to move*

White can hope for is to win both Black queen-side pawns for his one queen bishop pawn. But then his extra pawn on the king-side is probably insufficient for a win.

How about *1* R – B7ch and *2* RxRP? What follows is *2* . . . RxP, and material is even, but Black has a dangerous advanced passed pawn. This line is clearly inferior to the first.

Instead of either line, White plays

| *1* R – R1! | R – QR1 |

Clearly Black cannot permit RxPch, after which White would win both king-side pawns, get both rooks to the seventh, and hamstring Black by mating threats.

2 R(1) – R6	RxP
3 R – B7ch	K – B1
4 R – B6ch	K – N1

Black cannot escape the losses of tempo by *4* . . . K – K1, for after *5* RxNP the king has to move back to B1 to escape mate.

5 RxPch	K – R1
6 RxPch	K – N1
White wins	

Brief Tenure of the Seventh

A rook that reaches the seventh and can be maintained there is a strategic—i.e., long-term—force. But even the brief tenure of a rook on the seventh may have a powerful effect. It is a countable point in the system when it imposes time-wasting maneuvers on the opponent to oust it. For example, consider No. 170.

Morphy *v.* Seguin   1858

NO. 170. *White to move*

1	P – K5	QxQ
2	RxQ	N – R2
3	R – Q7	

Observe that this "pig" hits only the queen knight pawn, which can be protected. It exerts no mate threat nor attacking force upon the king. Yet it is a nuisance. It immobilizes the queen rook for the moment. Before Black can challenge it with his king rook, the bishop must move. Thus White gains several tempos to regroup his pieces usefully.

3	. . . .	QR – N1
4	N – Q5	B – B1
5	B – B2	KR – Q1
6	N – N6	RxR

Black is compelled to exchange, else White will move R(3) – Q3 and maintain a rook on the seventh.

7	NxR	R – B1
8	R – B3	R – B2
9	NxB	NxN
10	RxP and wins	

Gaining the Seventh Rank

The strategic process of gaining the seventh rank is the accumulation and concentration of force—e.g., doubling of rooks on an open file, decoy of enemy minor pieces away from protection of the invasion square, and exertion of collateral threats to prevent challenge by the enemy's rooks. The process is illustrated by No. 161, among others.

But tactical methods are sometimes available—e.g., the opponent is forced or induced to leave the invasion square momentarily bereft of all guard; then when the rook arrives, it exerts short threats that gain time for its reinforcement. Naturally, such an outcome must be largely due to adverse error, as the next two examples indicate.

In No. 171, Black has erred by not challenging the queen bishop file. The situation does not seem dangerous, for an immediate doubling of White rooks comes to nothing—e.g., *1* R – B2, QR – B1; *2* KR – QB1, RxR; *3* RxR, KN – K2 and Black will be able to play R – QB1.

But White finds a clever maneuver to nail down the file.

Capablanca *v.* Alekhine 1913

NO. 171. *White to move*

1 BxN!	PxB
2 Q – R5	P – QR3

The bishop cannot well retreat. If *2* . . . B – B3; *3* NxB, PxN, the backward pawn on the open file is a fatal weakness. Or *2* . . . B – Q2; *3* NxB, QxN; *4* R – B7.

3 Q – B7!

The forced swap of queens gets a rook to the seventh without loss of time.

3	QxQ
4 RxQ and wins	

If *4* . . . QR – N1; 5 N – N5 threatening both king bishop pawn and *6* N – K6ch. Black loses a pawn and the game.

In No. 172, Black is faced with the perennial Queen's Gambit problem of developing his queen bishop. He must contrive to move P – K4 or P – QB4. The recipe is no doubt N(4) – B3 and then P – K4. Instead, he makes a gross blunder.

Capablanca *v.* Vidmar   1922

NO. 172. *Black to move*

1	P – QN3?
2 NxN	BPxN

Unfortunately, he cannot play KPxN, for then 3 B – Q3 would win a pawn.

3 **B – Q3**	P – KR3
4 **Q – B7!**	

The queen is more of a "pig" than a rook! Black cannot continue normal development, and the queen is curiously difficult to oust. (E.g., *4* . . . R – K1 with the intention of moving the knight is met by 5 B – N5.) The tie-up eventually cost Black the exchange.

SUMMARY

Count a point plus for a rook on the seventh rank.

21. *The Passed Pawn*

IN this chapter and the next we will discuss certain points that are often the dominant factors in endplay. That fact does not mean, however, that they cannot arise at an earlier stage. On the contrary, their emergence in the midgame—or even the opening—is what launches the battle of simplification. The player with the point seeks to simplify, to swap off pieces, to precipitate the endgame: his opponent resists exchanges and tries to complicate.

Actual and Potential Passed Pawns

An actual passed pawn is one whose advance will not encounter an enemy pawn on either adjacent file. A potential passed pawn is one of a group that can be advanced (barring the interference of pieces) in such a way as to yield an actual passed pawn.

The difference is seen in No. 173. The White queen knight pawn is an actual passed pawn. Black's majority of three-to-two on the other side represents a potential passed pawn.

The actual passed pawn often enjoys a decisive lead in time over the potential. If not opposed by pieces, it queens in five

NO. 173.
Passed Pawn
White to move

moves at most. To promote the potential passed pawn usually necessitates the advance of two or more pawns, totaling well over five moves.

When the only pieces left are the kings, this matter of *time* is decisive. Thus White wins in No. 173:

1 P – KN4

To draw the Black king away by *1* P – QN4 would be useless, for the White king has no avenue of approach to the Black pawns. White must first break up the Black phalanx to create such an avenue.

1 . . . .   **P – B5ch**

If *1* . . . PxP; *2* PxP. The advance of White's queen knight pawn will then draw the Black king away from the defense of his pawns. White will win easily. The text move puts up a semblance of a defense.

2 K – Q3   **P – K5ch**

The only hope. Otherwise White's king reaches K4, draws the Black king to the queen-side and mops up all the pawns. Now, at least Black will have a passed pawn.

3 PxPch   **K – B4**

If *3* . . . K – K4, *4* P – N4, KQ3, *5* K – Q4 and Black cannot stop both passed pawns.

4 K – B3

A waiting move. Now Black has to commit himself.

4 . . . .   **P – B6**

If *4 . . . K – Q3; 5 K – Q4* wins.

5 **K – Q3**	**P – B7**	8 **P – N4**	**K – Q5**
6 **K – K2**	**K – Q5**	9 **K – B3**	
7 **KxP**	**KxP**		

White wins after picking off the enemy pawn.

The Midgame Passed Pawn

The commonest antidote to an attack on the king is to swap off pieces, so as to deplete the mating force available. The establishment of a passed pawn puts a damper on this method: the opponent must avoid swapping down to an endgame in which the passed pawn becomes decisive.

Even a few exchanges may fatally impair the opponent's power to block the passed pawn. The triumph of a pawn's "lust to expand" in the teeth of heavy pieces is illustrated in No. 174A.

Black has just played P – QB4. The attack on the queen pawn is strategically correct, but the move is premature. Black should first play N – B3 and O – O. The refutation:

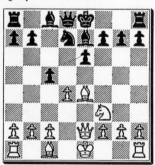

Unzicker *v.* Donner   1955

NO. 174A. *White to move*

1 **P – Q5**   **P – K4**

White keeps a positional plus after PxP or N – B3.

2 **B – B5**	**O – O**	6 **N – K4**	**B – N2**
3 **O – O**	**B – B3**	7 **R – Q1**	**P – N3**
4 **N – Q2**	**P – KN3**	8 **B – R6**	
5 **BxN**	**QxB**		

White seizes the opportunity to swap bishops, removing the piece that could blockade his pawn at Q3. Of course 8 . . . BxB cannot be played because of 9 N – B6ch. Observe, by the way, that White has avoided the routine move P – QB4, which would be a mere waste of time.

8	P – B4
9 BxB	QxB
10 N – B3	

NO. 174B. *Black to move*

The position seems to be anomalous with reference to the Point Count. Black has a bishop for a knight, and also greater space behind his own front lines. White has "only" the passed pawn. Are we to conclude that Black has the better game?

Decidedly, no! The foregoing count is purely pictorial. If we look at the position dynamically, we see that White has as much central space as he needs. Most important, his stay-at-home pawns are "yet to be heard from." When we study the effect of White wing advances, we see that the Black front line is in fact overextended; it presents targets for attack. Black's large central space is *too* large—his king stands exposed. White speedily demonstrates the reality of this dynamic appraisal.

| 10 . . . . | B – N2 |
| 11 P – QR4 | |

Threatening to loosen up the Black queen-side, leaving at least a backward pawn subject to attack by queen and knight. Since the file-opening would also lead to swaps, Black understandably prevents it, by accepting a backward pawn at once.

11	P – QR4	13 P – Q6	Q – Q1
12 Q – N5	Q – QB2	14 N – Q5	BxN

Forced, but with the disappearance of his last minor piece Black is hard put to restrain the passed pawn.

15 RxB	P – K5	20 R – Q6	R – R2
16 QR – Q1	K – N2	21 Q – B3ch	K – N1
17 P – Q7	R – B3	22 Q – B6	R – R1
18 P – R3	R – K3	23 QxR	Resigns
19 Q – B4	R – K2		

The Protected Passed Pawn

The passed pawn is so much the stronger when protected by another pawn because then, with pieces reduced to kings, the enemy king cannot even threaten to capture the pair. Thus, in No. 175, the White queen rook pawn is safe, since if the Black king goes to QN5 to attack it the knight pawn queens. The White king is free to go on a raid, provided that it stays within reach of the queening square of Black's potential passed pawn on the king-side.

So long as the Black pawns stand in phalanx, White cannot approach them: the Black king can prevent access to Black's KB2 by shuttling around K2, Q2, K3. One way for White to win is to compel the Black phalanx to advance, so that it will be more readily accessible to attack. At the same time, White must count moves carefully to see that Black does not get ahead in the race.

NO. 175. *White to move*

1 K – K3		K – Q4
2 K – B4		K – Q3
3 K – K4		K – K3
4 K – Q4		K – Q3
5 K – B4		

Now if the Black king gives way, White can play K – B5, P – N6, and capture the queen rook pawn if need be. He will get a queen in time to forestall a Black queen. So Black is constrained to move a pawn.

5	P – N3	8 K – Q4	P – R4
6 K – Q4	P – R3	9 K – K4	K – K3
7 K – B4	P – N4	10 P – N6	

White can draw the Black king away at the cost of his queen knight pawn because now his own king is near enough to prevent the exchange of both Black pawns for his king rook pawn.

10	K – Q3	13 KxP	K – B4
11 K – B5	K – B3	14 P – R4 and wins	
12 KxP	KxP		

The Outside Passed Pawn

When both sides have a passed pawn, and there is another group of pawns separate from the passed pawns, the player whose passed pawn is most remote from this group has an advantage that is often decisive. The situation is put schematically in No. 176. White wins because his passed pawn is "outside." After *1* K – B3, K – R4; *2* KxP, KxP, the White king stands nearer the queen-side. White will therefore win the Black queen knight pawn and queen his own.

NO. 176. *Outside Passed Pawn*
White to move

An illustration of the decisive effect of an outside passed pawn is No. 140.

The Crippled Majority

Consider the formation skeletonized in No. 177: the pawns are split into two wings; White has a majority on one wing and Black on the other.

NO. 177. *Either to move*

Each player has a potential passed pawn, which can be stopped only by the enemy king. In No. 177, neither player can ignore the other's potential passed pawn, since he cannot win a race in time against it. Therefore the White king is compelled to go to the king-side and the Black king to the queen-side. Barring an egregious blunder, the game is a draw.

This situation—inequality of White and Black pawns on one wing or both—is nevertheless packed with dynamite. If for any reason a player cannot mobilize his majority side, he stands to lose. The commonest cause of such a misfortune is that his majority is crippled by a doubled or a backward pawn.

Consider No. 178. Black's three-to-two on the queen-side is incapable of generating a passed pawn: if . . . P – R6, P – N3, or if . . . P – N6, PxP. Hence the White king is a free agent, while the Black king is tied to the king-side. White wins by raiding the queen-side. Black can liquidate the king-side—

NO. 178. *White to move*

1 K – B2	K – K3
2 K – K3	K – B4
3 P – N6	PxP
4 PxP	KxP

but does not get to the queen-side in time to stop White's queen knight pawn after 5 K – Q4.

An illustration of how to win a game by crippling an adverse majority is given by No. 179. To maintain equality of material, White has had to capture a pawn on his QR5. Now his knight is in a predicament. Any time it retreats to N3, then BxN doubles the queen knight pawn, crippling White's majority. But the knight must retreat soon or go lost.

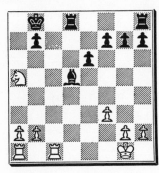

Ed. Lasker *v.* Capablanca   1915

NO. 179. *Black to move*

1	R – QB1
2 P – QN3	RxRch
3 RxR	R – QB1
4 RxRch	

To evade the exchange is useless.

4	KxR
5 K – B2	K – B2
6 K – K3	K –N3
7 N – B4ch	BxN
8 PxB	

Black wins

The White queen-side is crippled by the splitting of the pawns. Black develops a king-side passed pawn to draw the White king away, then captures both queen-side pawns.

(8 . . . K – B4; 9 K – Q3, P – K4; 10 P – N4, P – B3; 11 P – KR4, P – KN3; 12 K – K4, K – Q3; 13 P – B4, PxP; 14 KxP, K – B4; 15 P – R5, KxP; 16 K – K4, P – QN4; 17 P – R3, K – N6; 18 Resigns.)

SUMMARY

Count a point plus for a passed pawn.

If both sides have a passed pawn, the plus points may cancel. But in this situation, count a point for the outside passed pawn (if it is sufficiently remote).

Count a point plus for a protected passed pawn.

Count a point minus for a majority wing crippled in such a way that it cannot generate a passed pawn.

22. *King Position and Offside Majority*

WE have not finished with pawn play—even yet!—but let us pause to consider the role of the king in endplay.

Mobility of the King

When a sufficient number of pieces are swapped off, particularly heavy pieces (queens and rooks), the kings may emerge from their hideaways and take active part in the combat. In fact, it is often incumbent on the kings to do so, for neither player can afford to let the other alone gain this great increment to his striking power.

In No. 180, the Black king wins his battle almost singlehanded.

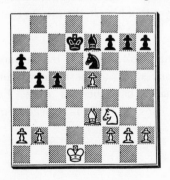

Johner *v.* Euwe   1934

NO. 180. *White to move*

1 N – Q2

White seeks to strengthen his light squares so as to prevent the approach of the Black king.

1 . . . .   **P – N4!**

With the long-range object of forcing a breach in the White king-side when he eventually plays P – KB4 to protect his advanced king pawn.

2 P – B3	K – B3	6 N – B1	K – K5
3 P – KN3	K – Q4	7 K – Q2	N – B4
4 P – B4	PxP	8 N – N3ch	NxN
5 PxP	N – Q5	9 PxN	K – B6

and Black wins

Among other things, Black's king rook pawn decides.

Many an endgame hinges on what is called the *king position:* the nearness of the king to the center, to the adverse pawns, to his own pawns, or his position vis-à-vis the enemy king. The ability of one king to bypass or force back the other depends on the opposition and suchlike tactical matters that we will not discuss. The strategical aspects of king mobility may be summarized as

A] the relative freedom of the kings from obstruction by their own forces;

B] the avenues open, by reason of the pawn formations, for advance and penetration into enemy territory;

C] the "head start" held by either king in the race to reach critical squares.

A review of the endgames in this book will show that in most of them the winner achieved a superior king position, without which the outcome would probably have been a draw. For instance: avenues of penetration, Nos. 62, 140, 141; head start, No. 179, possibly No. 139.

Improving the King Position

The foregoing citations teach the lesson that you should compare the mobility of the kings before swapping off to an endgame. You do not want to leave your opponent with a winning superiority in king position.

Generally speaking, the king gains in power with every step he takes toward the enemy first rank. Of course, many exceptions can be cited; they do not invalidate the rule that, when the kings stand opposed in the center, the more advanced king has the advantage, if any.

If wholesale exchanges are in prospect, you should look for opportunity to better your king position first. On occasion, this precaution makes the difference between a win and a draw.

In No. 181, White's king-side attack has been contained. The Black king is safe.

White has a protected passed pawn, but there is hardly a way to shepherd this down to the eighth rank at the moment. To tip the scale in.his favor, White fortunately can use his king.

White therefore first improves the position of his king.

Tarrasch v. Walbrodt   1898

NO. 181. *White to move*

1 K – R2	B – K3
2 R – N5	B – Q2
3 K – N3	B – K1
4 K – B4	B – Q2
5 P – R5	B – K1

After 5 . . . PxP, White would swap off all the heavy pieces, capture the king bishop pawn and the forward king rook pawn. He would then return with his king to KB4 and play P – K4. Afterward, he would experience little trouble in picking up

Black's king rook pawn and/or forcing through a pawn to the eighth rank.

6 PxP	BxP	10 RxR	RxR
7 B – K2	Q – Q1	11 QxR	Q – KB1
8 B – R5	BxB	12 P – K6	Resigns
9 QxB	RxR		

The Offside Majority

A consideration that pervades the midgame and even the opening, because of its endgame significance, is the "queen-side majority," more accurately described as the *offside majority*.

This is a pawn majority on the wing remote from the enemy king. The situation is set forth schematically in No. 182. As in No. 177, each player has a pawn majority on one wing. The White king stands on the side of the Black majority, while the Black king stands remote from the White majority. Now, since the passed pawn inherent in a majority wing can be stopped from queening only by the adverse king, White has a "head start" in king position. In No. 182 this lead is just enough to give White the victory.

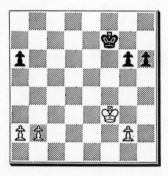

NO. 182. *White to move*

1 P – QN4

The plan is rapidly to establish a passed pawn, draw the adverse king to its side and raid the other wing.

1	K – K3
2 K – K4	P – KR4

Black's only hope is to force an exchange of king-side pawns.

3 P – R4	P – N4	6 P – N6	K – Q3
4 P – N5	PxP	7 K – B5	
5 PxP	P – R5		

The pawns must fall.

If both kings castle on the same side, the player whose pawn majority is on the *other* wing has a potential endgame advantage. Since king-side castling is usual, this advantage is commonly called the "queen-side majority." We prefer the term *offside*, since the same situation obtains when both sides move O – O – O and one then establishes a king-side majority.

An example of the offside majority in operation is No. 183.

White has two-to-one in the center. The question is, can he get sufficient counterplay in the center to prevent Black from ramming through a passed pawn on the queen-side?

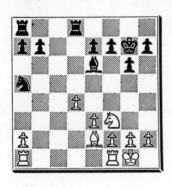

Eliskases *v.* Flohr   1937

NO. 183. *White to move*

| 1 P – K4 | B – N5 |

It is interesting that Black avoids the exchange of bishop for bishop (by B – B5), seeking rather to get the knight. One reason is that the center pawns are going to be stopped on light squares, after which the White knight would be more useful than the bishop in remobilizing them.

| 2 KR – Q1 | P – K3 | 4 BxB | QR – B1 |
| 3 K – B1 | BxN | 5 R – Q2 | P – K4 |

Letting White get his protected passed pawn—because it can be impregnably blockaded by the knight, while the White bishop becomes bad.

6	P – Q5	N – B5
7	R – K2	N – Q3

Black wins

Black can count three points under the system for offside majority, control of the only open file, and strong outpost (even though the knight is not very far "out"!). White has merely a pictorial point for a protected passed pawn. Black can force a rook to the seventh, since if White challenges and swaps rooks the offside majority races down.

(8 R – N1, R – B5; 9 P – N3, R(1) – QB1; 10 B – N2, R – B8ch; 11 RxR, RxRch; 12 R – K1, RxRch; 13 KxR, P – B4; 14 P – B3, PxP; 15 PxP, P – QN4; 16 K – Q2, P – QR4; 17 K – Q3, K – B3; 18 B – B3, K – K2; 19 P – KR4, P – R3; 20 B – Q1, K – Q1; 21 P – R4, PxP[?]; 22 BxP, K – B2; 23 B – B2, K – N3; 24 K – B3, K – N4; 25 K – N3, K – B4; 26 K – R4, N – B5; 27 B – N3[?], N – Q7; 28 B – B2, N – B8; 29 KxP, NxP; 30 K – R4, N – R4; 31 K – N3, K – Q5; 32 K – N4, N – B3; 33 P – Q6, P – N4; 34 PxP, PxP; 35 K – N5, P – N5; 36 B – Q1, P – N6; 37 B – B3, K – K6; 38 B – R1, K – B7; 39 K – B6, P – N7; 40 BxP, KxB; 41 P – Q7, NxP; 42 KxN, K – B6; 43 Resigns. At 21 Black could have assured the win by P – N5 and at 27 White could have drawn by B – N1.)

The Four-to-Three Wing

An additional factor enters into No. 183 and many other instances of the offside majority.

A majority of two-to-one or three-to-two readily generates a passed pawn. But when the wing grows to four-to-three and beyond, the passed pawn does not come so readily. Chances abound for the weaker party to bring about a pawn stalemate. Even with help of the king, the victory on that side is not easy, and in any event it is time-consuming. Therefore, in No. 183, quite apart from the position of the kings (which favors Black), White's four-to-three on the king-side is by no means compensation for Black's two-to-one on the queen-side. White cannot live long enough to get a king-side passed pawn; his only chance for counterplay is through center control—which here is easily nullified.

Another instance of the same is No. 184A. The queens being still on the board, White might develop his center superiority into a direct attack on the Black king. Unfortunately, his proud center is wobbly under the attack of the Black pieces.

Kostic *v.* Gruenfeld   1922

NO. 184A. *White to move*

1 R – N1	N – R4
2 P – Q5	KR – B1
3 B – Q4	

Again because of the excellent Black development, White can have no hope of moving P – K5 and holding the phalanx. E.g., *3* P – K5? R – Q1 or *3* Q – Q3, P – K3; *4* KR – Q1, PxP and White emerges with an isolated pawn that cannot live long. Nor can White treasure his bishop, to aid the center pawns, since N – B5 impends.

3	BxB
4 QxB	P – N3
5 N – K5	Q – Q3
6 N – N4	Q – B5

White would enjoy *6* . . . R – B5?; *7* N – R6ch, K – B1; *8* Q – R8 mate.

| 7 N – K3 | R – B4 |

Thus Black is able to double rooks and keep command of the open file. A later stage of the game is No. 184B. The rook on the

NO. 184B. *White to move*

seventh is murderous. Observe that counterplay by White based on P – Q6 is squelched by the fact that the Black king stands within range to stop a passed queen pawn. This is a necessary consequence of the fact that White's majority wing is "onside."

Gaining the Offside Majority

No. 185A is a regular position of the defense to the Ruy Lopez. As is well known, the logical course for White is to strive for a king-side attack, based usually on P – KB4 – B5. Black should strive for queen-side counterplay based on P – QB4. White departed from this orthodox procedure—to his cost.

Chajes *v.* Tarrasch   1923

NO. 185A. *White to move*

1 B – B2	P – B4
2 N – N3? ·	

While the "book" says that Black can hold his own after 2 PxP e.p., if White does not make this move he has nothing to show for his pains. His king-side advance is blocked for a long time, and Black can hit soon on the queen-side, as witness:

2	Q – Q2
3 QN – Q4	NxN
4 NxN	P – B4

The same move would have followed *4 PxN*.

5 NxB	QxN
6 P – B3	N – N4
7 BxN	BxB
8 P – KB4	B – Q1
9 Q – B3	B – N3

NO. 185B. *White to move*

Now Black has an offside majority that is a mighty threat, even though four-to-three! White has a protected passed pawn, but it is effectively blockaded. Of this position (Chajes *v.* Tarrasch, 1923), Marozcy commented that White, without making a single bad move, now has the inferior game. We venture to say that *2 N – N3* was a very bad move indeed. Be that as it may, No. 185, like No. 183, indicates the superiority of the mobile offside majority to the blockaded though protected passed pawn.

Offside Majority v. Minority Attack

In Chapter 18, we discussed the *minority attack* based on a half-open file. Now, if you have a (noncrippled) majority pawn wing, your opponent necessarily has a half-open file bearing upon it. The question may arise in your mind, do you have an advantage because of the majority, or does he have the advantage because of the half-open file?

This is often a very real question over the board. It cannot be settled by a general rule but only by the dynamics of the particular position. All that can be said is: the majority triumphs if it can be set in motion; the minority attack triumphs if it can immobilize the pawns in a defensive salient.

The minority attack operates, if at all, early in the game, on a crowded board. The more pieces are exchanged, the better is the chance of mobilizing the majority wing.

A tactical point in advancing a majority wing is to keep the unopposed pawn ahead or abreast of its fellows; if it falls behind, it may become backward. This consideration is the key to many positions that might be studied on the question of majority wing *v.* minority attack. If the unopposed pawn can reach the fourth rank, the whole wing can generally be kept mobile; if it cannot, the wing is apt to be paralyzed. The second condition is seen in the remarkable No. 154. The first obtains in the two following examples—the key pawn is already at the fourth.

In No. 186, the game continued

Capablanca *v.* Villegas   1914

NO. 186. *White to move*

1	KR – Q1	KR – Q1

Forced; he cannot stand R – Q7.

2	P – QN4	RxR
3	QxR	P – QN3
4	P – N3	R – QB1
5	R – QB1	R – Q1
6	Q – K3	K – B1
7	P – B5	PxP
8	Q – K4!	

To prevent Q – B3, blockading the pawn.

8	R – Q4
9 PxP	P – N3

Of course not 9 . . . RxP; 10 Q – QN4.

10 P – B6	K – N2
11 P – QR4	

To deny the rook access to QN4.

11	R – Q3
12 Q – K5ch	Resigns

13 QxR follows.

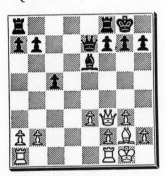

Marshall *v.* Capablanca   1909

NO. 187. *White to move*

In No. 187, White's best chance is a center advance, say P – K4,
Q – K3, and P – KB4. Instead:

1 KR – B1?	QR – N1	7 BxR	R – Q1
2 Q – K4	Q – B2	8 B – B3	P – N3
3 R – B3	P – QN4	9 Q – B6	Q – K4!
4 P – QR3	. P – B5	10 Q – K4	QxQ
5 B – B3	KR – Q1	11 BxQ	
6 R – Q1	RxRch	Black wins	

(11 . . . R – Q8ch; 12 K – N2, P – QR4; 13 R – B2, P – N5; 14
PxP, PxP; 15 B – B3, R – N8; 16 B – K2, P – N6; 17 R – Q2,
R – QB8; 18 B – Q1, P – B6; 19 PxP, P – N7; 20 RxP, RxB; 21

R – B2, B – B4; *22* R – N2, R – QB8; *23* R – N3, B – K5ch; *24* K – R3, R – B7; *25* P – KB4, P – R4; *26* P – N4, PxPch; *27* KxP, RxRP; *28* R – N4, P – B4ch; *29* K – N3, R – K7; *30* R – B4, RxPch; *31* K – R4, K – N2; *32* R – B7ch, K – B3; *33* R – Q7, B – N7; *34* R – Q6ch, K – N2; *35* Resigns.)

SUMMARY

Count a point plus for better king position if the kings are actually free to roam.

Count a point plus for an offside pawn majority, provided that it is not immediately under an immobilizing minority attack.

23. *Relative Values*

THE Point Count System has been presented as a method of comparing the White and Black positions to determine which is superior strategically, and why. Such evaluation is of more than academic interest; it is the very essence of learning to play chess well.

The points enumerated stand as *limited objectives* you should strive for as a means to the eventual objective of checkmate.

In general, a net plus of four points is equivalent to more than a pawn and so to a readily "won game." Yet, a single plus point is often the initial capital for a victorious campaign: it facilitates the acquisition of additional points. Advantage begets advantage.

In the practical business of playing a game, you are repeatedly confronted with two questions:

A] If I can establish one of two points in my favor, but not both, which should I choose?

B] How much of a minus can I afford to incur to gain a plus point?

Unfortunately, it is not possible to arrange the points in a scale of relative values. Much depends on the particular positions. In early play, the major considerations are no doubt development, space, and the center. Superiority in any of these aspects is most likely to lead to further acquisitions. Yet any of them may turn out, on occasion, to be inconsequential, and some minor point, such as a doubled pawn, may prove decisive.

This chapter will give a number of examples to show how master players have dealt with the foregoing questions. So far as any generalization is safe, we may infer from the examples:

A] Pawn weaknesses are endurable when they enhance the scope of the pieces.

B] An advantage you can exploit immediately is a safer choice than one that must await a considerable change in the position (e.g., reduction to endplay).

C] To win a "won game" often necessitates transforming one point into another.

D] The effort to perpetuate an adverse point of weakness may be misguided; surer progress may come from transformation.

E] A single point can at times outweigh all others, and to gain such a point may be worth the sacrifice of material.

Acceptable Doubled Pawn

The least of all weaknesses, perhaps, is the doubled pawn. We have already discussed its acceptability to gain a half-open file (Chapter 18) and to gain the bishop-pair (the "Ruy Lopez question," Chapter 17 and elsewhere). Another instance is No. 188. Black moves *1* . . . B – B4. He (Tarrasch) considers that to exchange his bad bishop for White's good bishop is worth the doubled king bishop pawn. His king-side is somewhat weakened, but the pawn capture toward the center strengthens him there. White evidently agreed with this estimate, for he delayed exchanging until forced to do so.

Schwarz *v.* Tarrasch 1932   Burn *v.* Tarrasch 1911

NO. 188. *Black to move*   NO. 189. *Black to move*

Acceptable Isolani

No. 189 is a position arising from the Sicilian Defense. The "book" move is *1 . . . P – Q4*. White can isolate the Black queen pawn, but Black finds this acceptable to gain free play for his pieces, particularly the queen bishop. A tactical point is that White must take immediate measures to forestall P – Q5, where the pawn would be as safe as on Q4 but would cramp the White development.

No. 190A is a position arising from the Ruy Lopez. Black (Tarrasch) plays

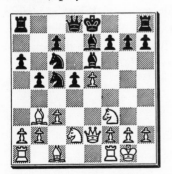

O. Bernstein *v.* Tarrasch 1914

NO. 190A. *Black to move*

1 . . . .   P – Q5!

He thereby incurs an isolated king pawn. But the pawn is not noticeably weak, being masked from frontal attack, and above all, Black gains free play for his pieces. The continuation was:

2	BxB	PxB
3	PxP	NxP
4	NxN	QxN
5	N – N3	

White is embarrassed by the dominating Black queen. If 5 N – B3, Q – Q6 and after the exchange of queens Black's queen-side pawns would descend fast. White accepts a doubled and isolated queen knight pawn, perhaps with the hope of making some use of the half-open queen rook file.

5	....	NxN
6	PxN	O – O

NO. 190B. *White to move*

The outcome of the transaction is that Black's isolani is negligible, while his swap of a center pawn for a wing pawn has given him the ominous queen-side majority. White is unable to develop naturally; his bishop cannot emerge without loss of something, and he cannot move R – Q1 to chase the queen—but he did:

7	R – Q1?	RxP!

Black wins

Acceptable Doubled Isolani

A game, Teichmann *v.* Tarrasch, 1894, opened:

1	P – K4	P – K4
2	N· – QB3	N – KB3

3	B – B4		B – B4		7	P – KR3		B – K3
4	P – B4		P – Q3		8	B – N5		P – QR3!?
5	N – B3		N – B3		9	BxNch		PxB
6	P – Q3		B – KN5		10	PxP		PxP

Teichmann *v.* Tarrasch 1894

NO. 191. *White to move*

Black accepts a doubled, isolated queen bishop pawn. In return he gets the bishop-pair, two half-open files, and a lead in development. Tarrasch considers this more than ample compensation, amounting almost to a "won game." (Note that White cannot play *11* NxP, for then Q – Q5 wins a piece.)

No. 192 is a regular position in the Sicilian Defense. The usual continuation is B – K2, so as to follow with B – K3 without being bothered by Black's N – KN5. Ivkov (White) is skeptical of the sting in that move, so plays at once

Ivkov *v.* Taimanov 1955

NO. 192. *White to move*

1	B – K3		N – KN5
2	B – QN5		NxB
3	PxN		

White considers that his doubled, isolated king pawn is easily offset by his lead in development, which is intensified by the half-open king bishop file. The continuation bears him out:

3	B – Q2		
4 O – O	N – K4		

The analysts have found nothing better.

5 N – B3	BxB	8 QxQch	KxQ
6 NxB	Q – Q2	9 RxP and wins	
7 NxN	PxN		

Transforming Adverse Weakness

In Chapter 9 we saw several examples of the classical operation against the isolated queen pawn—"blockade, attack, destroy!" We should expect to see this operation attempted in No. 193. But White perceives tactical difficulties. His blockading knight is attacked; to reinforce it by B – K3 invites B – QB4, while P – K3 permits Black to bring the White pawn to Q4 by

Rubinstein v. Salwe   1908

NO. 193. *White to move*

swaps. If *1* N – B2, Black can answer P – Q5, for *2* BxNch, QxB does not win the queen pawn, the White king rook being loose.

So White concedes that he cannot maintain the blockade; he plays *1* NxN, and after PxN the queen pawn is no longer isolated. But White is satisfied, for a pawn weakness remains—a backward queen bishop pawn or a hanging phalanx.

An analogous but more surprising transformation was wrought in No. 194. Here we can see no tactical bar to the routine process: QN – Q4, B – K3, Q – Q2, R – Q1, etc. But Botvinnik (White) had a different idea:

Botvinnik *v.* Boleslavsky 1941

NO. 194. *White to move*

1 **B – K3!?**	**BxB**
2 **BxNch**	**PxB**
3 **PxB**	

White has deliberately given himself an isolated king pawn while "de-isolating" the Black queen pawn. Part of the idea is the familiar one that the Black weakness does not disappear: it is merely transformed. But the idea of shunting the king bishop pawn into isolation on the king file, rather than using it as a battering-ram on the king bishop file, is astonishing. The subsequent play reveals that the purpose is to nail down outpost stations for the knights at Q4 and QB5, whence they dominate the advanced center. Black's bishop is largely useless.

In No. 195, Black threatens Q – R3, winning a pawn. White makes the best of a bad bargain with

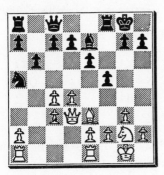

Gilg *v.* Tarrasch 1926

NO. 195. *White to move*

1 **P – B5**

Now one might expect PxP, saddling White with a doubled isolani. But Tarrasch (Black) is not satisfied with that. The queen bishop file is not open for frontal attack. If Black wants to advance his queen pawn, he will have to give White a chance to undouble anyhow. So—

1 . . . .   P – Q4!

letting White undouble at once.

2 PxP e.p.   PxP

3 B – Q2   P – Q4

Black is satisfied with the transaction; he gains a strong station for his knight.

4 P – B3   Q – B5!

Aimed against the liberating advance P – K4.

5 Q – K3   Q – B3

6 Q – Q3   N – B5

Black wins

Transforming a Plus

The preceding examples suggest that you should not be too dogmatic in the exploitation of adverse weaknesses. There is more than one way to skin a cat. The same lesson applies with even greater force to the conservation of your own plus points. The transformation of such points is dealt with in Chapter 24; here let us interject one example.

Look again at No. 23 and read what is said of the demerits of P – Q5. Then play out this game (Tarrasch *v.* Showalter, 1898):

Tarrasch *v.* Showalter   1898

1 P – K4   P – K4

2 N – KB3   N – QB3

3 B – B4   B – K2

4 P – Q4   P – Q3

NO. 196A. *White to move*

5 P – Q5

Doesn't this move deserve a query? Doesn't it close the beautiful diagonal of the bishop and make that bishop bad?

No. 196A is a little different from No. 23—yet what a *big* difference! The Black king bishop is on K2, not B4. Consequently, P – Q5 confers no favor upon it; rather, the move helps to keep it locked in. The White advance is the launching of a grand long-range plan to suffocate the whole Black army.

5	N – N1
6 B – Q3!	

The bishop still serves well by preventing P – KB4.

6	N – KB3
7 P – B4	O – O
8 P – KR3!	

To restrict the Black queen bishop.

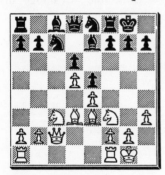

8	P – B3
9 N – B3	N – R3
10 B – K3	N – B2
11 O – O	KN – K1
12 Q – B2	PxP
13 BPxP	

NO. 196B. *Black to move*

Black must still strive for P – B4 to escape the toils.

13	P – KN3	17 R – KN1	B – Q2
14 B – KR6	N – N2	18 R – N2	R – B1
15 P – KN4!	N(B2) – K1	19 QR – KN1 and wins	
16 K – R2	K – R1		

The strategy of constriction has succeeded. Black is trussed up for the kill.

(*19* . . . P – N3; *20* Q – Q2, N – B3; *21* N – K1, N – N1; *22* B – K3, P – KN4; *23* N – B3, P – B3; *24* P – KR4, P – KR3; *25* R – KR1, K – R2; *26* K – N1, K – N3; *27* N – R2, R – QB2; *28*

N – B1, Q – B1; *29* Q – K2, K – B2; *30* B – R6, Q – N1; *31* N – N5, BxN; *32* BxB, KR – B1; *33* PxP, RPxP; *34* B – B6, B – B1; *35* Q – B3, RxB; *36* PxR, N – K3; *37* R – R7ch, B – N2; *38* N – N3, RxP; *39* N – B5, Q – QB1; *40* R(2) – R2, N – K2; *41* NxB, NxN; *42* BxKNP, Q – K3 and Black resigned before White's next move, since *43* B – R6 wins a piece.)

Pawns for Points

The majority of sacrifices are tactical: they depend upon an exact calculation of the outcome, mate, or regaining of the material sacrificed. But there are also strategic sacrifices, for the purpose of gaining points. Since a pawn is worth, on the average, three points, it might seem that you must gain at least that number to warrant sacrifice of so much as a pawn. Not so, because points beget points. A single countable advantage may actually be worth much more in potential gains.

A simple case is No. 197.

Marshall *v.* Capablanca   1918

NO. 197. *White to move*

1 N – Q4	Q – K4!

Of course not QxRP, for then R – R1 wins the queen.

2 NxP	QxQ
3 RxQ	R – Q7!

Black has submitted cheerfully to loss of a pawn, because he gets a rook to the seventh. No exact calculation is required to warrant the belief that this advantage is sufficient to win back the pawn in due time.

4	R – N1	R – K1
5	P – K5	P – KN4
6	P – KR4	PxP
7	R – K1	R – K3
	Black wins	

In No. 198, Black threatens the king knight pawn. There are obvious objections to the defenses P – KN3, B – B1, K – B1. So—

Fuderer *v.* Milic   1955

NO. 198. *White to move*

1	N – B3!	QxP
2	K – K2	

White has lost a pawn and forfeited castling. In return he has gained a half-open king knight file against the castled king, and a huge lead in development. That this was enough was quickly demonstrated.

2	....	Q – R6	9	RxPch	RxR
3	QR – KN1	P – KB4	10	BxPch	K – R1
4	R – N3	Q – R4	11	RxR	KxR
5	R(1) – KN1	R – B2	12	Q – K7ch	K – R1
6	Q – R3	N – Q2	13	N – K5	PxP
7	K – K1	PxP	14	P – B4	Resigns
8	BxQBP	P – B5			

White threatens 15 Q – Q8ch, etc.

In No. 199, Black clearly stands better. His king-side pawns hold the White bishops at bay and threaten eventually to roll down against the castled king. Still, how is he to continue? P – K5 loses a pawn, and P – B5 reduces the chance of breaking through. Preparatory maneuvers behind the lines cannot solve the problem of how to push the pawns on without letting the White bishops come to life.

Black finds an elegant solution:

Pilnik *v.* Geller   1955

NO. 199. *Black to move*

1	P – K5!
2 BxB	QxB
3 PxP	P – B5!

At the mere cost of a pawn, Black gains the strong station K4 for his knight, establishes a mobile three-to-two majority on the tender king-side, and leaves the White bishop staring at a stone wall. White must hurry to bolster his king-side.

| 4 R – B2 | N – K4 |

Naturally not . . . QxNP, Q – N4 with counterplay.

| 5 QR – KB1 | Q – R5 |

Threatening N – N5.

6 B – Q1	R – B2
7 Q – B2	P – N4
8 Q – B3	QR – KB1
Black wins	

The Black steamroller cannot be halted.

(9 P – KR3, P – R4; 10 B – K2, P – N5; 11 RxP, RxR; 12 RxR, RxR; 13 P – KN3, N – B6ch; 14 K – B2, QxRP; 15 PxR, P – N6ch; 16 KxN, P – N7ch; 17 K – B2, Q – R7; 18 Resigns.)

A colorful example of installing a strong outpost at cost of a pawn is No. 200. White has greater space on the king-side, and an outpost at Q5 How can he exploit these points? The knight actually discommodes Black little, and it can be swapped off at will, since it has no retreat. For once, a bishop on Q5 would be stronger than a knight, since it would crowd the Black king uncomfortably. Wherefore:

Ojanen *v.* Liflaender   1955

NO. 200. *White to move*

1 P – N4!	N – B2
2 NxN	QxN
3 PxP	PxP
4 P – KR4!	P – KR3
5 P – K5!	QxP
6 B – Q5ch	K – R2
7 Q – B3 and wins	

Black is now helpless against an attack on the king rook file. (7 . . . PxP; *8* B – B4, Q – K2; *9* QR – K1, Q – Q1; *10* R – K2, R – K1; *11* R – R2, Q – K2; *12* RxP, B – Q2; *13* K – B2, B – B3; *14* R(1) – KR1, BxB; *15* RxPch, BxR; *16* RxBch, K – N2; *17* R – N6ch, K – R1; *18* Q – R3ch, Q – R2; *19* R – R6, B – N1; *20* Q – R4, R – KB1; *21* P – N5, K – N2; *22* P – N6, Resigns.)

The Intangible Point

All other things being equal, confidence wins games. Allied to the will to win, it sparks the mental ignition, brings forth ideas, dispels doubts, promotes clear thinking. In contrast, Milquetoast timidity, befuddles, inhibits and defeats itself.

By all means use the psychological weapon. Move with alacrity, capture with impunity and play with dignity!

If you can do all this, credit yourself with a point.

24. Practical Value and Application of Point Count

WHEN you are conversant with all the plus and minus points, as given in Point Count, you have added a minimum of thirty-two plans of action to your strategic arsenal. You have learned, for example, that certain factors, like control of the center, or superior development, or greater space, or outpost pieces, or any one of the many other plus points, are assets. Conversely, the cramped position, the bad bishop, and the intrinsic weaknesses of certain pawns and pawn configurations, among others, are liabilities. An isolated pawn no longer is just a pawn, as far as you are concerned. It is a plan. It is something to foist upon your opponent and avoid for yourself. The same holds true of all the plus and minus points. They are plans. The plus points are to be amassed. The minus ones you are to inflict upon your opponent. Minus points in the enemy camp are tantamount to plus points in your own.

As the factors of Point Count become your second nature, you become an expert trader, for Point Count guides you in making profitable trades. It debunks aberrated ideas, provides you with a sound measuring rod. You are even willing to accept weaknesses so long as you net compensating advantages. Indeed, the basic art of evaluating and appraising, as given in Point Count sharpens your judgment. You not only know whether you are ahead or behind, but also by what margin and for what reasons. By knowing the margin, you know what risks you can afford; by knowing the reasons, you know what lines of play to exploit. For example, you have heard time and again that control of the center is valuable. But have you ever been told *how* valuable? Is it worth a knight? Is it worth two pawns? One pawn? Point Count answers this as well as many other similar questions for which you are constantly having to make decisions.

This is how your appraisal of a position via Point Count will determine your course of action:

You Are More Than Four Net Points Plus

You examine the position and find that you are blessed with a preponderance of, say, sixteen net plus points. In material value, this is equivalent to five pawns and one plus point, or one rook and one plus point, or a knight, two pawns and one plus point. Your advantage is so great, the game nearly plays itself. Between experts, such a game terminates. The eventual loser resigns at once. Between amateurs, any number of alternative actions are possible. Above all, however, the prospective winner must be circumspect.

First, provide for the safety of your king. You undoubtedly recall many instances were inadequate precautions led to unexpected disaster. Remember that all your net pluses vanish into thin air the moment you are checkmated.

Then define the position sharply in your mind. Expand upon your advantages and aggravate your opponent's weaknesses. Whatever you do, bear in mind that, with so many points behind, your opponent can offer only token resistance. Usually, you can overwhelm his king by superior force, though this is not necessary. You can add to your points by advancing your pawns to new queens, or capturing more material. Because your lead is so great, the mere exchange of a unit increases that lead proportionally and hastens the end. You can even afford to be liberal and sacrifice a few points in exchanging for the sake of expediency, so long as you maintain a certain winning advantage.

When you have five or more net plus points, you follow the above outlined campaign. If you have only something approaching the minimum five-point lead, you must, of course, be less liberal, lest you jeopardize victory.

If you are in the unhappy predicament where you are many, many net points behind, your actions will depend upon your best judgment. If you are playing an expert, resign. If you are certain that you are going to lose to your opponent, resign. If you think there is a ghost of a chance, continue. Then all depends upon your opponent, though you can assist in rattling him. He must blunder or you must swindle him. You weigh the probabilities. Generally, complications, even unsound ones, offer the greatest hope. And have no qualms about winning by a trap. A victory by an unsound combination is scored equal to that of the finest artistic effort.

When you are far ahead or far behind in points, the actions almost suggest themselves. The problem before you is relatively easy. When the point gap narrows, the problem grows. Let us take case number two:

You Are Four Points Plus or Minus

After checking the Point Count, you find a net difference of four points, plus or minus. Four points is the equivalent of one pawn and one point. Between masters, one net pawn plus or three net points is adequate to insure victory.

Let us assume you are on the plus side of the board. You know you have a theoretical win. What course of action should you pursue? As in case number one, be circumspect, secure your king, evade traps and pitfalls and define your pluses and minuses.

Your general plan, as before, is to expand on your pluses and/or aggravate your opponent's minuses. If your plus is the material pawn and a point, the pawn and the point ought to decide the game in your favor. The process of converting the pawn to victory, however, is a long one, and you must gird your loins for it. When you are ready—that is, when everything else is in order—you will advance your extra pawn, or you will advance on the wing where you have the extra pawn and force a passed pawn. The passed pawn must win the game.

If you encounter obstacles in this action, such as the necessity of exposing your king, you are, of course, to remove these obstacles. This can be accomplished by prudent exchanges. Here, too, every exchange enhances the value of the extra pawn. And every exchange which cuts down the force of your opponent militates against an unpleasant surprise. If your opponent runs from exchanges, all well and good. He will then be ceding important, dominating squares.

In an encounter between masters, the extra pawn often decides before the endgame is reached. Observing inevitable defeat, the master will speculate on a desperate diversion or unsound attack. When this fails, as it should, and his position is in tatters, he resigns, thereby capitulating quickly.

When your four net points plus are of the positional variety as against the material ones, victory is within your grasp. Here, however, you must convert these points into material or into decisive demonstrations against the enemy king.

Let us take a case where you have control of the center (one point), you enjoy better development (one point), your opponent is cramped (one point), and you are in possession of a useful, half-open file (one point). This makes for a net plus total of four points. What course should you follow?

To be sure, it is difficult to map a specific course for a general position. Yet, with all these plus points, the win must be there. When you control the center, for example, you can usually expand on either wing and further cramp your opponent. And when he is trussed up, you can strike at his king or win material.

Be that as it may, just such a position occurs in the game, Horowitz-Martin (see illustrative games, page 323). Here, White smashed through on the half-open file for a quick win.

It is certainly pleasant to be on the plus side of a position. Unfortunately, even the greatest masters suffer the fate of being on the minus side. When you are four points minus, what ought you do?

First, you must realize that with perfect play you are inevitably lost. In a lost position, the best and most artistic moves will still lead to a loss. Hence, you must rely on the human factor, your opponent. Size him up. If you believe that he is weak on defense, by all means attack, even unsoundly. Enjoy the last fling. Something may come of it, possibly only the gain of time to repair your own minuses.

The alternative course is to mark time and pray for a blunder.

You Are Two Points Plus or Minus

When you are two points plus, you are theoretically on the brink of victory. But you must find ways and means of increasing your plus. Here again, your course of action will depend upon the nature of your advantage. If, for example, your two points consist of control of the center (one point) and your opponent has an isolated pawn (minus one point), you may have a long row to hoe. Your long-range plan then is to capitalize on his chronic weakness, the isolated pawn. At the same time, your short-range plan should be to increase your plus points by expanding on your center control. If your plus points are intrinsic ones, like the protected passed pawn or the outside passed pawn, you should seek an ending. If your plus points are transient ones, like your opponent's king in the center (minus one) and weak-square complex (minus one), you should attempt to capitalize these in the middle game, or convert to an endgame with something more tangible to show for your pluses.

Even though you have a long-range plan, it doesn't follow that capitulation will necessarily come in the endgame. The specter of a losing endgame may evoke desperate action by your opponent, which ought to bring a favorable decision sooner.

Again, let us examine the other side of this picture. You are two points minus. You are theoretically on the brink of defeat.

This is really the moment for you to undertake some counter-action—desperate action, if need be. Do not wait until your position deteriorates beyond repair. Rely on tactical swindles, bluff attacks, anything and everything that may throw the opponent off balance. Do something before the ax falls.

You Are One Point Plus or Minus

Let us examine the last case. The difference between both sides is one net point. This can hardly be viewed as serious, though the side with the minus point must exert every effort to contain his opponent.

In the usual course of any well-played game, White, by virtue of his first move, enjoys a certain initiative. If this were to be measured in terms of points, it would be fractional. Black's problem usually is to keep this fractional point from growing into a full one, while White concentrates into building it up. With perfect play, White reaches his maximum position after a while and is contained. Black equalizes.

A net difference of one point rarely decides a game. To say never, however, would be a misstatement. The very first game in Chapter 25, Illustrative Games, shows how a single point can be nursed along to the endgame, where it is decisive.

Thus, to summarize, we observe that Point Count helps us evaluate our position, after which we determine our course of action. When we are on the plus side of the board, with due circumspection, we continue to increase our pluses. At times when we are preponderantly plus, we can afford to be liberal by sacrificing some points in order to reach our goal quickly.

Point Count is of exceptional value when we are on the minus side of the board. For then it will dictate a policy of action rather than lethargy, action which in time may save the game from a desolate fate.

Before closing this chapter, it may be well to restate that chess is a competitive game played by human beings. It is subject to human foibles, and it is perfectly ethical to garner points by playing upon these foibles.

25. *Illustrative Games*

THE following games illustrate in action the strategic points discussed in this book.

Certain aspects of strategy cannot well be illustrated in less than complete games, and the following are selected with these particular aspects in mind. They are:

A] How the possession of a single major plus point may lead to the acquisition of additional points.

B] How points must frequently be transformed, one to another, to maintain equality or to conserve a winning preponderance.

Game I

Within the first six moves, White acquires a minus point, which, however, seems unimportant and may well be transient. Black nevertheless precipitates the exchange of queens, nurses the White weakness through sixty moves of endplay, and finally triumphs. This is a rare type of game! It requires not only consummate tactical skill but also supreme self-confidence.

CARO-KANN DEFENSE

ATKINS *v.* CAPABLANCA, 1922

1 P – K4	P – QB3	5 QxB	P – K3
2 P – Q4	P – Q4	6 N – K2	Q – N3
3 P – K5	B – B4	7 O – O	
4 B – Q3	BxB		

NO. IA. *After 7 O – O*

As a result of his inferior third move, White is weak on the light squares, being left with a semi-bad bishop. Black stakes all on this weakness.

7	Q – R3	10 N – Q2	PxP
8 Q – Q1	P – QB4	11 PxP	Q – Q6
9 P – QB3	N – QB3		

Now the swap cannot be evaded.

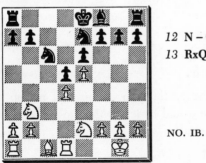

12 N – QN3	QxQ
13 RxQ	KN – K2

NO. IB. *After 13 . . .*
KN – K2

Black's task is to restrict the scope of White's minor pieces—above all, to avoid the swap of bishops. At the same time, he must not let the open file go to White by default.

14 B – Q2	P – QR4	17 N – B3	N – R2
15 QR – B1	P – QN3	18 K – B1	KN – B3
16 P – QR4	K – Q2	19 K – K2	R – B1

NO. IC. *After 19 . . .*
R – B1

White has nearly reached the limit of mobilization yet can do nothing but defend. Black has the possibility of bringing his king rook to the queen-side for assault there, and even of a king-side expansion.

20 B – K1	B – K2
21 N – N1	P – B4
22 PxP e.p.	

The backward White queen knight pawn, formerly too negligible to be counted, now becomes a real weakness. But it is understandable that White does not relish the prospect of a king-side steamroller.

| 22 . . . . | BxP |
| 23 B – B3 | N – N5 |

At last White has a chance to swap off his bad bishop—and cannot afford to do so. He would be left with a queen rook pawn subject to frontal attack and a weak queen pawn, and denied access to his QB3.

24 B – Q2   N(2) – B3
25 B – K3

NO. ID. *After 25 B – K3*

Having obtained use of the outpost station at QN5, Black next prepares to gain command of the open file.

| 25 . . . . | N – R7 | 27 N – R3 | KR – QB1 |
| 26 R – B2 | R – B2 | | |

Preventing 28 N – N5, to which the answer would be NxPch.

| 28 R(2) – Q2 | N – R2 | 30 R(3) – Q2 | R – B3 |
| 29 R – Q3 | N – N5 | 31 R – QN1 | B – K2 |

Intending to get rid of the knight at R3 so as to gain access to the seventh rank.

32 R – QR1   B – Q3
33 P – R3   R(3) – B2
34 R(1) – Q1   N – R7
35 R – QR1

NO. IE. *After 35 R – QR1*

Black's patient preparation has enabled him to get rid of the knight without even giving up his mighty bishop.

| 35 . . . . | BxN | 37 R – Q1 | R – B5 |
| 36 RxN | B – N5 | 38 R – QB1 | N – B3 |

Threatening NxPch and so forcing the reply. Observe that to the bad White bishop Black added a plus for command of the open file, which he now transforms into an offside pawn majority plus an outpost station at his Q4.

| 39 RxR | PxR |
| 40 N – Q2 | |

NO. IF. *After 40 N – Q2*

Black simplifies to knight *v.* bad bishop.

40	BxN!	44 P – B3	R – QN1
41 KxB	K – Q3	45 R – R3	P – QN4
42 K – B3	K – Q4	46 PxP	RxP
43 R – R1	P – N3	47 B – B2	N – N5

Heading for Q6. Useless is 48 B – K3, N – Q6; 49 R – R2 because of R – N6ch. As the final accretion, Black now gets a passed pawn.

NO. IG. *After 47 . . .*
       N – N5

48 P – QN3	PxP
49 KxP	N – B3ch
50 K – B3	R – N8
51 R – R4	R – B8ch
52 K – Q2	

He cannot maintain the guard of QB4, for if 52 K – Q3, N – N5ch, and at the very least the rook can get to B7 with a check, then go to R7.

52	R – B5	56 R – QN1	K – B3
53 R – R1	P – R5	57 K – Q3	R – B6ch
54 R – R2	N – R2	58 K – Q2	R – N6
55 R – R1	N – N4	59 R – B1ch	

The futility of the bishop persists to the end. If RxR, the passed pawn will draw the White king away so that the Black king can march to KB8 via K6 and raid the pawns.

59	K – N2	64 R – B8	N – B3
60 R – B2	P – R6	65 R – QR8	R – N7ch
61 B – N3	NxP	66 K – K3	RxP
62 R – B7ch	K – N3	67 B – B2	N – N5
63 R – B4	K – N4	Resigns	

Game II

Black holds back his center pawns, letting White take greater central space. White turns this point into center control, nurses it through a long series of transformations, reduces to a king-and-pawn ending where it becomes a one-step better king position, and wins after both players get new queens.

This type of game is at the opposite pole from Game I. Black's inferiority lies, not in a permanent weakness, but in a net deficit. The White plus is continually transient and can be conserved and exploited only by judicious transformation.

RETI OPENING

HOROWITZ *v.* PRZEPIORKA, 1931

1 N – KB3	N – KB3	9 R – Q1	P – B4
2 P – B4	P – K3	10 P – K4	Q – N1
3 P – KN3	P – QN3	11 P – N3	PxP
4 B – N2	B – N2	12 NxP	P – QR3
5 O – O	B – K2	13 B – N2	Q – B2
6 P – Q4	P – Q3	14 P – B4	QR – B1
7 N – B3	O – O	15 Q – K2	KR – Q1
8 Q – B2	QN – Q2	16 QR – B1	B – B1

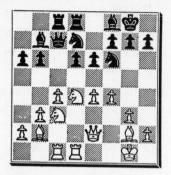

NO. IIA. *After 16 . . .*
B – B1

White has the greater central space. Black's position is cramped but solid. True, his queen pawn is backward on an open file, yet it can be defended more times than it can be attacked. How is White to proceed? One idea is P – KN4 with the intention of P – N5. But the immediate P – KN4 is answered strongly by P – K4. Without going into tactical details, we can see that a king-side pawn storm is not practicable so long as Black has the option of a center break by P – K4 or P – Q4. This circumstance leads to the idea of destroying the option. The Black center phalanx must be forced into a chain, thus reducing its mobility.

17   **P – KB5**   **PxP**

Black rightly judges that stabilization of the center by P – K4 would allow a king-side pawn storm.

18   **N – Q5**

An important *Zwischenzug* to gain the bishop-pair.

18 . . . .   **BxN**

Practically forced, since NxN would remove an important defender from the king-side and would leave the queen bishop locked in behind the White pawns.

19   **BPxB**   **Q – N2**

20   **NxP**

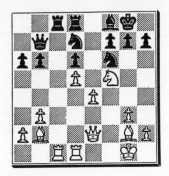

NO. IIB. *After 20 NxP*

The center is stabilized, but White has acquired the slight edge of two-to-one. Both sides have a weak center pawn, but White's "fights back" a little more than Black's. While both sides have outpost stations, White's knight on the fifth is more menacing than Black's will be on the fourth. The most important point, however, is White's bishop-pair, the more ominous for Black because his own bishop is locked in.

Black's position remains solid enough to repel all lighthorse attacks. There ensues a period of jockeying in which White seeks to cause a deterioration of the Black position.

20	N – K4	23 B – R3	RxR
21 B – QR3	N – K1	24 RxR	R – B2
22 Q – K3	R – Q2	25 K – N2	

White contemplates Q – N5, but first must forestall the fork, N – B6ch.

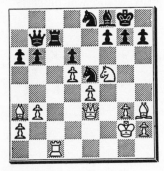

NO. IIC. *After 25 K – N2*

The swapping of rooks is two-edged. Black thereby lessens the danger from direct attack but also enhances the significance of the bishop-pair.

25 . . . .   P – N3

Was this move necessary? Possibly not, but it is understandable that Black finds the outpost intolerable. Now Black gets rid of his bad bishop, yet thereby becomes weak on the dark squares.

26	N – R6ch	BxN
27	QxB	N – Q6
28	RxR	QxR
29	Q – Q2	N – K4
30	Q – B1	QxQ
31	BxQ	

NO. IID. *After 31 BxQ*

Black threatens to win the king pawn in two moves. The king cannot go to its defense, for K – B2 allows a knight fork. But now the faster action of the bishops begins to tell.

31	. . . .	N – B3
32	B – B8	P – QR4
33	B – K3	N(3) – Q2

Black cannot let a queen-side pawn go for the White king pawn, for then White's offside majority would win quickly.

34	B – Q4	K – B1
35	K – B2	K – K2
36	K – K2	K – Q1
37	KBxN	NxB

NO. IIE. *After 37 . . . NxB*

White changes his point for the bishop-pair into good bishop *v.* knight. The preceding maneuvers have created an avenue of penetration to the queen-side for his king; the reduction of forces facilitates its use.

38	K – Q3	N – K4ch	
39	BxN	PxB	

Now the second bishop goes, but White gains a protected passed pawn. At the same time, Black gains a king-side majority. White stakes all on his lead in king position. But before the king continues his journey, the king-side pawns must be disposed to prevent an unsupported breakthrough.

40	P – KN4	P – B3	

Of course he must prevent the crippling P – N5.

41	P – KR4	P – R4	43	K – B4	K – Q2
42	PxP	PxP	44	K – N5	K – Q3

If 44 . . . K – B2; 45 P – R3, K – N2; 46 P – Q6 and wins. But now if White captures the knight pawn, Black gets a passed pawn too.

45	KxP!	P – B4	
46	PxP	P – K5	

He has no time for 46 . . . KxP, for 47 P – B6, K – K3; 48 KxP and the White king gets back in time to catch the king pawn.

47	P – B6	P – K6	
48	P – B7	K – K2	
49	P – Q6ch	KxBP	
50	P – Q7	P – K7	
51	P – Q8(Q)	P – K8(Q)	

NO. IIF. *After 51 . . .*
P – K8(Q)

White's forty-fifth move was made on the conviction that he can now escape perpetual check and eventually win by his pawn plus.

52 Q – Q5ch	K – N2	57 Q – B3ch	K – R2
53 QxKRP	Q – B7ch	58 Q – KN3	Q – R6
54 K – N5	QxQRP	59 K – B6	Q – N5?
55 Q – N4ch	K – R2	60 Q – Q3ch	K – N1
56 Q – QB4	K – N2	61 Q – Q8ch	Resigns

For White will be able to force the exchange of queens by a check at Q6 or QN7.

Game III

This game and the next bear upon the "Ruy Lopez question" (see this topic in Chapter 17). In the present game, Black has his cake and eats it too: he gets the bishop-pair, then contrives to undouble his queen bishop pawn. He gives a classic demonstration of what to do with the two bishops.

RUY LOPEZ

RICHTER *v.* TARRASCH, 1888

1 P – K4	P – K4	6 BxN	QPxB
2 N – KB3	N – QB3	7 QxPch	Q – K2
3 B – N5	N – B3	8 R – K1	QxQ
4 O – O	NxP	9 RxQch	B – K2
5 Q – K2	N – Q3		

NO. IIIA *After 9 . . .*
B – K2

Here is the question: Does Black's bishop-pair weigh more or less than the weakness of his doubled pawn?

10 P – Q3	P – B3
11 R – K1	K – B2
12 B – B4	P – KN4

Observe how, throughout the game, Black plays to restrict the scope of the White pieces.

13 B – Q2	B – N5
14 N – Q4	P – QB4
15 N – K2	N – N4

Threatens BxN and then N – Q5, winning the queen bishop pawn.

| 16 B – B3 | |

With NxB Black could now obtain the two bishops *v.* two knights. But he wants that—and more!

| 16 . . . . | QR – Q1 |
| 17 N – Q2 | N – Q5 |

White must take this intruder. Thus Black not only reduces White to two knights but also undoubles his pawn.

18 BxN   PxB

NO. IIIB. *After 18 . . . PxB*

Black has acquired preponderant space and control in the center. White's next move prevents B – N5, which would interfere with his plan to double rooks on the king file, but it creates a weakness that tells in the end.

| 19 P – QR3 | P – QB4 | 21 P – KB3 | B – Q2 |
| 20 N – KN3 | P – KR4 | 22 R – K2 | P – N4 |

Black intends to break through on the queen-side, which his bishops can rake while the knights can find no good posts for defense.

| | 23 QR – K1 | B – KB1 |

Much better than R – K1, leading sooner or later to a swap of rooks. Black needs a rook to back up his queen-side advance. The White rooks are no menace: the bishops neutralize the file.

| | 24 N(3) – K4 | R – KN1 |

Preparing to oust the knight by P – B4.

| 25 N – QN3 | R – B1 | 27 N – K4 | B – B1 |
| 26 N(4) – Q2 | B – Q3 | 28 N(4) – Q2 | P – B4 |

NO. IIIC. *After 28 . . .*
P – B4

Inviting White to commit hara-kiri by 29 R – K5, B – Q3; 30 R – Q5? R – N3, followed by QR – B3 and B – K3. The helplessness of the White rooks is noteworthy.

| 29 R – K5 | B – Q3 |
| 30 R(5) – K2 | R – QR1 |

Black wants to enforce P – R4, after which the steamroller will be irresistible.

| 31 N – R5 | QR – N1 | 33 K – R1 | R – KN3 |
| 32 N(5) – N3 | P – R5 |

In order to post his queen bishop at K3.

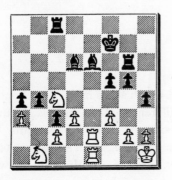

34	K – N1	B – K3
35	R – B2	R – QR1
36	R(2) – K2	P – R4

NO. IIID. *After 36 . . .*
          P – R4

To check this move by *36* N – R5 was no longer feasible, e.g.,
36 N – R5, B – B2; *37* N(5) – N3, B – N3; *38* R – K5, R – QB1
or even P – QB5.

37	N – N1	P – R5
38	N(3) – Q2	P – QB5
39	N – B1	

If *39* PxP, PxP and the queen knight pawn is bared to frontal
attack.

39	. . . .	R – QB1
40	K – R1	P – B6
41	PxP	PxP
42	N – K3	P – QN5

Finally obtaining a passed pawn, which is deadly.

43 N – B4

NO. IIIE. *After 43 N – B4*

Nothing avails. The passed pawn must soon cost White a piece.

43	BxN
44 PxB	RxP
45 R – K3	PxP
46 NxBP	B – N5
Resigns	

Game IV

Again, Black obtains the bishop-pair in return for a doubled queen bishop pawn. But White soon captures a bishop for a knight, then maneuvers into an endgame and exploits the Black weakness to win.

FOUR KNIGHTS OPENING

CAPABLANCA *v*. JANOWSKY, 1913

1 P – K4	P – K4	4 B – N5	P – QR3?
2 N – KB3	N – QB3	5 BxN	QPxB
3 N – B3	N – B3	6 O – O	B – KN5

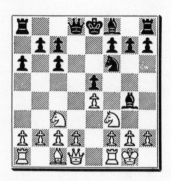

NO. IVA. *After 6 . . .*
B – KN5

The position is analogous to that which arises in the "Ruy Lopez question," with an important difference. Here the Black king pawn is under fire, and its protection is curiously awkward. If 6 . . . B – Q3; 7 P – Q4 is troublesome; Black can scarcely avoid the exchange of one of his bishops, if not worse. His actual move

commits him to BxN sooner or later. He gets into worse trouble
by avoiding this swap.

7 P – KR3	B – R4?
8 Q – K2	B – Q3
9 P – Q3	Q – K2
10 N – Q1	O – O – O
11 N – K3	

NO. IVB. *After 11 N – K3*

To forestall N – B5 Black should now play BxN and P – KN3.

11	B – N3?	13 N(3) – B5	Q – K3
12 N – R4	KR – N1	14 P – KB4	

Threatening NxBch and P – B5.

14	BxN	17 B – K3!	B – B1
15 NxB	PxP	18 Q – B2	R – Q2
16 BxP	B – B4ch	19 B – B5!	

One might think that White would want to retain his bishop
to defend his weakened dark squares. But Black lacks the means
to exploit that "complex" once his bishop disappears. The swap
brings nearer the time when White can exploit his superior pawn
formation.

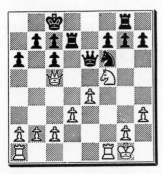

19	BxB
20 QxB	

NO. IVC. *After 20 QxB*

The positive aspect of White's advantage is the half-open king bishop file plus the strong outpost station at KB5. After he doubles rooks on the file, he will threaten NxKNP, if Black leaves his knight on KB3. But if the knight retreats, KB2 and KR2 come under attack. It is foreseeable that Black must hasten to swap knights, and probably queens also, to lessen the pressure. But both the points will remain intact.

20	K – N1	24 R – B4	NxN
21 R – B2	N – K1	25 QxN	QxQ
22 QR – KB1	P – B3	26 RxQ	R – K1
23 P – QN3	N – Q3		

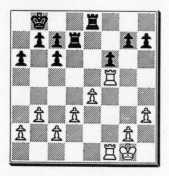

NO. IVD. *After 26 . . .*
R – K1

The next step is to force off the king bishop pawn, both to make the king pawn passed and to permit invasion of the seventh rank.

| 27 P – KN4 | P – QN3 |

Useless is 27 . . . P – R3, for 28 P – KR4 renews the threat. Black's only hope is to get queen-side counterplay, but White can squelch the advance, thanks to the doubled pawn.

28 P – N4!	K – N2
29 K – B2	P – QN4
30 P – QR4!	

To prevent Black from playing P – QR4 to get an open queen rook file.

30	R – Q5
31 R – QN1	R – K4
32 K – K3	R – Q2
33 P – R5	R – K3
34 R(1) – KB1	R(2) – K2

NO. IVE. *After 34 . . .*
R(2) – K2

Having locked up the queen-side, White can now continue the king-side breakthrough.

35 P – N5	PxP
36 RxP	R – R3
37 R – N3	R(3) – K3

Holding back the queen pawn as long as he can.

38 P – R4	P – N3	41 P – Q4	K – B1
39 R – N5	P – R3	42 R – B8ch	K – N2
40 R – N4	R – N2		

If K – Q2, the rook goes over and annexes the queen rook pawn.

43 P – K5	P – N4
44 K – K4	R(3) – K2
45 PxP	PxP
46 R – B5	

NO. IVF. *After 46 R – B5*

"To them that hath shall be given." White's two-to-none center has culminated in a passed pawn, and now he wins a pawn, the last of Black's former king-side majority. The rest is silence.

46	K – B1	51 K – Q3	R – R6ch
47 R(4)xP	R – R2	52 K – Q2	P – B4
48 R – R5	K – Q2	53 NPxP	R – R6
49 RxR	RxR	54 P – Q5	Resigns
50 R – B8	R – R5ch		

Game V

Here is the siege of a backward pawn. The pawn is not in danger of capture and must be held back by unremitting frontal pressure. The attacker is thus almost as tied down as the defender—but not quite. By patient, laborious maneuver he forces small deteriorations in the adverse position until, after nearly fifty moves, he can transform his advantage into a passed pawn—which wins after thirty moves more.

NIMZOVICH ATTACK

CANAL *v.* RUBINSTEIN, 1929

1 N – KB3	N – KB3	5 B – N2	B – N2
2 P – QN3	P – KN3	6 O – O	O – O
3 P – N3	P – N3	7 P – B4	P – B4
4 B – QN2	B – KN2	8 P – Q3?	

Probably intending 9 P – K4. But he merely hands over the initiative to Black.

8	P – Q4!
9 PxP	NxP
10 BxB	KxB
11 Q – Q2	N – QB3
12 N – B3	NxN
13 QxNch	K – N1

NO. VA. *After 13 . . .*
K – N1

Black threatens to get a pawn on the fourth (P – K4) v. pawn on third. White should therefore make immediate preparations to enforce P – Q4, beginning with *14 P – K3*.

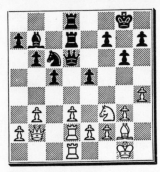

14	Q – N2	Q – Q3
15	KR – Q1	QR – Q1
16	R – Q2	R – Q2
17	QR – Q1	KR – Q1
18	P – KR4	P – K4

NO. VB. *After 18 . . .*
P – K4

There it is. The Black knight threatens to take the outpost station, after which P – K3 is unplayable and NxN hopeless. White therefore excludes the knight at the cost of a backward queen pawn.

19	P – K3	P – KR3
20	B – R3	

Hereabouts, P – Q4 is no good because after KPxP Black moves Q – KB3, eventually winning a pawn.

20	. . . .	R – K2	23	N – B3	N – N5
21	B – N2	Q – B3	24	N – K1	BxB
22	N – R2	P – KR4	25	KxB	P – R4

To forestall any attempt to relieve the pressure by P – QR3 and P – QN4.

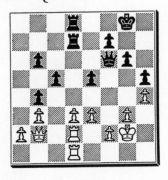

26	N – B2	KR – Q2
27	NxN	RPxN

NO. VC. *After 27 . . . RPxN*

White is now so trussed up that he can only temporize. But Black finds it not easy to break through.

28 Q – B2	Q – B3ch	31 K – N2	P – B4
29 P – B3	R – Q4	32 Q – B4	K – N2
30 K – B2	Q – Q2	33 K – B2	R – KB1

Threatening P – B5.

34 P – B4	R – Q1
35 PxP	RxKP

The picture is changed a little. Black has made a dent in the White king-side, but the disappearance of his king pawn requires increased vigilance to hold back the queen pawn.

36 Q – B4	R – Q4	39 Q – B4	Q – B3
37 Q – B4	Q – B3	40 Q – B2	P – QN4
38 Q – B2	Q – B3		

At last a new threat, eventually to advance the queen bishop pawn.

41 R – QB1   R(1) – Q3

NO. VD. *After 41 . . .*
R(1) – Q3

White can finally play P – Q4 and decides to do so, else he scarcely has a move.

42 P – Q4	Q – Q2!
43 R(1) – Q1	K – B2

Not 43 . . . PxP; 44 Q – N2.

44 Q – N2	Q – Q1
45 K – N2	R – Q2
46 K – R2	K – N1
47 K – N2	K – R2
48 K – R2	

NO. VE. *After 48 K – R2*

Black has tucked his king into safety to prepare the following tactical stroke.

48	**P – KB5!**
49 KPxP	

Of course if 49 NPxP, QxPch and the king is in trouble.

49	**RxP**
50 RxR	**PxR**

The backward pawn has disappeared, but in its place has blossomed a Black passed pawn.

51 R – Q3	Q – B3	55 K – N2	Q – Q4ch
52 Q – Q2	Q – Q3	56 K – R2	Q – K5
53 K – N1	K – N2	57 K – N1	K – B3
54 K – R2	Q – B4	58 K – B2	K – K3

NO. VF. *After 58 . . .*
K – K3

The king threatens to come to Q4, after which the rook can take the queen bishop file and go to QB6. White attempts a diversion on the king-side.

59	R – KB3	R – QB2
60	P – B5ch	K – Q4!
61	R – B4	R – B7!
62	RxQ	RxQch
63	K – B3	PxP
64	R – K8	RxP
65	R – KB8	

NO. VG. *After 65 R – KB8*

It might seem that Black's two extra pawns do not count for much, since he is going to lose them in a hurry. But the fact is that Black has an easy win, based on these points: (a) his pawns are nearer queening than White's king rook pawn, and (b) he has the better king position—near the pawns that need protection to go forward.

65	. . . .	R – QN7!
66	RxPch	K – B3

Against continued checks the king will walk to QR4.

67	RxRP	RxPch
68	K – K4	

If K – B4, the queen knight pawn marches right down.

68	. . . .	RxP	70 R – KN5	R – KR6
69	KxP	K – N3	71 R – N1	

If he tries to save his last pawn, the queen knight pawn marches down. White could now resign honorably.

71	. . . .	RxPch
72	K – Q3	R – QB5

It is, of course, important to prevent the king from reaching the queen knight file.

73 R – QN1	R – B6ch	77 R – R8	R – KN6
74 K – Q4	K – R4	78 K – B5	R – QB6ch
75 R – R1ch	R – R6	79 K – Q4	R – B5ch
76 R – R1	K – R5	80 K – Q3	P – N6
		Resigns	

Game VI

Black accepts an extreme pawn weakness—a doubled, isolated pawn—to obtain a half-open queen rook file. He demonstrates that this, if you know what to do with it, is more than adequate compensation.

QUEEN'S GAMBIT

JANOWSKY *v.* CAPABLANCA, 1916

1 P – Q4	N – KB3
2 N – KB3	P – Q4
3 P – B4	P – B3
4 N – B3	B – B4

Bring on your bears! The theoretical drawback to this cavalier solution of how to develop the queen bishop against the Queen's Gambit is that after 5 PxP, PxP; 6 Q – N3 the defense of Black's QN2 as well as Q4 poses problems.

5 Q – N3?	Q – N3
6 QxQ	PxQ
7 PxP	NxP
8 NxN	PxN

NO. VIA. *After 8 . . . PxN*

So the Black queen-side is a shambles, but he has free play for his pieces, particularly his queen rook. All the more remarkable is the following maneuver, by which the bishop that so boldly sought freedom now retires behind his own pawns.

9	P – K3	N – B3
10	B – Q2	B – Q2!!
11	B – K2	P – K3!

The self-immolation is accomplished. The idea, of course, is to use the bishop to support a queen-side attack based on the open files.

12	O – O	B – Q3
13	KR – B1	K – K2
14	B – B3	KR – QB1

NO. VIB. *After 14 . . .*
KR – QB1

Hereabouts White might have moved B – N5, in order to swap bishops after a knight move. But it is hard to believe that the exchange of a good bishop for a bad bishop would bring permanent relief.

15	P – QR3	N – R4

Black bares his teeth: the knight eyes the outpost station at QB5. If *16* BxN, PxB, Black has undoubled his pawns and enjoys the bishop-pair.

16	N – Q2	P – B4

To prevent counterplay by P – K4.

17	P – KN3	P – QN4
18	P – B3	N – B5
19	BxN	NPxB

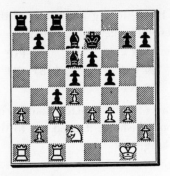

NO. VIC. *After 19 . . . NPxB*

So the pawns straighten out. Black emerges with three points net—plus points for his bishop-pair and half-open queen rook file, a minus point to White for his bad bishop.

20	P – K4	K – B2
21	P – K5	B – K2
22	P – B4	P – QN4
23	K – B2	

Observe that if White here (or previously) gets rid of his bad bishop by B – N4, he loses a pawn, e.g., 23 B – N4, BxB; 24 PxB, R – R5; 25 RxR, PxR; and after 26 . . . R – QN1 the pawn goes.

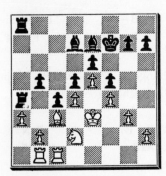

23	. . . .	R – R5
24	K – K3	KR – QR1
25	QR – N1	

NO. VID. *After 25 QR – N1*

Black was threatening P – N5. If now 25 . . . P – N5; 26 PxP, BxP, White does not play BxB, which would bare his queen knight pawn to frontal attack, but sits tight and lets Black play BxB, so that after PxB Black still has to find a way to penetrate. Black therefore switches to a king-side break, taking advantage of the preoccupation of the White pieces with queen-side defense.

25. . . .	P – R3	28 K – B3	PxP
26 N – B3	P – N4	29 PₓP	R(5) – R1
27 N – K1	R – KN1	30 N – N2	

If the knight goes the other way (N – B2), Black doubles on the king knight file and brings both bishops, if need be, to the king rook file to drive the White king back.

30	R – N5
31 R – N1	QR – KN1
32 B – K1	

NO. VIE. *After 32 B – K1*

The situation is ripe for combinative play. Black sacrifices a pawn for the moment, in order to hurl his queen bishop behind the White lines.

32	P – N5!	35 B – N3	B – K5ch
33 PxP	B – QR5	36 K – B2	P – R4
34 R – QR1	B – B7		

White must lose at least the exchange. If 37 N – K3, P – R5 just the same, for after 38 NxR, RxN the bishop goes.

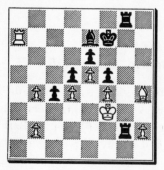

37 R – R7	BxN
38 RxB	P – R5
39 BxP	RxRch
40 K – B3	

NO. VIF. *After 40 K – B3*

Now the Black rooks penetrate behind the White lines and mop up.

40	RxRP	44 R – K7	RxPch
41 BxB	R – R6ch	45 K – B3	R – QR1
42 K – B2	R – QN6	46 RxPch	K – R2
43 B – N5ch	K – N3	Resigns	

Game VII

"Occupation of the center by pawns does not spell center control," we have said. After all, the function of a pawn center is to gain posts and lines for the *pieces*. In this game, White lets his advanced chain disappear, then occupies the vacated squares with pieces, which not only blockade the Black pawns but also menace the heart of the Black territory. At the time this game was played, this procedure was so unorthodox that it was greeted with hoots of derision and incredulity.

FRENCH DEFENSE

NIMZOVICH *v.* SALWE, 1911

1 P – K4	P – K3	4 P – QB3	N – QB3
2 P – Q4	P – Q4	5 N – B3	Q – N3
3 P – K5	P – QB4	6 B – Q3	

Better is 6 B – K2. True, Black cannot now win the queen pawn: 6 . . . PxP; 7 PxP, NxP?; 8 NxN, QxN; 9 B – N5ch and wins the queen. But White's Q4 still needs the protection of the queen.

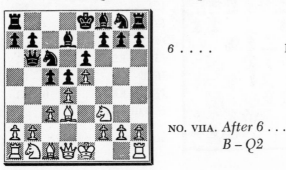

6 . . . .   B – Q2

NO. VIIA. *After 6 . . .*
B – Q2

Now the queen pawn really is threatened. To maintain it, White would have to lose a tempo with B – K2. Instead—

7 PxP

Utterly antipositional—in the opinion of the day.

7	BxP
8 O – O	P – B3
9 P – QN4	

Leaving a backward pawn on the open file—horrors! But this is necessary to let the queen bishop sally forth, and White is confident that the dominance of his pieces will shield the weakling.

9	B – K2
10 B – KB4	PxP
11 NxP	NxN
12 BxN	

NO. VIIB. *After 12 BxN*

Clearly the bishop is a tower of strength, hitting both wings of the Black camp, blockading the king pawn, and protecting the queen bishop pawn. An important tactical point is that *12 . . . B – KB3* fails against *13 Q – R5ch* (*13 . . . P – N3; 14 BxPch, PxB; 14 QxPch, K – K2; 15 BxBch, NxB; 16 Q – N7ch*).

12	N – B3
13 N – Q2	O – O
14 N – B3	B – Q3
15 Q – K2	QR – B1
16 B – Q4	Q – B2
17 N – K5	B – K1
18 QR – K1	

NO. VIIC. *After 18 QR – K1*

White has achieved the desired position. He has ensconced pieces in place of his center pawns; the Black center pawns are immobilized. Since the White pieces are admirably posted for a king-side attack, Black gets rid of the pestiferous knight, giving White the bishop-pair.

18	....	BxN
19	BxB	Q – B3
20	B – Q4	B – Q2
21	Q – B2	

Gaining a tempo to bring the rook forward, by the threat against the king rook pawn.

| 21 | .... | R – KB2 |

To meet BxN with PxB, maintaining guard of the king rook pawn.

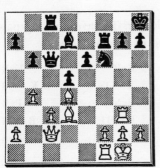

| 22 | R – K3 | P – QN3 |
| 23 | R – N3 | K – R1 |

NO. VIID. *After 23 . . . K – R1*

The king rook pawn was again threatened. But this move turns out to be no defense.

| 24 | BxRP |

Since *24 . . .* NxB; *25* Q – N6, K – N1; *26* BxKNP would win quickly.

| 24 | .... | P – K4! |

So that if *25* BxKP, NxB, after which the Black queen guards KN3.

25	B – N6!	R – K2
26	R – K1	Q – Q3
27	B – K3	

Thus White gets away with his pawn. Black continues to mix it up, but White dexterously evades trouble.

27	....	P – Q5
28	B – N5	RxP
29	RxR	PxR
30	QxP	

NO. VIIE. *After 30 QxP*

Black has no more shots in his locker. To save his king pawn, he himself soon has to propose the exchange of queens.

30	....	K – N1	35	RxR	KxR
31	P – QR3	K – B1	36	B – Q3	K – Q3
32	B – R4	B – K1	37	BxN	PxB
33	B – B5	Q – Q5	38	K – B1	B – B3
34	QxQ	PxQ	39	P – KR4	Resigns

Game VIII

This game is a warning—if warning be needed—that the acquisition of a lead in strategic points does not of itself win a game. You still have to play chess. Your points are meaningless if you cannot steer through the tactical complexities of exploiting them. White gains the lead, though it is not so great as perhaps he imagined. He vacillates between two plans, then commits a blunder of dogmatism, burying a bishop alive rather than permit dissolution of his proud bishop-pair. Black patiently consolidates a somewhat ragged position, develops what seemed to be a very

remote resource, then sweeps the field in a burst of tactical fireworks.

PETROFF DEFENSE

PILNIK *v*. OLAFSSON, 1955

1	P – K4	P – K4	*7*	O – O	O – O
2	N – KB3	N – KB3	*8*	R – K1	N – Q3
3	NxP	P – Q3	*9*	N – B3	P – QB3
4	N – KB3	NxP	*10*	B – KB4	B – N5
5	P – Q4	P – Q4	*11*	P – KR3	B – R4
6	B – Q3	B – K2	*12*	B – R2	P – KB4

NO. VIIIA. *After 12 . . .*
P – KB4

A bold move, leaving himself weak on K3 and K4. Still, he
establishes K5 as a station for his knight, and prevents P – KN4.

13	N – K2!	P – KN4

"He who says A must say B." Black cannot permit the knight to
reach K6 via KB4.

14	N – N3	B -- N3
15	N – K5	

White has won the first skirmish. His king knight has been un-
pinned, and now takes a strong station, though it cannot remain
there long. Still, it will serve to gain the bishop-pair.

15 . . . .   N – Q2
16 NxB   PxN

NO. VIIIB. *After 16 . . .*
                PxN

Let us apply the Point Count. White has a plus for his two bishops, another for the outpost station at K5, a third for command of the open king file. Black's only solid plus is the outpost station at his K5. He has a half-open king rook file, but whether he can make any use of it is a question. The king-side pawns are also a question: Do they represent a "mobile pawn wing" or a "compromised king-side"? They might turn into either. At present we shall have to regard them as neutral.

How should White continue? One plan is to bring the knight to the outpost station N – B1 – Q2 – B3 – K5. Another is to double rooks on the king file: P – QB3, Q – B2 (the queen is posted here, not on Q2, in view of Black's N – K5), R – K2, QR – K1. Doubling faces the fact that Black can plug the file by N – K5; the Black knight can then be ousted by P – KB3, but this move will prevent the White knight's tour to K5. It seems that White must choose one plan or the other: he cannot execute both. Yet there actually is a chance for both, by doubling rooks first, then sending the knight on his travels, and playing P – KB3 only after the knight has arrived at K5. Of course, by a prompt N – K5 Black will have two opportunities to swap knights, but then the king file remains open. The greater hazard is that the Black knight may support disruptive threats during the time it remains on K5.

17 Q – K2?

A move that fits into neither plan, and so is a waste of time. Much better is P – QB3, as played a few moves later.

17	R – B2
18 N – B1	N – K5
19 P – KB3	

Inconsistent. There was no point in *18* N – B1 if he was re-solved to make this move immediately. Much better was *19* N – Q2, putting the question.

| 19 . . . . | N – Q3 |
| 20 P – B3 | |

Belatedly going for the formation he should have established earlier.

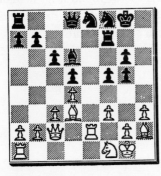

20	N – KB1
21 Q – QB2	N – K1
22 R – K2	B – Q3

NO. VIIIC. *After 22 . . . B – Q3*

In contrast with White, Black has lost no time in regrouping his pieces to best effect. His king rook and king knight are posted to prevent invasion by the White rooks. Now he gets rid of the White queen bishop that bores into his central space, thus gain-ing dark squares for his queen.

23 P – KN3??

"One doesn't believe one's eyes" (Euwe). White would rather play a piece down, in effect, than swap bishops. This is carrying the fetish of two bishops beyond reason!

| 23 . . . . | N – N2 |
| 24 QR – K1 | Q – B3 |

White has at last nailed down the open file—too late to do any-thing with it.

25 K – N2   N(2) – K3

The crowning insult—Black even posts a piece on the beleaguered file. White proceeds to use the moribund queen bishop
in the only way he can, to guard Q4 in preparation for P – QB4.

26 B – N1   R – Q1
27 R – Q1   R – R2

Who said the half-open king rook file was a "remote" plus!

28 P – QB4

So, counterplay. It is true that Black loses ground if he snatches
at the queen pawn: 28 . . . NxP; 29 BxN, QxB; 30 BxP. But 28
P – QB4 threatens nothing; Black can simply ignore it.

28 . . . .   P – N5!

NO. VIIID. *After 28 . . .*
P – N5

A bolt from the blue! The point is that Black wants to remove
the White king knight pawn, to gain access to his KB5. If at once
28 . . . P – B5, White can lock up the king-side by 29 P – KN4.
Hence Black first prevents this advance, at the cost of a pawn if
need be—e.g., 29 RPxP, P – B5.

29 BPxP   BxP

Now Black can afford this more expeditious way of removing
the pawn.

30 NxB   RxP!

The rook is immune: 31 KxR? N – B5ch; 32 K – R2, Q – R5

mate. Subsequent analysis indicates that White's best chance was *31 N – R5*, but Black should still win.

31	NPxP	N – B5ch	37 K – B3
32	K – B3	Q – R5	38 NxN
33	B – B2	N – R2	39 RxPch
34	R – KN1	N – N4ch	40 Q – B1
35	K – K3	R – K1ch	41 N – B4
36	K – Q2	N – B6ch	Resigns

NxRch
QxB
K – R1
R – K6
R – K8

Game IX

With the advent of hypermodernism, players have been taking exceptional liberties in ceding the center. Their general idea is to set up the opponent's mid-section as a target and strike at it. Here the strategy boomerangs. The target not only encroaches on the enemy domain but actually strikes first! Black beats a retreat and finds himself in close quarters. An effort to extricate himself leaves him subject to a tactical blow.

YUGOSLAV DEFENSE

HOROWITZ *v.* BEAN, 1957

1	P – K4	P – Q3	5 B – QB4	O – O
2	P – Q4	N – KB3	6 P – KR3	P – B4
3	N – QB3	P – KN3	7 PxP	PxP
4	N – B3	B – N2	8 Q – K2	N – B3

NO. IXA. *After 8 . . .*
N – B3

White's superior center and mobile king pawn force a rout.

9	P – K5	N – K1
10	P – K6	P – B4

After *10 . . .* PxP; *11* BxPch, Black's king pawn is isolated and his king position weakened.

11	B – B4		N – Q5
12	NxN		PxN
13	N – Q5		N – Q3?

NO. IXB. *After 13 . . .*
   N – Q3

14	NxPch		**Resigns**

After *14 . . .* QxN; *15* BxN, QxB; *16* P – K6ch decides. Or *14 . . .* K – R1; *15* NxPch, PxN; *16* P – K7, forking queen and rook.

Game X

A titanic struggle for the center opens the following game, and Black succeeds in his goal of compelling White to relieve the tension on White's eighteenth. In doing so, however, the defender makes a play on his sixteenth which apparently will have no bearing on the future course of the game. He parts with a bishop for a knight and half-opens White's king rook file. Quickly, however, the scene shifts to the half-open file, where by a deft tactical stroke the file is completely opened. White penetrates on this avenue and Black finds himself in a mating net.

RUY LOPEZ

HOROWITZ *v.* MARTIN, 1938

1	P – K4	P – K4	9	B – B2	Q – K1
2	N – KB3	N – QB3	10	P – KR3	R – Q1
3	B – N5	P – QR3	11	R – K1	K – R1
4	B – R4	N – B3	12	QN – Q2	N – KN1
5	O – O	B – K2	13	N – B1	B – B3
6	Q – K2	P – Q3	14	Q – Q1	QN – K2
7	P – B3	B – Q2	15	N – K3	P – B4
8	P – Q4	O – O			

NO. XA. *After 15 . . .*
P – B4

Up to here, Black hasn't granted an iota in the center. But he has left himself open to a small concession.

	16	N – N4	BxN
	17	PxB	

The position has hardly changed. Who would believe that the decision soon comes on the half-open king rook file?

	17	. . . .	N – B3
	18	P – Q5	N – N1
	19	P – KN3	Q – Q2
	20	P – N5	B – K2
	21	N – R4	P – KN3
	22	K – N2	P – B3
	23	R – R1!	K – N2

NO. XB. *After 23 . . .*
K – N2

A brief summary of the position discloses: (1) material is relatively even, save that White has the bishop-pair, a long-term consideration; (2) White has the center and the greater space; (3) White's king is presently secure, whereas some of White's men are poised for action in the direction of the Black king; (4) White enjoys the half-open king rook file. Hence, with the advantage of center, space, king security and half-open file, White enjoys a lead of more than four points, sufficient to produce a win. Yet, where is it? To quote grandmaster Tarrasch, it is there, but you must see it!

24 N – B5ch!

This is it. White relies on tactical considerations to bring home the strategically won game.

24 . . . .   **PxN**

If 24 . . . K – R1; 25 RxPch, KxR; 26 Q – R1ch, and mate in two.

25	RxPch	KxR
26	Q – R5ch	N – R3
27	QxNch	K – N1
28	Q – N6ch	K – R1
29	B – K3	Resigns

Game XI

A commentary on the strength of salient *v.* reverse salient is the essence of the next two games. In Game XI White provokes Black into establishing the advanced salient, thinking that some time during the future course of the game he will find some way of attacking and demolishing it. In Game XII Black provokes White into taking the advanced salient. In both cases the salient is in juxtaposition to the reverse salient. Curiously, in the first game, the salient is supreme, and in the second game the reverse salient takes the honors. All of which is a bit confusing. What, therefore, is the lesson?

As previously enunciated (see Chapter 3, "Advanced Chains and Salients"), the advanced salient offers the better prospects. The difference between the two in potency, however, is significantly slight. There is no cut and dried formula that will alert the player to a decisive course of action. The advanced salient, being a bridgehead in enemy territory, calls for prompt and courageous exploitation, sometimes involving great sacrifice to force capitulation. The reverse salient is essentially defensive. It is a defiant bulwark to rapid enemy incursion. It calls for precise defense on a move-to-move basis, with a long-term plan of whittling away the adverse pawn projection.

RETI OPENING

KASHDAN *v.* HOROWITZ, 1936

1 N – KB3	P – Q4	6 P – K4	B – N5
2 P – QB4	P – Q5	7 P – KR3	B – K3
3 P – KN3	P – QB4	8 P – Q3	P – B3
4 B – N2	N – QB3	9 N – R3	Q – Q2
5 O – O	P – K4	10 K – R2	

Black has the advanced salient. From here on and for the next several moves Black's plan is to smoke out the White king even,

NO. XIA. *After 10 K – R2*

if need be, at tremendous sacrifice. Soon, all his forces will be directed at the monarch.

10	P – KN4	13 B – Q2	N – N3
11 N – B2	P – KR4	14 P – R3	B – N5
12 N – N1	KN – K2		

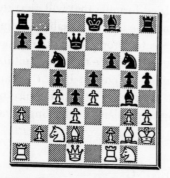

NO. XIB. *After 14 . . . B – N5*

The offer of the bishop is based on obtaining the open rook file which will provide a sweep·to the enemy king.

15 PxB

White believes that he has adequate defense by the return of the piece on his sixteenth. Better would be *15 P – B3, B – K3*, after which, in due time, Black would launch the battering-ram . . . P – N5.

15	PxPch
16 N – R3	

NO. XIC. *After 16 N – R3*

16 . . . .   N – B5

This is what White failed to anticipate. He must now accept the knight, and in doing so he creates a new station for Black at Black's K4, from which point of vantage Black's other knight will join the fray. Black's king-side pawns, moreover, now become alive and mobile.

17	PxN	KPxP	24	P – R5	P – N5
18	P – B3	PxN	25	BxP	NxPch
19	B – R1	N – K4	26	BxN	BxBch
20	Q – K2	B – Q3	27	K – R1	P – N6
21	R – KN1	O – O – O	28	RxP	RxR
22	P – N4	P – N3	29	RPxP	KR – N1
23	P – R4	QR – N1	30	PxRP	

All the foregoing play has netted Black the exchange—a rook for a knight. Black, however, appears to be in extreme jeopardy. Fortunately, all is not what it seems.

NO. XID. *After 30 PxRP*

30 . . . .   QxP!

The queen is immune.

31	B – N4ch	R/6xB	34	N – K1	R – KB7
32	QxRch	RxQ	35	K – N1	P – R7ch
33	RxQ	R – N7	36	KxR	P – R8(Q)
				Resigns	

Game XII

BENONI DEFENSE

RESHEVSKY *v*. HOROWITZ, 1956

1	P – Q4	N – KB3	8	P – KR3	N – R3
2	P – QB4	P – B4	9	B – N5	N – B2
3	P – Q5	P – K4	10	Q – Q2	Q – K1
4	N – QB3	P – Q3	11	P – KN4	P.– QR3
5	P – K4	P – KN3	12	N – N3	P – N4
6	B – Q3	B – N2	13	P – N3	R – N1
7	KN – K2	O – O	14	P – B3	N – Q2

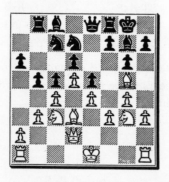

NO. XIIA. *After 14 . . .*
N – Q2

Observe the similarity of Black's formation to White's of the previous game.

15	K – B2	N – N3	18	B – K3	R – B2
16	QR – QN1	B – Q2	19	P – R3	B – KB1
17	P – KR4	P – B3	20	N – R2	

White's last is inferior. Better is *20* P – R5, P – N4; *21* N – B5, BxN; *22* KPxB, establishing a station at K4 for ready occupancy by the knight.

20	B – K2
21 P – R5	P – N4
22 N – B5	BxN
23 KPxB	

NO. XIIB. *After 23 KPxB*

Momentarily, all the points are in White's favor. White enjoys (1) the bishop-pair, (2) the center, (3) space, and threatens, moreover, to occupy the station at K4 by returning with his knight. Should he succeed in doing so, the preponderance of points will be overwhelming. But it is Black's move.

$$23 . . . . \qquad P – K5!$$

This pawn sacrifice changes the complexion of things. It plugs White's station at K4 and, in turn, creates one for Black at Black's K4. True, Black has parted with a pawn. Yet, it was a question of do or die. To boot, the outpost knight (when it gets to K4) will serve as a great measure of compensation.

24 PxP	N – Q2	29 R – N3	P – N5
25 B – K2	B – Q1	30 PxP	PxP
26 N – B3	N – K4	31 Q – B2	N – R3
27 P – N4	BPxP	32 N – N5	R – Q2
28 RxP	P – R4	33 R – R1	N – B4

Black's well-posted knights just about balance White's extra pawn. But White wants more and falls victim to a well-concealed and attractive countercombination.

$$34 \ \text{NxP?}$$

NO. XIIC. *After 34 NxP*

| 34 . . . . | NxPch |
| 35 BxN | Q – K4!! |

A stellar move, attacking rook and threatening to win queen by Q – R7ch.

36 R – QB1	NxR	40 Q – K6	Q – R7ch
37 QxN	QxN	41 K – B3	R – R2
38 P – B5	Q – K4	42 P – Q7	B – K2
39 P – Q6ch	K – B1	43 P – B6	

White's pawns are assuming enormous proportions. Black must act quickly.

NO. XIID. *After 43 P – B6*

| 43 . . . . | R/1 – R1 |

Black now threatens R – R7 with a mating attack. *43* . . . R – R7 at once would lose after *44* QxR, followed by P – B7.

44 P – B7	RxP
45 RxR	QxR
46 P – R6	Q – Q3
47 Q – B4	

White cannot afford to trade queens on account of Black's passed queen knight pawn.

47		QxP
48	B – R5	B – Q3
49	K – N4	

White is lost. The rest is a matter of time.

49		R – B1
50	Q – Q5	Q – K2
51	B – Q4	R – Q1
52	K – R3	B – K4
53	B – B5	RxQ
54	BxQch	KxB
55	PxR	P – N6
56	B – B3	K – Q3

White sealed 57 B – K4 but did not resume play when he discovered he could not hold the game. The finale is the triumph of the passed pawn.

Glossary

advanced group   a group of pawns, the foremost of which has reached the fifth rank or farther.

advanced pawn   one that has reached the fifth rank or farther.

backward pawn   a pawn that cannot be guarded by a fellow pawn, and which is effectively prevented from advancing by an enemy pawn on an adjacent file.

bad bishop   one that moves on squares of the same color as those on which the owner's center pawns, or most of his pawns, are fixed; thus the bishop duplicates the work of the pawns and is also hampered by them.

base of pawn chain   the rearmost pawn(s) of a salient or reverse salient; in a chain of three or more pawns, any behind the van may be regarded as a base.

bishop-pair   two bishops belonging to one player, especially when his opponent has only one bishop or none.

bishops of opposite colors   one bishop on each side, one moving on light squares and the other on dark.

blockade   to prevent the advance of an enemy pawn by posting a piece directly in front of it.

blockade game   the policy of restricting the movement of enemy pieces to such an extent that the

	opponent is in danger of loss by *Zug-zwang*.
"book" move	a move recommended as best, or as play-able, in the given position, by current books on the openings.
center	strictly, the four squares: White's Q4, Q5, K4, K5; loosely, the area in and around these squares; see *subcenter*.
centralization	the policy of posting pieces in the center or where they command central squares.
chain	two or more pawns on adjacent files and in a diagonal line.
closed center	a center so occupied or commanded by pawns that pieces are effectively ex-cluded from it.
combination	a planned sequence of moves in which every important adverse move is foreseen and provided for; a tactical series of moves as distinguished from an over-all strategic plan.
command	attack on a square such as to preclude its occupation by the enemy; broadly, the total number and values of the squares attacked by one's own forces.
compromised king (or king-side)	the situation of the castled king after one or more of the pawns originally on the second rank in front of him has disap-peared or moved, thereby seriously jeop-ardizing the king.
connectedness	a phalanx or other pawn group is con-nected when accompanied by friendly pawns on either or both adjacent files, capable of guarding some member of the group.
control of the center	(a) sufficient command of the center to exclude adverse pieces from it; or (b) significantly greater command of the cen-ter than is enjoyed by opponent; but

see the qualifications explained in Chapter 2.

crippled majority
(or wing)
a majority pawn wing so disposed (as by the doubling of pawns) that it cannot force a passed pawn against the minority wing facing it.

dark square
one of the so-called "black" squares of the board.

development
(a) the earliest phase of a game, when the player strives to bring his minor pieces and queen off the first rank, and usually to castle; (b) in this book, the disposition of a player's pieces at any time, with reference to their total mobility and command.

diagonal
a line of squares connected diagonally, as QB1, Q2, K3 . . . KR6.

doubled pawn(s)
two or more pawns of the same color on one file.

exchange
two captures, one by each player; a player *wins the exchange* when he captures a stronger piece while losing a weaker, as gaining a rook for a bishop or knight; to *win the minor exchange* is to capture a bishop for a knight.

expansion
the advancing of pawns to increase one's space for maneuver and command of the board.

fianchetto
the posting of a bishop at QN2 or KN2.

file
a line of squares extending from the White side to the Black, as KR1, KR2, KR3 . . . KR8.

frontal attack
(or pressure)
attack, particularly on a pawn, by an enemy rook or queen on the file.

guard
to guard a piece or pawn is to "attack" it with a friendly piece or pawn, so as to make a retaliatory capture if it is captured; to guard a square is to attack it

	so as to inhibit its occupation by enemy forces.
half-open file	a file from which only the player's own pawn has disappeared; the file is said to be half-open *for him.*
hanging pawns	a phalanx on the fourth rank, not connected on either side; broadly, any pawn group that is under frontal attack and cannot safely be advanced.
hole	a square on the third rank, in front of an unmoved pawn, that cannot be guarded by a friendly pawn, and so is open to occupation by an enemy piece; broadly, any important square on which a piece can settle without being attacked by an enemy pawn.
hypermodernism	a school of chess theory and practice that emphasizes delay in advancing center pawns, fianchetto of bishops, the avoidance of routine moves, etc.; avowed adherents of the school include Dr. Savielly Tartakover, Aron Nimzovich, Ewfim Bogolyubov, and Richard Reti.
isolani	= *isolated pawn.*
isolated pawn	one that cannot be guarded by a fellow pawn because the pawns on both adjacent files have disappeared.
isolated phalanx	one that is not connected; see *connectedness.*
king in the center	the situation of the king after the owner has forfeited the right to castle; often a dangerous situation.
light piece	= *minor piece.*
light square	one of the so-called "white" squares of the board.
line	a file, rank or diagonal of the board.
major piece	a rook or queen.
majority attack	an attack by advancing a majority pawn

wing against the minority facing it, usually with threat of establishing a passed pawn.

majority wing a group of two or three (possibly four) pawns on adjacent wing files, faced by fewer enemy pawns on that wing.

mating net the situation of a king beset by enemy forces when he has little or no prospect of escaping checkmate.

minor exchange see *exchange*.

minor piece a knight or bishop.

minority attack an attack by advancing a minority pawn wing, supported by pieces, usually with a threat of creating a serious weakness in the opponent's majority on that wing.

minority wing a group of two or three pawns on adjacent wing files, faced by a greater number of enemy pawns on that wing.

mobile wing a pawn wing able to advance because not blocked, and because the advance would not seriously impair the player's defense of his own king.

mobility freedom to move; the scope of a piece measured by the number of squares it can reach, the lines open to it, its freedom from obstruction by friendly forces, etc.

offside majority a pawn majority on the wing away from that in which the two kings are posted (when both are in the same wing); if both kings castled on the king-side, the offside majority is on the queen-side.

open file one containing no pawns of either color.

outpost (a) a piece (often a knight) established on an advanced square from which it can be ousted only with difficulty, or not at all, by an enemy pawn, and (usually) guarded by a friendly pawn; (b) the square occupied by such a piece: in this book, distinguished as *outpost station*.

passed pawn   a pawn not opposed by an enemy pawn on the same file or either adjacent file; it is *outside* when more remote than the opponent's passed pawn from a group of White and Black pawns on the other wing (see page 251). A majority pawn wing normally contains a *potential* passed pawn, which becomes *actual* when it is forced past the opposing minority wing.

pawn storm   an attack spearheaded by an advancing group of pawns.

pawn wing   a group of two or three (possibly four) pawns on adjacent files, usually (always, in connection with the terms "majority" and "minority") separated from their fellow pawns by at least one open or half-open file.

phalanx   two or more pawns on the same rank and adjacent files; a phalanx of three is occasionally called a *triple* phalanx.

piece   loosely, any of the chessmen, but in this book and most others the term means a man other than a pawn.

pin   the situation of a piece or pawn that cannot legally move off a line or from a square, because such move would expose its own king to check; the term is extended to situations where a move is not illegal but is inadvisable because it would expose a superior piece to capture.

Point Count   the system of evaluation of strategical advantages and disadvantages set forth in this book. For plus and minus points, see page 8. For dynamic and pictorial points, see page 14.

positional   largely synonymous with strategic, as distinguished from tactical; *position play*

	is a strategic move or plan as distinguished from a tactical (combination).
qualitative majority	a pawn wing able to force a passed pawn against an equal number of enemy pawns opposing it, because the enemy wing is crippled.
queen-side majority	an offside majority on the queen-side (both kings having castled king-side).
rank	a line of squares parallel to the White and Black sides of the board, as QR4, QN4, QB4 . . . KR4.
reverse salient	a formation of three pawns in a "V" pointing toward the owner, as White pawns on QB4, Q3, K4.
rook on the seventh	a rook that has reached the seventh rank away from the owner, thus attacking the enemy second rank laterally.
salient	a formation of three pawns in a "V" pointing away from the owner, as White pawns on QB4, Q5, K4. See also *reverse salient*.
space	loosely, the total number of squares available to a player for posting or maneuvering his pieces; in this book, such squares behind the player's front-line pawns.
station	= *outpost station*.
steamroller	a mass of advancing pawns; a pawn storm.
stopped pawns	a White and a Black pawn adjacent on the same file, blockading each other.
strategy	long-range planning; the theory and practice of obtaining slight but lasting advantages (points) which in accumulation may result in the decisive gain of material or in checkmate.
subcenter	the squares immediately adjacent to the center, particularly those on the fourth and fifth ranks.

tactics   where strategy is concerned with setting goals and formulating short- or long-range plans, tactics deal with the immediate and concrete execution of the plans, usually by means of combinations.

tempo   a gain of time in development, as by compelling opponent to make a move that does not contribute to his development.

two-for-one   the possession of two pawns on the center files, where the opponent has only one; *two-for-none, three-for-two* similarly refer to the count of opposing pawns in the center files.

van   the foremost pawn(s) of a salient or reverse salient.

weak pawn   one in danger of being lost, because it is isolated, backward, too far advanced, etc.

weak square   = *hole* in the broad sense. *Weak-square complex* is a series of connected holes, as on a diagonal when the bishop moving on squares of that color has disappeared.

wing   the area on either side of the center, designated as king-side or queen-side; a *pawn wing* is a group of pawns lying predominantly aside from the center.

Zugzwang   (German *compulsion to move*), the situation of a player whose moves are so restricted that any move he chooses will impair his defense seriously or fatally.

Zwischenzug   (German *intermediate move*), a move interpolated before a necessary or expected move (such as a retaliatory capture), exerting a threat that the opponent cannot ignore.

ABOUT THE AUTHORS

I. A. HOROWITZ, *three-time United States Open Champion and three times a member of the United States World Championship Teams (Prague, 1931, Warsaw, 1935, and Stockholm, 1937), has been playing, writing, lecturing and breathing chess for nearly half a century! In 1933, he founded* Chess Review, *now the world's leading chess magazine. Thousands of American chess players from coast to coast have met Horowitz over-the-board in friendly combat during his transcontinental tours.*

GEOFFREY MOTT-SMITH *is the author of many books on card games, chess, checkers and other board games, puzzles, mathematical recreations and hobbies. He is a consultant to card manufacturers on the rules of games and chairman of the committee that writes the laws of contract bridge. He manages annual bridge tournaments conducted by mail for college undergraduates, for the personnel of the U.S. State Department and for private companies. As an avocation, he composes chess problems.*